FINDING MEANING IN AN IMPERFECT WORLD

FINDING MEANING IN
AN IMPERFECT WORLD

Iddo Landau

OXFORD
UNIVERSITY PRESS

OXFORD
UNIVERSITY PRESS

Oxford University Press is a department of the University of Oxford. It furthers
the University's objective of excellence in research, scholarship, and education
by publishing worldwide. Oxford is a registered trade mark of Oxford University
Press in the UK and certain other countries.

Published in the United States of America by Oxford University Press
198 Madison Avenue, New York, NY 10016, United States of America.

© Oxford University Press 2017

Library of Congress Cataloging-in-Publication Data
Names: Landau, Iddo, 1958– author.
Title: Finding meaning in an imperfect world / Iddo Landau.
Description: Oxford ; New York, NY : Oxford University Press, [2017] |
Includes bibliographical references and index.
Identifiers: LCCN 2016039724 (print) | LCCN 2016047250 (ebook) |
ISBN 9780190657666 (cloth : alk. paper) | ISBN 9780190657673 (pdf) |
ISBN 9780190657680 (ebook) | ISBN 9780190657697 (online course)
Subjects: LCSH: Life.
Classification: LCC BD431 .L257 2017 (print) | LCC BD431 (ebook) |
DDC 128—dc23
LC record available at https://lccn.loc.gov/2016039724

1 3 5 7 9 8 6 4 2
Printed by Sheridan Books, Inc., United States of America

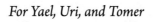

For Yael, Uri, and Tomer

CONTENTS

Acknowledgments   *ix*

1. Introduction   1

2. Implications   17

3. Against Perfectionism   31

4. Anticipations of Nonperfectionism   49

5. Death and Annihilation I   65

6. Death and Annihilation II   85

7. Life in the Context of the Whole Universe   93

8. Determinism and Contingency   101

9. Skepticism and Relativism   117

10. The Goal of Life   135

11. The Paradox of the End   145

CONTENTS

12. Suffering   163

13. Human Evil   173

14. Why We Are Blind to Goodness   191

15. Identifying I   205

16. Identifying II   217

17. Recognizing   229

18. Conclusion I   249

19. Conclusion II   267

Bibliography   281
Index   291

ACKNOWLEDGMENTS

This book owes much to many, but the most to those who shared with me their qualms and views on the meaning (or meaninglessness) of life. Some of these were terminal cancer patients whom I met while volunteering for the Israel Cancer Association. Many others were registered students who took my classes over the years, and yet others, usually older than regular students, sat in these classes as auditors. Their stories, arguments, and questions, in class and very often after class, taught me very much.

Many have also generously given of their time to read and comment on parts or the whole of the book. I am very grateful to my colleagues and friends Aliza Avraham, Stephen M. Campbell, Peter Hacker, Mane Hajdin, Aviv Hoffmann, Ivor Ludlum, Menachem Kellner, Ariel Meirav, Avital Pilpel, Eli Pitcovski, Bracha Oren-Simon, Saul Smilansky, Daniel Statman, Moti Suess, Lior Tal, Rivka Weinberg, and Irad Yavneh, as well as to two anonymous referees for Oxford University Press. Their very helpful comments and criticisms alerted me to many problems and allowed me to improve the book in many ways. I am especially indebted to my friends Peter

Hacker, Daniel Statman, Rivka Weinberg, and Saul Smilansky, who not only read and commented on two drafts of the manuscript but also offered invaluable practical help and advice. Their input is greatly appreciated.

At different stages of the development of the manuscript, Marion Lupo, Dana Rothman-Meshulam, Belina Neuberger, Richard Isomaki, and especially Marie Deer have made many excellent linguistic and stylistic suggestions. The text now reads much better thanks to their proposals, some of them not only linguistic but also philosophical.

I owe a special gratitude to Lucy Randall, the philosophy editor at Oxford University Press, who very helpfully commented on the whole of the book, making numerous important suggestions on both form and content. Her wise and experienced counsel changed the character of the book much for the better. Many thanks also to Hannah Doyle and Sasirekka Gopalakrishnan for their very patient and efficient administration of the production of the book.

Certain chapters in the book make use of materials from my articles. I gratefully acknowledge the permission of the editors and publishers to use materials from the following articles: "The Paradox of the End," *Philosophy* 70 (1995): 555–565; "The Meaning of Life *Sub Specie Aeternitatis*," *Australasian Journal of Philosophy* 89, no. 4 (2011): 727–734; "Immorality and the Meaning of Life," *Journal of Value Inquiry* 45, no. 3 (2011): 309–317; "Foundationless Freedom and Meaninglessness of Life in Sartre's *Being and Nothingness*," *Sartre Studies International* 18, no. 1 (2012): 1–8; "Sartre's Absolute Freedom in *Being and Nothingness*: The Problem Persists," *Philosophy Today* 56 (2012): 463–473.

FINDING MEANING IN AN IMPERFECT WORLD

Chapter 1

Introduction

1

A few years ago one of my students asserted, out of the blue, in the middle of an introduction to philosophy class, that it was pointless to discuss the issue we were then deliberating about (causal necessity) since life is completely meaningless. For a second I considered ignoring her statement and just continuing with the discussion. I even thought of telling her that the issue she raised was irrelevant to the theme of that session. Her face and body language, however, suggested that I do otherwise, so I asked her whether she would like to elaborate on the issue. She said that she did not have anything more to say about it; that is just the way life is. Silence followed. I was not sure what to say.

I asked whether she would agree that we should do in class what we learned philosophers often do before they even start considering arguments for and against various positions: they try to clarify more precisely what these positions are. Might I ask some questions that would help me better understand her position? She agreed. I asked whether she believes that all people's lives are meaningless or that only her own life is meaningless. She thought a bit, and then said that in her view not all people's lives are meaningless, although hers was.

I asked whether she thought that her life was meaningless necessarily, or was meaningless only because of certain events that happened to be true of her life, so that if these events were not to occur, her life would have not been meaningless. She replied that the latter was the case. My third question was whether she thought that her life was irredeemably meaningless, so that it must continue to be so also in the future, or that, in her view, if she would do some things, her life might turn out to be meaningful. Again she thought a bit, and again picked the latter alternative. She then said that she retracted, for the time being, her initial statement, and would like to think about it more and come to speak with me after class. I was impressed to see how helpful a few simple, clarifying questions, so typical of the way philosophers routinely address new issues, had been.

Another student raised his hand and said that that discussion was very interesting for him. Other students nodded. He added that he always thought that Hamlet's question, "To be or not to be," that is, whether to continue "to suffer the slings and arrows of outrageous fortune" or "to die," was a very important and relevant question. I said that I always found it odd that Hamlet presents only these two options, failing to discuss the third alternative, that of improving the way things are. Again, this rather simple observation, typical of the way philosophers enumerate alternatives, seemed to have had an effect on him and, as I could judge from body language, the class.

It then occurred to me for the first time that many people may find rational, philosophical discussions of the meaning of life quite helpful.

2

This book aims to present and critique some presuppositions about the meaning of life that lead many people to believe, unnecessarily in my view, that their lives are meaningless; to reply to recurring arguments made by people who take their lives to be meaningless; and to offer strategies that may help people identify what is meaningful, and increase meaningfulness, in their lives. The assumptions and arguments I criticize here are ones I have found in the literature or have heard from people who have told me, sometimes with considerable pain, that they do not take their lives to be sufficiently meaningful. I have been surprised to find that most people I have spoken to on the subject take a much bleaker view of the meaning of their lives than, I believe, need be, and that many refrain from asking questions or taking action that could make their lives more meaningful. People who regard their lives as meaningless or insufficiently meaningful will not usually entertain *all* the presuppositions and arguments criticized here, or need to employ all the strategies for increasing life's meaningfulness proposed ahead. Most readers, then, are likely to find several of the discussions in this book irrelevant to their own thoughts on the meaning of their life. As many of these discussions are independent of each other, the book is not built as one long argument, with each chapter building on the previous one. Instead, the book consists of a series of relatively self-contained discussions, although they do share some suppositions and a common theme. In most cases, one can agree with some of the views the book suggests while disagreeing with the others.

3

The rest of this introductory chapter focuses on clarifying the term "meaning of life," and suggests that it has much to do with value. Chapter 2 points to some general implications that can be drawn from the relation between meaning and value. Many of these implications undermine commonly held presuppositions about the meaning of life that lead some people to believe that their lives are meaningless or not meaningful enough. Chapter 3 presents the perfectionist presupposition about the meaning of life, according to which meaningful lives must include some perfection or some rare and difficult achievements, and criticizes it. Nonperfectionism about the meaning of life is not new; versions of it already appear in works of earlier writers as well as in religion, poetry, prose, and film. Chapter 4 describes some such anticipations of nonperfectionism.

Chapters 5 through 14 present commonly heard arguments that lead some people to wonder whether their lives can be meaningful (or to hold that they cannot). Chapters 5 and 6 discuss the claim that life cannot be meaningful because of our eventual death and annihilation. Chapter 7 replies to the argument that claims that life is meaningless because whatever we do is negligible when examined in the context of the universe at large. Chapter 8 starts out by discussing the view that because there is no free will, life cannot be considered meaningful, and then deals with arguments suggesting that life is meaningless because blind chance affects much of what happens to us and even who we are. Chapter 9 inquires whether we can hold life to be meaningful even if nothing is absolutely certain, and then moves to the relativist challenge: some people fear that life is not meaningful because nothing is objectively true or valuable.

Some people feel that their lives are meaningless because they do not have answers to questions such as "What am I living for?" or "What is the purpose of my life?" Chapter 10 answers these concerns, and chapter 11 discusses the paradox of the end, that is, the cases in which we work hard toward achieving an end, but then, once we attain it, feel that its meaning has vanished. Some also hold that life is meaningless because it, or the world, is so full of suffering and evil. Chapters 12 and 13 criticize arguments claiming that life is, or must be, extremely painful and vicious. Chapter 14 focuses on several dynamics that bring some people to turn a blind eye to the better parts of reality.

Many people fail to engage with what is meaningful to them because they do not know how to identify it. Chapters 15 and 16 discuss ways of identifying what is meaningful to oneself, and chapter 17 elaborates on ways of sensitizing ourselves to the meaning that we already have. Chapters 18 and 19, the concluding chapters, deal with some general questions, such as whether it is possible to lead a meaningful life without religion; whether issues of meaning should be discussed only by psychologists; and whether the claims in this book clash with existentialist thought, as well as with many people's descriptions of their meaningless lives.

The discussions ahead could have been elaborated more than they are here. However, since this is an introductory book, designed to interest and be of practical use for nonacademics as well as academics, I have usually kept the discussions short, sometimes summarizing more detailed arguments, at other times hoping that future work will consider in more detail the suggestions presented here. I anticipate that further elaborations of the themes discussed here will indeed follow.

4

As many other philosophical discussions, this one begins with an effort to clarify the main terms of the discussion. When we talk about the "meaning of life," the word "life" can be understood in more than one way: it may be taken to refer to individual lives, like yours or mine; or to human life overall; or even to biological life in general, including human, animal, and plant life. Although some of what will be said here about the meaning of individual lives could easily be extrapolated to considerations of the meaning of human life or of biological life, this book focuses on the meaning of individual human lives.

"Meaning," too, can be understood in more than one way. In regular speech, "meaning" has two main senses. One sense relates to a family of notions such as interpretation, explanation, and understanding, as in "The meaning of *bonsoir* in French is 'good evening.' " The other sense belongs to a family of notions such as importance, worth, and value, as in "This means a lot to me." Along with many others, I take the meaning of life to have to do mostly with meaning in the second sense, that is, with worth or value.[1] People who take their lives to have no meaning, or to have insufficient meaning, are saying that they do not take their lives, or central aspects of their lives, to be of sufficient worth. People who wonder what would

1. See, e.g., Harry Frankfurt, "On the Usefulness of Final Ends," *Iyyun: The Jerusalem Philosophical Quarterly* 41 (1992): 8; Susan Wolf, "Happiness and Meaning: Two Aspects of the Good Life," *Social Philosophy and Policy* 14, no. 1 (1997): 208–213; Wolf, "Meaning and Morality," *Proceedings of the Aristotelian Society* 97 (1997): 304; R. W. Hepburn, "Questions about the Meaning of Life," in *The Meaning of Life*, ed. E. D. Klemke, 2nd ed. (New York: Oxford University Press, 2000), 264–265; Kai Nielsen, "Death and the Meaning of Life," in Klemke, *The Meaning of Life*, 237, 242–247; W. D. Joske, "Philosophy and the Meaning of Life," in Klemke, *The Meaning of Life*, 287–290; John Cottingham, *On the Meaning of Life* (London: Routledge, 2003), 31; Berit Brogaard and Barry Smith, "On Luck, Responsibility and the Meaning of Life," *Philosophical Papers* 34, no. 3 (2005): 443.

make their lives meaningful, or more meaningful, are wondering what would insert more value, or worth, into their lives.[2] People who think that their lives are meaningful are people who think that a sufficient number of aspects of their lives are of sufficient value.

Consider a few examples. In his *Man's Search for Meaning*, Viktor Frankl describes how some concentration camp prisoners retained meaning in their lives, while others did not.[3] As Frankl describes it, those who retained meaning in their lives did so, for instance, by helping others (despite the scarcity of food and the harsh circumstances) or by planning and hoping for a better future after the war. Those who were able to hold on to meaning in their lives even in the conditions of the camps could do so because they knew that some aspects of life still held value for them, or could hold value in the future, and focused on them.

Thomas Nagel, similarly, argues that if we consider our lives from the objective, wide perspective, they seem to lack meaning, since any life has only a negligible effect on the universe. If we had not lived, nothing much would have changed for the world at large in the long run.[4] Put differently: from the wide perspective, our lives are inconsequential. When Nagel presents such arguments for the diminished meaning of life, he is telling us that our lives do not have enough value; he is discussing the insufficient worth of human beings (seen from that wide perspective). Again, meaning has to do with value.

Likewise, Tolstoy recounts in his semiautobiographical *Confession* how at a certain point in his life, he came to see it as meaningless.[5] He knew that he was considered the greatest Russian novelist and one

2. I henceforth use "worth" and "value" interchangeably.
3. Viktor Frankl, *Man's Search for Meaning* (New York: Washington Square Press, 1985), 86–98.
4. Thomas Nagel, "Birth, Death, and the Meaning of Life," in *The View from Nowhere* (New York: Oxford University Press, 1986), 208–231.
5. Leo Tolstoy, *Confession*, trans. David Patterson (New York: Norton, 1983), 27.

of the greatest authors in the history of humankind; his estate was thriving; his family was healthy and loved him. Yet at a certain point he started looking at all of that and asking himself, "So what?" He was the greatest Russian author. "So what?" There may be ways of improving people's condition that would allow them to prosper. "What concern is this of mine?" These "So what?" and "What concern is this of mine?" questions are questions about worth. What troubled Tolstoy was the feeling that everything he had accomplished or planned lacked sufficient value. As long as he thought that what he had was valuable, he did not sense that life was meaningless. And he would have returned to seeing life as meaningful if he could once again have seen his art, his family, and his possessions as having worth, or had he found other aspects of life that seemed to him worthy.

And when Thoreau tells us in *Walden* that he left his former, urban life for some time and "went to the woods because I wished to live deliberately," we take this to have to do with the meaning of life because people usually conduct themselves deliberately (rather than, say, carelessly or indifferently) with regard to issues that are valuable to them.[6] This is also why we associate living intensely and passionately with meaningfulness: people are usually intense or passionate about what they take to hold much importance or value. The same is true of very early statements. When Ecclesiastes says, "Then I considered all that my hands had done and the toil I had spent in doing it, and behold, all was vanity and a striving after wind, and there was nothing to be gained under the sun," the writer is saying that, in his view, all his actions have been worthless or futile since they do not bring about anything valuable.[7] A few verses later he declares: "Then I said to myself, 'What befalls the fool will befall

6. Henry D. Thoreau, *Walden: Or, Life in the Woods* (Mineola, NY: Dover, 1955), 59.
7. Ecclesiastes 2:11, Revised Standard Version.

me also; why then have I been so very wise?' And I said to myself
that this also is vanity. For of the wise man as of the fool there is no
enduring remembrance, seeing that in the days to come all will have
been long forgotten. How the wise man dies just like the fool!"[8] The
argument is that because we all ultimately disappear and are forgotten, there is no real difference between the life of the (worthy) wise
and that of the (worthless) fool. Much of what seems to have value,
the author suggests, in fact has none.

Discussions I have had with people who think that their lives are
meaningless or who are searching for what would make them more
meaningful also confirm that they are preoccupied with issues of
worth and value in their lives. What had been of worth in their lives
was taken away, or they no longer saw what could be of sufficient
worth in their lives, or they had not found something of sufficient
value in their lives. For instance, two bereaved parents with whom
I talked had lost their child—one of the worst things, if not the
worst, that can happen to anyone. They once had something very
valuable in their lives, but she was gone, and hence they felt that life
was meaningless. Another person was a devout Communist who
had managed to retain his loyalty to Communism notwithstanding
all the information about the many purges and gulags. But when the
Eastern Bloc was dissolved in 1989, he felt that his life had become
meaningless. Something that had been of great value to him ceased
to be so. A gifted and ambitious biologist I knew confided that
she felt her life to be meaningless because she had not succeeded,
despite many efforts, to reach the very top of her profession. What
was of extreme value to her was that recognition; when it became
clear to her that she would not achieve it, she felt her life to be meaningless. For all these people, life will feel meaningful again only if

8. Ecclesiastes 2:15–16, Revised Standard Version.

they succeed in creating or finding something else of sufficient value to take the place of some of what was lost, was proven unworthy, or was not achieved.

This is true as well of some other notions that are employed synonymously with "the meaning of life" or in conjunction with it. Some discuss self-realization or the fulfillment of one's potential as what makes life meaningful. But those who employ these notions in this context are not looking for the realization of just any part of the self, or for the fulfillment of just any type of potential; they are looking for the realization of what is of *value* in life. If we were told that a certain Mr. Smith realizes himself by acting out his pedophilic inclinations or his obsessive tendency to fill his house with towels, we would not see him as having a meaningful life, even if we accepted that he had succeeded in realizing the potential of these long-repressed and very central aspects of his psyche. This is true also of Smith's own evaluation of the degree to which his life is meaningful: he would understand his actions as making his life meaningful only if he considered them worthy; if he saw them as unworthy and regrettable behaviors, he would not think that they made his life meaningful even if he accepted that they were the realization of (problematic) parts of his psyche.[9] We distinguish, then, between self-realizations that make life meaningful, and those that do not, by the value of what is realized; the pivotal question continues to involve the value of what one does. The same is true for authenticity. There are, of course, several understandings of this difficult notion, but the example of Smith's towel collecting shows

9. Questions relating to relativism and objectivism are frequently raised in this context: Worthy to whom? Who decides what is valuable? Is what is of worth, and therefore meaningful, objectively so, or do different people just have different opinions that cannot be resolved about worth and meaningfulness? I take up this discussion of objectivity and relativism in chapter 9.

that we take authentic behavior to make life meaningful only when we take it to be of *value*. Likewise, some people wonder about the goal, aim, or purpose of life, or ask what they are living for. However, they are not looking for just any goal, but rather for a *worthy* one. They will accept that they have found a goal or purpose that makes life meaningful, or that they have something to live for, when they accept some end as of sufficiently high value. The means-end structure in itself is not sufficient for a meaningful life; just stating a purpose will not be of help if the purpose is not of sufficient value.

Some also claim that life becomes meaningful if we relate to, or are part of, something "greater" than us. They are searching for something greater because they think that what they already have is insufficiently valuable. But again, to fulfill its function, the greater has to be considered of *value*. Thomas Nagel has pointed out that just being greater, without also being of sufficient value, is unhelpful. If "we learned that we were being raised to provide food for other creatures fond of human flesh, who planned to turn us into cutlets before we got too stringy [just as many of us treat chickens today] . . . that would still not give our lives meaning."[10] I have also heard it said that if a person has nothing that she is ready to die for, her life is meaningless. I am not at all sure that I agree with this claim, but the intuition behind it is the one discussed here: meaningfulness has to do with value or importance. The saying supposes that if one is ready to die for some issues, there are things in one's life that are very important to one, and thus make one's life meaningful.

Alienation of the type that leads to feeling meaninglessness also has to do with perceived lack of worth. When one is alienated in such a way, the value of things does not, so to say, touch one. Things

10. Thomas Nagel, "The Absurd," in *Mortal Questions* (Cambridge: Cambridge University Press, 1979), 16.

are not fully present to one in several ways, including that one does not sense their worth. The boredom that has to do with meaninglessness also issues from a sharp sensation of worthlessness. This is not the type of boredom produced by repetition (say, of a piece of music or of a story) or by lack of stimuli. This is the type of boredom in which there are stimuli, but one finds them boring because they are not important: "They are all the same. Who cares." Likewise, some people mention, as related to the meaning of life, that they are looking for "the point of it all." We can know that they are looking for what is of sufficient worth in life because they accept that they know what "the point of it all" is when they consider what is proposed to them as indeed being of sufficient worth. The same is true for those who ask themselves with despair whether "this is all there is to it" or whether "this is as good as it gets." These people, too, are expressing their concern that there is nothing of sufficient value beyond what they see around them—which to them seems to be of inadequate value. They stop asking these questions and fearing that "this is all there is to it" and that "this is as good as it gets" when they engage in something that they consider to be sufficiently valuable.

What is common to all discussions of the meaning of life is concern with sufficient worth or value. Indeed, I have not yet encountered a discussion—written or oral, scholarly or personal—in which the discussion of the meaning of life does not translate well to a discussion of what is of sufficient value in life.

5

Earlier I mentioned another sense of "meaning": that which has to do with understanding or interpretation. Lack of meaning in this other sense, too, can bring about meaninglessness. But I believe

INTRODUCTION

it does so via loss of worth. In some cases this happens because understanding is something that one greatly values, and when it is undermined, one feels that one has lost something of great worth in life. In other cases undermined understanding brings about meaninglessness because some understanding or conceptualization is a necessary condition for the attribution of value and, thus, for meaningfulness. Attribution of value presupposes some worldview or categorization of how things are or should be, of what is of value and what is not. A loss in comprehension undermines the attribution of value, and then one feels meaninglessness.[11] This sometimes happens to people who move to another culture, or who move between subcultures. This is why immigrants sometimes feel a sense of meaninglessness: some of what has been taken to be of value in their previous culture is not taken to be so in the new one, and they are less certain in their evaluations of what is worthy and what is not.[12] Adolescents, who are moving between two frameworks, that of childhood and that of adulthood (one hour they behave as though they were eight years old and the next as though they were twenty-five), are also sometimes similarly disoriented, and this is

11. Cf. Cottingham, *Meaning of Life*, 21–22. It might be objected that mystical experiences pose counterexamples, since they are meaningful but ineffable or incomprehensible (see, e.g., William James, *The Varieties of Religious Experience* [New York: Modern Library, 1902], 371; Evelyn Underhill, *Mysticism: A Study in the Nature and Development of Man's Spiritual Consciousness* [New York: Noonday, 1945], 73–75). But I think that research on mystical experiences, as presented by James, Underhill, and other scholars of mysticism, as well as discussions of the topic by many mystics, should be seen as ways of interpreting or understanding the experience. We do have theories of mysticism and do know quite a few things about it, such as that it has to do with a feeling of elation; the distinction between self and world (or God) disappears or the self disappears; and the experience transcends categories. We also know, for example, that a person who says that the gastronomic pleasure of eating a steak is a mystical experience does not understand what he is talking about (or is speaking metaphorically). Thus, the meaningfulness of mystical experiences, too, presupposes some interpretation or understanding.
12. Other factors that often enhance immigrants' feeling of meaninglessness are diminishment of social status and estrangement from the new environment.

one reason why they are frequently very interested in issues of the meaning of life and sometimes feel that meaning is lacking for them.

Likewise, in the case of the Communist acquaintance mentioned above, the fall of the Eastern Bloc led to the undermining of meaning in his life in several ways. The demise of the USSR obliterated something that he took to be, with all its faults, very valuable. But it also suggested to him that the Marxist ideology he believed in was wrong. That left him in a state of incomprehension, since up until then he had used Marxist categories to conceptualize whatever happened in the world. When he lost his faith in Marxism, he also lost a way of comprehending what was around him. His ability to intellectually understand what was around him was valuable to him itself, but it was also a way of attributing positive and negative worth to many events and issues around him, and that way now collapsed; the events lost the value and identity they had had.

Some people who are bereaved of a person dear to them also feel a sense of incomprehension. They have a wrong, sometimes implicit, supposition about life: that to good or prudent people only good things happen (a preconception that is sometimes buttressed by an overly protected childhood).[13] Thus, such people sometimes cannot understand how it is that such a thing happened to them. The world, or central segments of it, becomes incomprehensible and alien since it is unclear to them how to make sense of the dire event they have experienced. This makes life meaningless in yet another way, because it diminishes another highly valued quality— its comprehensibility. If the bereaved could accept, instead of the presupposition that only good things happen to prudent and good people, the more modest notion that being prudent and good does

13. For an interesting discussion of this topic see Harold S. Kushner, *When Bad Things Happen to Good People* (New York: Schocken, 1983).

not guarantee that good things will happen to oneself, but only increases (in liberal democracies) the statistical probability that this will be the case, their life would not seem to them to have become meaningless in that further way.

Thus, although injury to one's understanding and loss of meaningfulness can come together, the critical issue remains that of worth. Note that a diminution of comprehension that is not accompanied by a decrease in value (as may happen if one is content not to comprehend too much when submerged, say, in deep love or in a mystical experience) does not obliterate meaning. On the other hand, a decrease in value that is not accompanied by a diminution in comprehension (for example, when one loses a child or a job but is totally alert to all facets of the situation and understands it well) does obliterate meaning.

The meaning of life, then, has to do primarily with value, and this is how I will treat it in the remainder of this book.[14] Complaints that there is no meaning in life are complaints that there is insufficient value in life. Questions about the meaning of life are questions about what is of sufficient worth in life. A meaningful life is one in which there is a sufficient number of aspects of sufficient value, and a meaningless life is one in which there is not a sufficient number of aspects of sufficient

14. Some authors distinguish between meaning *of* life and meaning *in* life, preferring to use the second term. See, e.g., Susan Wolf, "The Meanings of Lives," in *Introduction to Philosophy*, 4th ed., ed. John Perry, Michael Bratman, and John Martin Fischer (New York: Oxford University Press, 2007), 63; Wolf, *Meaning in Life and Why It Matters*, with commentary by John Koethe, Robert M. Adams, Nomy Arpaly, and Jonathan Haidt (Princeton, NJ: Princeton University Press, 2010); and Thaddeus Metz, *Meaning in Life: An Analytic Study* (Oxford: Oxford University Press, 2013). However, since most authors and interlocutors continue to use "the meaning of life," I often do so here as well. I sometimes use also "meaningfulness" or just plain "meaning," treating all of them here as interchangeable and moving from one to the other for the sake of stylistic variety.

value.[15] This is one reason why people who take their lives to be meaningless sometimes say that they sense emptiness, although they occasionally find it difficult to explain what their lives are empty of. When asked in discussions, they sometimes reach the view that their lives are empty of issues of sufficiently high value.

Accepting that the meaning of life is based on worth or value is an important move for several reasons. First, it facilitates thinking about the meaning of life: that notion is rather vague and burdened, while "worth" and "value" are somewhat clearer (although they, too, require further elucidation). Second, we know quite a lot about worth and value from previous work in value theory, as well as from our own experience. If meaning in life is based on the overall worth achieved in life, then we can use what we already know about values to understand the characteristics of meaningful lives. Third, accepting the relation between meaning and value allows us to draw many implications about the meaning of life. Many of these are relevant both for those who strongly believe that their life is meaningless and for the larger group of those for whom meaninglessness of life is like a buzz, always there in the background, at times softer, at times louder.

---

15. Thus, lives and aspects of lives can be valuable without being meaningful. This will happen if we do not take them to be of a sufficiently high value.

Chapter 2

Implications

1

Many important implications can be drawn from the relationship between the meaning of life and value, established in the previous chapter. One is that as with other values, so with the meaning of life, we should not expect to reach conclusions that are as precise as those in the exact sciences. Aristotle claims in his *Nicomachean Ethics* that it is a mistake, in discussions of matters of value, to expect to reach the degree of precision typical of discussions in, for example, mathematics.[1] Yet he does believe that we can make philosophical progress and reach plausible, viable conclusions even in these less precise spheres of research. Today, too, discussions of matters of value—notwithstanding their contribution and helpfulness—cannot attain the same standards of precision as in the exact sciences. This difference between value theory and the exact sciences will henceforth be presupposed.[2]

---

1. 1094b13ff; 1098a26ff.
2. See also David Schmidtz, "The Meanings of Life," in *Life, Death, and Meaning*, ed. David Benatar, 2nd ed. (Lanham, MD: Rowman and Littlefield, 2010), 94. Much of the advanced research in the exact sciences, such as modern physics, is also less precise and certain than it may at first seem, and yet in this field, too, we make progress and increase our knowledge.

2

Another implication of the relation between the meaning of life and value is that people can be mistaken about the meaning of their lives. This is plausible, since people can be wrong in their evaluations, including their self-evaluations. For example, I may believe myself to be a good parent or spouse although in fact I am not (and vice versa). You may wrongly think that your scientific work is lacking when in fact it is not (and vice versa), or that you are a terrible pianist when you are not (and vice versa). We sometimes think that people are too hard on themselves—that they in fact write better literature or philosophy than they think they do—while at other times we think that people judge themselves too highly. But if we accept that people can be wrong in the evaluation of specific aspects of their life, it would be inconsistent to believe that they cannot be wrong in their estimation of the overall worth of all of the aspects of their life. It would be surprising if the meaning of life were the exception: that is, if people could be wrong in their evaluation of various aspects of their life but not in their evaluation of the meaning of life.[3]

But this means that in this sphere, too, we cannot just rely on immediate feelings or sensations and thus just "know" whether life is meaningless or not. Here, too, we can gain much from learning and thinking about the issue, evaluating arguments, uncovering our implicit presuppositions and reconsidering them, comparing and talking with others about the issue. Impressions, even when powerful and clear, may be erroneous. The claim that we can be wrong

3. Cf. Susan Wolf, *Meaning in Life and Why It Matters*, with commentary by John Koethe, Robert M. Adams, Nomy Arpaly, and Jonathan Haidt (Princeton, NJ: Princeton University Press, 2010), 125.

about the meaning of our lives is an important presupposition in this book, since much of the discussion in it deals with what I take to be mistakes that many people make about the meaning of their lives. Not all of these mistakes are explicitly and clearly held; some relate to implicit suppositions that can profitably be brought into the open and considered.

3

Many presuppose that the degree of meaning in life is a given or a constant that they just have to learn to live with. But the relation between meaning and value suggests that the degree of meaning in life can be decreased or increased. If we can frequently increase or decrease the grade of our moral behavior, the beauty to which we are exposed, our artistic sensitivity, our knowledge, our happiness, and so many other things we value, it would be odd if we could not do so with meaning as well. The degree of meaning in life, then, is something that we can often change.

4

Understanding the relation between meaning and value directs us toward what we need to do to increase meaning in life if we feel that it is insufficient. If we want to make an insufficiently meaningful life more meaningful, we should look for what is valuable and try to enhance it in our lives. For example, if we think that artistic activity is worthy, then engaging in it is likely to increase the meaning in our life. If we think that knowledge is valuable, then learning will make our lives more meaningful.[4] (Some specific actions that we can take to identify what may improve the meaning of our lives are discussed in chapters 15 and 16.) Many people dedicate much time and energy to pursuing what they do *not* in fact see as meaningful, perhaps because they have not spent enough time identifying what is valuable to them.

5

Almost all lives should not be considered as either absolutely meaningful or absolutely meaningless; there is a continuum from the highest to the lowest degree of meaningfulness. We accept this for all other values. Beauty, happiness, morality, and love all come in degrees; houses and landscapes are not either absolutely beautiful or absolutely ugly, but are usually somewhat beautiful and somewhat ugly, somewhere on the continuum between the two extremes. People are frequently neither entirely happy nor altogether miserable, but happy to a certain extent. They are not completely interesting or completely boring, not completely moral or completely immoral, but somewhere along the continuum between the two extremes. We can expect the extent of general value in life, and hence the degree of meaning in life, to be the same. In all

---

4. I disagree here with Wittgenstein's observation that "those who have found after a long period of doubt that the sense of life became clear to them have then been unable to say what constituted that sense." Ludwig Wittgenstein, *Tractatus Logico-Philosophicus*, trans. D. F. Pears and B. F. McGuinness (London: Routledge and Kegan Paul, 1966), 6.521, 149–151. Many people I know have been able to say what increased (or diminished) meaning in their lives, and according to the analysis suggested here people may deliberately and consciously enhance valuable aspects of their lives to increase meaningfulness. Wittgenstein also suggests that "the solution to the problem of the meaning of life is seen in the vanishing of this problem," but this is not true of this problem more than of any other to which one has found a satisfying solution.

probability, almost all of us have at least *some* degree of meaning in our lives; almost none of us have absolutely none. Our lives are somewhere on the continuum between the poles of absolute meaningfulness and absolute meaninglessness.

As with many other values, we establish a threshold somewhere on this continuum and take meaning in our life to either fall below that threshold or be situated above it (and thus our life to be either meaningless or meaningful, respectively). But it is important to remember that even when we consider the degree of meaning in our lives to fall below the threshold and thus our lives to be meaningless, we are usually still somewhere on the continuum: our lives have an insufficient degree of meaning, rather than none at all. Remembering this is important, for several reasons. First, if we acknowledge that although we take it to be below the threshold of what would be sufficient for having a meaningful life, the degree of meaning in our life is not zero but, say, 20 or 80 percent, we have a truer representation of reality. Second, if we wrongly take our life to be absolutely meaningless, we are likely to feel more distressed than if we remember that our life is somewhat meaningful, even if insufficiently so. It allows us to see that even if our situation is not as good as we want it to be, we do have some meaning in our life rather than none at all, which is good news. Third, if we decide that we want to improve things, recognizing that we have some degree of meaning rather than none at all allows us to see that there is less work to be done; there is already something to begin with and build upon rather than start from scratch. Fourth, we can learn, from what meaning we do have in our life, what works for us and what does not, what our weaknesses and strengths are, and thus which directions we should best follow. Finally, remembering that we are on a continuum, and that the desired quality is thus not completely absent, gives us more of a chance to ask ourselves whether we have indeed drawn the demarcation line in the right place. Is what we have really insufficient, or is it only less than we would have wished it to be, or less than what some other people have? This last issue is discussed in some detail in the next two chapters, which deal with perfectionism, but it also reverberates in many other chapters in the rest of this book.

6

Some hold that if we change from time to time what is meaningful to us, our lives are not really meaningful. But when it comes to other values, we do not accept this view: for example, we do not believe that if something genuinely interests us it will always do so. Some issues interest us for part of our lives, and then we find some other issues that arrest our attention. We do not suppose, when this happens, that the former issues were not really interesting or that previously we were not truly interested in them. Likewise, if a friendship dries up over time, or if, unfortunately, a friend passes away, we can frequently find other friendships, after some time has passed, that can also be rich, deep, and satisfying. This does not mean that the former friendship, the present one, or both were shallow or untrue (nor does it mean that we will stop missing our late friend). Of course, too frequent changes in what one values indicate a lack of seriousness or some other problem: if one changes what gives meaning to one's life every other day, it may well be that one's involvement is superficial. But we would not say so about people who change their fields of interest or friends after lengthier stretches of time. A person who, say, was engaged in philanthropic work in a third-world country from the ages of twenty to thirty, focused on good parenting from thirty to fifty, wrote good literature from fifty to sixty-five, and ultimately spent years in meditation in a monastery would not seem to have led a meaningless life.

It is important to remember this point, especially for people who have lost what gave meaning to their lives. Unfortunately, things that are very meaningful to us are sometimes destroyed. The meaningful thing may be a child (losing a child is probably the most painful and terrible loss), a career that has ended, or a capability that is lost. Yet, notwithstanding our strong initial feelings, we are usually able to find meaning in other things, as time goes by. The first hours, months, or years are usually the most difficult. This is because we are then in an in-between period, when what was valuable is no longer present and something new of value has not yet been found or created. But this in-between period need not continue forever. If we can succeed in remembering that we are going through a crisis— that is, a temporary low in which we have to persevere and struggle till things become better again (even if differently than they were before)—we can frequently regain or recreate meaning. Of course, when one is within the crisis, it is difficult to identify it as such, that is, as a difficult period that will pass or be overcome. It is easy, in the crisis, to lose a sense of proportion and context, imagining that in the future things will always continue to be the way that they are during the crisis.

Some concede that what gives meaning to life can occasionally change, yet believe that *at each point in time* there must be only one thing that gives life meaning. But we do not regularly think that it is problematic to value various issues at the same time. For example, we do not think that there is anything wrong in taking aesthetic pleasure in many different paintings, in a variety of artistic styles, or in several different artistic fields (for example, both visual art and music). Nor do we think that there is anything inappropriate in performing various types of volunteer work (addressing various moral concerns, or benefiting different people), or in finding pleasure and happiness in different activities or hobbies. Thus, I may have a meaningful life thanks to my family life, my career, my hobby, my philanthropic activity, and my spiritual work at the same period of time. Of course, we would not want to spread ourselves too thin over too many aspects of life, but that is not the same thing as saying that we should focus only on one.[5]

Engaging with several valued relationships and activities in a number of spheres of meaning at the same time can even be advantageous. Note that we sometimes value those who can appreciate or create several types of art, or who care about a wider range of moral issues, more than those who limit themselves to only one. Moreover, since most people find many things worthy and, thus, meaningful in their lives, it is unhelpful to focus on one source of meaning only, as this would involve a denial of much that is potentially of worth to us and thus a denial of many aspects of meaning in our lives. A single aspect of life is also almost certain to become tiresome after some time. Finally, engaging with several spheres of meaning is helpful in cases in which one of them is lost or destroyed; it is easier to compensate for this loss if one already has other resources, since one has thus not lost everything and may rely on and enhance existing resources rather than start from scratch.

---

5. This is what makes the question about "the point of it all" problematic: it suggests to some people that there is *one* point that we should be looking for, while for many people there are, or should be, several points. This is also why it is more accurate to talk of (plural) meanings of, or in, life rather than of the (one) meaning of, or in, life. I am in disagreement here with Viktor Frankl's assertion that "to each question there is one answer—the right one. There is only one meaning to each situation, and this is its true meaning" (*The Will to Meaning* [London: Souvenir, 1971], 61).

7

It is untrue that if something is meaningful in our life, we would want
to devote all our time to it, so that if we do not want to engage with
only that particular thing, it cannot be seen as really constituting
the meaning of our life. For almost everyone, such an expectation is
unrealistic: there are many activities and experiences that we value
very much yet do not want to do or go through *all* the time. There
seems to be a mechanism in the human psyche that holds us back
from doing or experiencing the same thing incessantly, for a long
period of time, no matter how good it is. We must alternate, lest we
get bored and even suffer sharply. The loveliest and deepest music,
if listened to incessantly, will become unbearable not because it is
unworthy (now that we have listened to it over and over, we realize
that it is of poor quality), but merely because of the continuous repetition. One can listen to other pieces of music, or read a book, and
then return to the former piece to enjoy its beauty and depth again,
sometimes even more than before. Likewise, people who love their
baby very strongly and deeply will nevertheless feel, after constantly
being with the baby over a certain period of time, that they also want
to read a book, listen to music, or spend time alone or with friends
rather than continuing to interact lovingly with the baby. This does
not testify to a lack of love but, rather, to the mechanism mentioned
above; after a break, they continue to deeply enjoy being with the
baby.[6] This is also the case for lovers who—even when their love
is very strong—need to spend time not only with each other but
also alone, or in a conversation with friends, or with a book. It is

6. I have met mothers who felt unnecessary guilt for their occasional need to do something
other than interact with their baby, wrongly taking this need to show that there was something wrong with their mothering or with their love for their newborn.

similarly wrong to infer from our reluctance to engage ceaselessly with what is meaningful that it is not really meaningful.

8

We should not expect the degree of meaning in our lives to remain constant. Some believe that if a life is indeed meaningful, there should be no fluctuations in the degree of its meaning; in this view, if ups and downs occur (as they almost invariably must, to some degree), life is not really meaningful. This is a conception of meaning that looks at it as if it were a formal certificate; once I have earned my MD, or obtained citizenship in a certain country, I am always a doctor or a citizen: that will not change from day to day. But maintaining meaning is different from obtaining a formal title. We do not enjoy art or music to the same degree every day. The intensity of the love we feel toward loved ones, even when the love is strong and good, increases and decreases to some extent during the week. The same is true about what we find interesting, our enjoyment of and commitment to helping others, and our religious zeal, perhaps even more so the more genuinely religious we are. Since, as living creatures, we are dynamic and changing, our relationship to almost everything of value in our life ebbs and flows to a degree, so that there must be some fluctuations as we go along. It would be surprising if this were not also true of what we take to be meaningful.

9

Meaning does not solve all of life's problems. Some people suppose that if they suffer from any difficulties, their lives are not really meaningful. However, one can attain a high degree of value in some areas but not in others, thus suffering tribulations in those other aspects of life. One may, for example, enjoy a high degree of knowledge and moral stature while suffering from financial or health problems. Viktor Frankl, mentioned in chapter 1, discusses how some concentration camp prisoners managed to maintain the meaning of their lives in spite of the radically harsh conditions they experienced in the camps. However, their lives in the camps were not, of course, problem-free but full of horror. One can enjoy a meaningful life but still be bothered with problems in some, even many, aspects of one's life.

10

It is also incorrect that uniqueness in what one does is necessary for leading a meaningful life.[7] True, in some spheres of value uniqueness is important. For example, in scientific research and in creative writing, composing, painting, and so on it is important to be original, and this requires one to create something new, that is, different from what already exists. In such cases meaning does indeed have to do with uniqueness. But much of what we find of value does not have to do with uniqueness. For example, the value of the good relationship between a parent and a baby does not have to do with uniqueness, originality, or the difference of each such relationship from others, but rather with the closeness, intimacy, and love in the relationship. Knowing that other parents experience warmth or intimacy quite

7. I disagree here with Richard Taylor, who associates meaningfulness with what he calls "creative power," and holds that "to the extent that it is shared, such that what it brings forth is also brought forth by others, then it is not . . . creative power." Richard Taylor, "Time and Life's Meaning," *Review of Metaphysics* 40 (1987): 682.

similar to one's own does not decrease the value one finds in one's relationship. The same is true of other types of love: what is valuable in my love for my wife is not its difference from all other loves in all other couples; indeed, what is good and valuable in our love is probably quite similar, in its main details, to what is good and valuable in the love that other lucky couples experience. Likewise, the worth that we find in a moral activity, such as feeding the hungry, is not in the uniqueness of feeding this or that hungry person rather than another, or in any other unique details of the interaction. It has to do with relieving hunger or saving a life, and the fact that many similar acts have been, are, and will be done does not make it less valuable. The same is true of the worth found in understanding or in experiencing beauty. It does not have to do with the difference between what one understood or experienced and what others did.

Of course, it is important not merely to imitate others or act in a mechanical and alienated way. But I can act in an authentic, personal way, engaging in what is genuinely important to me, even if others act in similar ways. The value of what I do is no less if, in acting deliberately and authentically, I am also acting in ways that others commonly choose. Just as trying to be like everyone else can obstruct the pursuit of what is most meaningful, so can trying to be different from everyone else. We would do better to pursue what is meaningful rather than what is conventional *or* what is unconventional; conventionality and unconventionality are equally inadequate indicators of meaning.

11

The relation between worth and meaning allows us to see that several presuppositions about the meaning of life that lead some people mistakenly to believe that their lives are meaningless are incorrect. Readers may also have noted one of the characteristics of this discussion: it takes the meaning of life off its pedestal. Meaning is not only something up there in the sky, holy and exalted, the secular analogue of a mystical experience. One need not discuss it with a pounding heart, a choked-up throat, or a quivering hand. The meaning of life is just one more value, even if it is a supervening or a second-order value (and, of course, an important one). Most of what is true of other values is true also of it. Accordingly, it is a much more normal, mundane phenomenon than it may at first seem. Many people treat the meaningful life (and their own lives) in an overly dramatic way. But a life can be meaningful even without the bathos that sometimes accompanies thoughts and decisions about it. Nor is meaning more mysterious than other notions related to value. They are all, of course, far from being absolutely clear, and all require more philosophical work and reflection. But meaning is not special among them. Indeed, one of the aims of this book is to oppose the view that there must be something mysterious in meaning. The notion of meaning is often overromanticized, to the disadvantage of those who consider it. Meaning is a normal aspect of life.

Chapter 3

Against Perfectionism

1

Of all the presuppositions that bring people to believe that their lives are meaningless, the most common is probably the perfectionist presupposition.[1] According to this presupposition, meaningful lives must include some perfection or excellence or some rare and difficult achievements,[2] and lives that do not show this characteristic cannot be seen as meaningful. Meaningful lives, then, must transcend the common and the mundane.

1. My use of "perfectionist," "perfectionism," etc. differs from that of Thomas Hurka, George Sher, Steven Wall, and others in moral and political philosophy who employ these terms to refer to theories that present objective understandings of the good life defined in terms of human nature. Perfectionist theories in their sense of the term need not be perfectionist in the sense used here, and vice versa. See Thomas Hurka, *Perfectionism* (New York: Oxford University Press, 1993); George Sher, *Beyond Neutrality: Perfectionism and Politics* (Cambridge: Cambridge University Press, 1997); Steven Wall, *Liberalism, Perfectionism and Restraint* (Cambridge: Cambridge University Press, 1998).
2. Perfection or excellence need not appear together with rareness and difficulty. Perfect things can be common and easy to obtain. Likewise, things that are rare and difficult to obtain need not be perfect or excellent. However, since most people who feel that life is insufficiently meaningful group the notions together, holding that meaningful lives must show achievements that are both perfect or excellent *and* rare or difficult to obtain, and since most arguments regarding these notions are similar, I treat them here together as part of "the perfectionist supposition." Some of what I write ahead relates only to perfection and excellence or only to rareness and difficulty, but most of it relates to both.

A surprisingly large number of philosophers who write on the topic of the meaning of life endorse the perfectionist presupposition. To the extent that Nietzsche should be interpreted as calling for meaningful lives, he too presents ideals that are very difficult, or almost impossible, to achieve. Nietzsche distinguishes sharply between, on the one hand, his ideal Overman (and the very few "higher men" or "powerful human beings" leading to this ideal) and, on the other hand, all other human beings.[3] Becoming an Overman or one of the few "powerful" is extremely difficult and rare, and Nietzsche has deep contempt for those people he sees as "merely the experimental material, the tremendous surplus of failures: a field of ruins" or means for an ideal future.[4] Even people we usually see as geniuses are insufficient for him.[5] Camus takes our life to be absurd because we cannot attain perfect knowledge that would unify everything under one principle and recognize the eternal relations between things. According to Camus, anything less than that arouses a sense of absurdity.[6] But this suggests that we cannot have a nonabsurd life if we do not achieve perfect knowledge, close to

3. Friedrich Nietzsche, *The Will to Power*, trans. Walter Kaufmann and R. J. Hollingdale (New York: Vintage, 1968), §§ 859, 964, pp. 458, 506; *Thus Spoke Zarathustra*, trans. Adrian Del Caro (Cambridge: Cambridge University Press, 2006), 26, 34, 59, 232.

4. *The Will to Power*, § 713, p. 380.

5. Friedrich Nietzsche, *Daybreak*, trans. R. J. Hollingdale (Cambridge: Cambridge University Press, 1997), § 548, p. 220. Note, however, that although Nietzsche presents here a far-fetched ideal, elsewhere he points out that he is suspicious of ideals and of the rejection of reality as it is (*The Will to Power*, § 80, p. 50; *Ecce Homo*, in *"The Anti-Christ", "Ecce Homo", "Twilight of the Idols", and Other Writings*, ed. Aaron Ridley and Judith Norman, trans. Judith Norman [Cambridge: Cambridge University Press, 2005], 71, 86). Perhaps the solution to this inconsistency is that in Nietzsche's view *his* ideal, unlike those put forward by others, is not actually an ideal but simply a deeper grasp of reality.

6. Albert Camus, *The Myth of Sisyphus*, in *"The Myth of Sisyphus" and Other Essays*, trans. Justin O'Brien (New York: Vintage, 1991), 17–22. In Camus's terminology there is a difference between absurdity and meaninglessness, but I take much of what he says about the absurd to hold for meaninglessness as well, and I do not distinguish between the two concepts here or in the rest of this book.

that which has traditionally been attributed only to God. Likewise, Oswald Hanfling writes that since our lives lack permanence, they seem insignificant from a long-term perspective, and Robert Nozick claims that "a significant life is, in some sense, permanent; it makes a permanent difference to the world—it leaves traces."[7]

Some other writers, without stating or implying that only superhuman lives can be meaningful, still argue that in order to be meaningful, lives must show difficult or exceptional achievements. Plato cites (probably in agreement) in the final sentence of his *Greater Hippias* the Greek saying "All that is beautiful is difficult," and Spinoza, perhaps influenced by him, concludes his *Ethics* with "But all things excellent are as difficult as they are rare."[8] Berit Brogaard and Barry Smith claim that a meaningful life must consist in realizing ambitious and difficult plans.[9] Laurence James argues that conferring meaning on a life requires an achievement that would be difficult both for the average person and for the agent in question.[10] Thus, for James, if Mozart were to perform a task that is difficult for the average person, but not difficult for him (say, composing a very

---

7. Oswald Hanfling, *The Quest for Meaning* (New York: Blackwell, 1988), 24; Robert Nozick, *Philosophical Explanations* (Cambridge, MA: Belknap Press of Harvard University Press, 1981), 582; see also 594–595. Similar claims are made by William Lane Craig, "The Absurdity of Life without God," in *The Meaning of Life*, ed. E. D. Klemke, 2nd ed. (New York: Oxford University Press, 2000), 42; and Thomas V. Morris, *Making Sense of It All* (Grand Rapids, MI: Eerdmans, 1992), 25–27. Morris cites Leszek Kolakowski and Tennyson as making similar claims.

8. Plato, *Greater Hippias* 304e, in *Greater Hippias*, trans. Benjamin Jowett, in *The Collected Dialogues of Plato*, ed. Edith Hamilton and Huntington Cairns (Princeton, NJ: Princeton University Press, 1961), 1559; Baruch Spinoza, *Ethics*, in *The Collected Works of Spinoza*, ed. and trans. Edwin M. Curley, vol. 1 (Princeton, NJ: Princeton University Press, 1985), 617.

9. Berit Brogaard and Barry Smith, "On Luck, Responsibility and the Meaning of Life," *Philosophical Papers* 34, no. 3 (2005): 446.

10. Laurence James, "Achievement and the Meaningfulness of Life," *Philosophical Papers* 34, no. 3 (2005): 438–439. James does not think that achievements are the *only* things that can make life meaningful, but he believes that if they do make life meaningful, they have to be difficult to achieve.

beautiful piece of music), this would not make his life meaningful. Richard Taylor claims that a meaningful life must show powers that are not common and bring forth what no one else has.[11] And E. J. Bond suggests that what makes our life meaningful is the achievement of excellence.[12]

It is not only philosophers who find the perfectionist supposition to be intuitive. Most people who have told me that they found their life meaningless held one version or another of the perfectionist supposition. Many of them mention, among other issues, that they are not absolutely authentic, absolutely immune to peer pressure, absolutely truthful, absolutely unaffected by egotistic motivations, or absolutely courageous. Others mention their own deaths, the eventual destruction of the cosmos, their contingency, or their inability to measure up to achievements such as those of Churchill, Mother Teresa, Einstein, or Leonardo.

2

I suggested in chapter 2 that we should be aware of the continuum between the poles of complete meaningfulness and complete meaninglessness, even if we impose a demarcation line somewhere on that continuum. In imposing a demarcation line, we can draw it very close to the pole of complete absence of meaning (so that almost everything, except that which is almost totally meaningless, would be considered meaningful), or very close to the pole of absolute

11. Richard Taylor, "Time and Life's Meaning," *Review of Metaphysics* 40 (1987): 684, 682. However, Taylor seems to contradict himself, as he also claims that he is not praising "something rare, the possession of only a few," but rather a "capacity . . . sometimes found in quite mundane things" (683). It is unclear to me how this tension in his paper can be resolved.
12. E. J. Bond, *Reason and Value* (Cambridge: Cambridge University Press, 1983), 159–161.

meaning (so that everything, except that which is almost totally meaningful, would be considered meaningless), or somewhere in the middle. The perfectionist inclination in many people leads them to draw the line very close to the pole of absolute meaning, so that if life is not absolutely or almost absolutely meaningful, it is taken to be meaningless. Similarly, when they examine whether their lives show characteristics that can make them meaningful, such as moral behavior, good parenting, authenticity, courage, knowledge, or sensitivity to beauty, they again draw the line very close to the pole of absolute positive value, so that, for example, a life that is not absolutely or almost absolutely moral is not taken to be sufficiently moral and, thus, sufficiently meaningful.

Note that just like perfectionists, so also many nonperfectionists endorse ideals, believe that the ideal is better than the nonideal, would have liked to attain the ideal, try to do so, and are glad if ideals are achieved or if there is progress toward them. These characteristics are not what distinguishes perfectionists from nonperfectionists. What marks perfectionists is that they fail to see the worth that inheres also in the nonperfect; they despise and reject it. Both perfectionist and many nonperfectionist students think that receiving a grade of 100 percent on an exam is better than receiving any other grade, and both would be glad to receive it. But the perfectionists are those who, when they receive a 98, feel that they failed. For them, this 98 is like a zero. They do not want it; they fail to see the worth in receiving such a grade. Perfectionists believe that if our city is not the most beautiful in the world, it is disgustingly ugly; that if one is not Einstein one is a fool; and that if a person does not write as Shakespeare did, she had better just give up writing altogether. Noticing that our city is not the most beautiful in the world, criticizing what is wrong with it, wishing to improve it, and trying to do so does not make one a perfectionist. But we are perfectionists if, after noticing that our city is not the most beautiful in the world, we become blind to the beauty and value that it does have.

Thus, perfectionists are so busy with the search for the perfect that they neglect to see and find satisfaction in the good. And since it is rare, and sometimes impossible, to reach the perfect, perfectionists, who do not want to have anything to do with the good that is less than perfect, find satisfaction in nothing, continuing their desperate quest for the perfect. Some perfectionists even hate the good for being imperfect and want to destroy it. They reject the imperfect in their lives with the same detestation with which others reject crime, perhaps because they see the less than perfect as a crime.

3

I will argue here, however, that many considerations count against perfectionist views of the meaning of life. The first two considerations have to do with consistency. One is that most people reject perfectionism in other spheres of life. Most of us do not accept that if the city we live in is not the most beautiful city in the world, it is repulsive and not worth living in; or that we are ignorant if we do not know everything about everything; that we are villains if we are not Mother Teresa; that we are failures if we are not the very best in class; or that our food is tasteless unless it is prepared in the best French restaurant in town.[13] But if we reject the perfectionist move in other spheres of value, we should do so, under pain of inconsistency, also in the sphere of meaning of life. We should, for example, reject Craig's claim that if there is no God

13. For a similar claim see Kurt Baier, "The Meaning of Life," in Klemke, *Meaning of Life*, 127–128.

and no immortality, "It means that life itself is absurd. It means that the life we have is without ultimate significance."[14] But having no *ultimate* significance and having no significance at all ("absurd" in Craig's terms) are very different. A life can be significant even when it is not ultimately so.[15] Of course, this consideration is relevant only for people who are perfectionist about meaning in life but nonperfectionist in other spheres; if they are also perfectionists in other spheres, no inconsistency arises. However, the great majority of people are nonperfectionists, and thus endorsing perfectionism only when it comes to the meaning of life does involve inconsistency for them.

A second consideration is that many who are perfectionists about meaning in their lives are guilty of upholding double standards and discrimination, but because they are their own victims, do not realize that this is the case. When thinking about double standards and discrimination, we usually consider cases in which people discriminate and employ double standards against others and in their own favor. But many perfectionists discriminate against *themselves*, judging their own lives more harshly, or by higher standards, than they do the lives of others. They take their own lives to be meaningless because they are not Einsteins or Picassos but do not see the lives of their children, parents, siblings, or friends as meaningless, although those people are not Picassos or Einsteins either. They think that because in a thousand years no one will remember them, it does not matter if they live or die. But when they hear that their child, or another child, might be murdered, they feel that a terrible thing is

14. Craig, "Absurdity of Life," 41–42.
15. Likewise, Schopenhauer writes "Were it [the human organism] of any value in itself, anything unconditioned and absolute, it could not thus end in mere nothing," suggesting that only what is unconditioned and absolute can be of any value. Arthur Schopenhauer, *Complete Essays of Schopenhauer*, trans. T. Bailey Saunders, 7 books in 1 Vol. (New York: Wiley, 1942), 5:24.

about to happen and that something of great value will be lost (and are ready to resort to considerable effort in order to prevent it from happening) although in a thousand years no one will remember that child either. They think that their life is meaningless because it did not achieve perfection, but do not judge others' lives in the same way. However, if it is wrong to discriminate against people, it is also wrong to discriminate against ourselves, even if *we* are doing it. We too are people. If we believe that there is significant worth in others, it is odd that we should not consider the same to be true of ourselves. As with the previous consideration, of course, this one too is relevant only to those who think that their lives, but not the lives of others, are meaningless because imperfect.

4

A third consideration is that perfectionist demands are implausible. In his *Phaedo*, Plato criticizes people who have exaggerated, implausible expectations of their friends.[16] Such people, he writes, are continuously disappointed and end up hating their friends. Because their lofty expectations are frustrated—as indeed they must be—those who hold these implausible expectations often become misanthropes. Plato's description seems to me very perceptive. The idealization of people, or of humanity at large, can breed hatred of people and of humanity, since implausible expectations are bound to be disappointed, bringing about frustration and anger. The reader, too, may know some people who love humanity very much yet hate all the human beings around them (and not only around them) because they are so disappointing. But

16. *Phaedo* 89d–90a.

this move can also be directed inward. Some people adopt it not toward other people but toward themselves, demanding implausible achievements from themselves and hating themselves very much for not attaining them.

Usually, we refrain from criticism based on implausible expectations.[17] When someone admires a certain dog, we do not point out in response that it cannot drive, since it is implausible to expect a dog to drive. We do not disapprove of a chair because it cannot be used to boil water for a nice cup of tea, nor of a kettle because it is inconvenient to sit on. It is unreasonable to have such expectations. It would be similarly odd to criticize someone for not being able to walk through walls or fly like Superman. But Camus, Kolakowski, and the other authors I have mentioned in section 1 criticize people, including themselves, for being inferior to God Almighty, who knows everything and lives forever. It is indeed no wonder that when people measure themselves or others by standards appropriate only to God, they fail, since they are measuring people by standards that are not appropriate for people. They set the rules of the game in a way that ensures that they will lose, and then, when they do indeed lose, they experience despair. It is also implausible, for almost all people, to demand of themselves that they be a Michelangelo, a Mozart, or an Einstein. It is no coincidence that such people are so rare. There have only been a few dozen such people in the entire history of humanity, and the probability that any one of us would turn out to be one of them is very slim. This consideration against perfectionism as regards the meaning of life—that perfectionist demands are implausible—also points to an inconsistency, since

---

17. See Brooke Alan Trisel, "Futility and the Meaning of Life Debate," *Sorites* 14 (2002): 76; Robert Audi, "Intrinsic Value and Meaningful Life," *Philosophical Papers* 34, no. 3 (2005): 346.

many of those who endorse perfectionism as regards the meaning of life regularly reject mythical or fairy-tale thinking and have very realistic expectations in all other spheres of their lives.

5

Fourth, holding perfectionist standards when evaluating the meaning of life frequently involves a great deal of cruelty. It might sound wrong to say this about people who treat the meaning of their lives in a perfectionist manner, since many of them are extremely benevolent and forgiving toward others. But cruelty is frequently object-specific: one can be cruel to one's children but not to one's employees, or vice versa; one can even be cruel to a specific child or employee but not to another. By the same token, many people who see their lives as meaningless are compassionate toward the world yet very cruel, even vicious, toward themselves, constantly flogging themselves emotionally for not having the qualities of a Leonardo, a Shakespeare, a Kant, or even of God. We could identify such cruelty if we heard them talking that way to others: "You are not as wise as Aristotle, hence you are an idiot, and I despise you"; "Since you are not as talented as Mozart, you are just one big zero"; "Because you do not write like Shakespeare, what you write is rubbish." But for some reason, such cruel (and unjust) utterances are allowed to pass as acceptable when people direct them at themselves.[18]

Cruelty is one of the worst evils one can engage in. It is appalling and base. It is unacceptable and should be curbed whenever it arises. Those who find themselves acting cruelly should stop. It is

---

18. Thus, the issue of inconsistency comes up here as well. In this particular discussion, however, I focus on the wrongfulness of cruelty.

morally forbidden to be cruel to any person or animal, and since one, too, is a person, it is equally forbidden to be cruel to oneself. When we are cruel to ourselves, we are oftentimes being cruel to a defenseless creature, as most people do not know how to defend themselves from this self-inflicted abuse. We do not hear any complaints, of course, since the objects of this cruelty just continue to bear the thrashing silently, sometimes even believing they deserve to be humiliated and oppressed. But this failure to complain does not make the cruelty legitimate.

One of the aspects of Kant's moral philosophy that I find most impressive is his bringing to the forefront the notion that we have duties not only toward others but also toward ourselves. These are indeed *duties*, not recommendations or suggestions; it is a moral sin and failure for one to neglect duties toward oneself. One might disagree with some of the examples of duties Kant discusses, but the notion itself is of great importance. There are some things that one is not allowed to do to oneself, and others that one has an obligation to do for oneself. Although we usually do not complain about vile behaviors when people direct them toward themselves, they are nonetheless very harmful and should not be tolerated. If I were asked to present the gist of this book in only one sentence, it would be: "Do not be cruel to yourself."

6

A fifth consideration against the perfectionist attitude toward the meaning of life is that, in some cases, the position that one's life is meaningless unless it shows absolute, or at least superlative and exceptional, qualities is tacitly based on conceited and narcissistic attitudes. This too may sound wrong, since many people who think that their lives are meaningless despise themselves, which is the very opposite of conceit and narcissism; the claim that I have just made here seems to suggest that people who believe their lives to be worthless are conceited. But rejecting oneself because one is not God or Einstein can in fact issue from great conceit. The process that leads to this self-loathing has to do with the adoption of very high, even impossible standards for oneself, frequently in conjunction with the attitude that those others, the riffraff or hoi polloi, may continue on with *their* inferior standards, if they so wish, but *I* endorse mine.

Thus, although the perfectionist position may seem very meek, its deeper nature is frequently immersed in conceit. Similarly, some people's perfectionist standards for meaning in life result from a narcissistic or egotistic urge to adore and aggrandize themselves. They want to feel that they, and therefore their lives, are ideal. Their frustration in failing to attain some degree of meaning frequently has to do with the simple aggravation of failing to see themselves as superior and of being unable to worship themselves.[19] Indeed, an important question one should consider is whether one can appreciate and respect oneself without adoring or worshipping oneself.

---

19. It is a curious phenomenon that some people who feel that their life is meaningless stop feeling so when their life is endangered or when they are in pain, in prison, or under various types of stress. This sounds odd, as one would imagine that worsening the quality of life would enhance, rather than decrease, the feeling that life is meaningless. There are several possible explanations for this fact. One might refer to an automatic psychological, perhaps even instinctual, reaction of self-preservation that is strong enough to take over one's mind, perhaps even gearing one psychologically toward a constructive mood, so that one does not think at all about problems of the meaninglessness of life, but only of survival. But another explanation is that when people's lives are endangered, they are in prison, etc., they no longer feel that they are at fault for not having attained certain achievements; instead, they feel that it is external, objective conditions that are keeping them from attaining achievements, and thus not their own fault, so that their smugness and narcissism can be preserved.

7

My sixth consideration against perfectionism about meaning in life is that it is often based on hypercompetitiveness. It bears mentioning that, in the right context and to the right degree, competitiveness is legitimate and can be beneficial and fun. But it is easy to take it too far. Some perfectionists cannot settle for anything that is less than perfect since they interpret each situation in terms of a competition, and the thought that some people may win against them in some imagined or real competition is too difficult for them to bear. Moreover, because they are hypercompetitive and interpret situations only in competitive terms, once they do not see themselves as winning the real or imagined competition, they feel they have nothing to continue to live for. Brooke Alan Trisel presents the analogy of competitive long-distance running.[20] If we see life as nothing but participation in that harsh race, where the only thing that matters is to win the gold, silver, or bronze medal, then once others have won those prizes and it is clear that we will not win a medal, there indeed is no longer any point in continuing to run. Some of those interested only in the gold, silver, or bronze medals will go on running because it is not considered polite or good form to stop running; but they will see their running as pointless.

Others, however, run not only to compete for the gold, silver, or bronze medals; they run because there is something to be proved by coming in seventh, by the time that they achieve, by racking up a certain number of races they have been in, and other reasons. Yet others run not only to compete; they also, or only, run every morning in the park because it is fun, it gives them a good feeling for the whole day, the park is beautiful in the morning, and running is healthy. The latter,

20. Trisel, "Futility," 71.

too, frequently make efforts to run well and often try to improve their running to make it better and healthier. One way of looking at what has been presented in this chapter is as a suggestion for people to consider running not (or not only) for the gold, silver, or bronze medals, or to consider not running (only) in races but (also) in the park.

Hypercompetitiveness numbs perfectionists to the great value of what is not competed for. They are insensitive to what might be called *noncompetitive value*, such as the value of jogging for fun in a park. To understand the distinction between competitive and noncompetitive value, consider the following example. I value philosophy. I like thinking about philosophical issues and enjoy reading and talking philosophy with friends and colleagues. Having worked in philosophy for some years, I can tell myself that I know philosophy better than most people in my hometown. When I stroll along one of its streets, I can tell myself that it is likely that I know more philosophy than the average person walking along that street at that time, even perhaps more than any other person walking along that street at that time. Now suppose, as a thought experiment, that a hand came down from heaven and touched the foreheads of everyone so that they all knew as much philosophy as I do. The extent to which I would now value philosophy less is the extent to which philosophy has competitive value for me. This is the extent to which I find philosophy to be of worth because I can tell myself, perhaps secretly or even subconsciously, things like "Ha! *I* know so much philosophy— and *others* don't!" The extent to which I continue to value philosophy under these new circumstances is the extent to which the value of philosophy for me is noncompetitive rather than competitive.[21]

---

21. Under the new circumstances the noncompetitive value of philosophy should even *increase* for me since I will have many more potential partners for discussion, who are likely to have many new good and interesting ideas. And in a version of this thought experiment in which

Noncompetitive value is the value something has when it is not considered in a competitive setting, that is, a setting in which we compete against each other and feel that we are winning or losing.[22] Accordingly, noncompetitive value may well also be found in what is common and easy to achieve. Competitive value, on the other hand, must be at least somewhat rare and difficult to achieve. If everyone could achieve it, no competition could be had; for a competition to take place, many must try to achieve something that only *some* can attain. (The others have to fail.) In most cases, the rarer and more difficult to achieve something is (when demand is stable), the higher is its competitive value. Likewise, in open market settings (which are, of course, also competitive), low supply of a product, when demand is stable, increases its price.

Competitive and noncompetitive value may, but do not have to, coincide. Gold, for example, has a low noncompetitive value; it is not a very useful metal in itself. It is its rareness, and thus the ability of some people to feel that they own it *while others do not*—they have won in the competition for gold—that gives gold its competitive value, and makes it valuable to its owners (and also to the others, who do not own it but are still in the competition and would like to own it), and thus also makes it expensive. Similarly, rubies and diamonds have a low noncompetitive value. They are not all that beautiful, certainly not more so than many crystals or other

the heavenly hand makes everyone a *better* philosopher than I am, the competitive worth of philosophy for me might decline even further, but the noncompetitive worth will rise further, since there will be so many better philosophers around for me to explore interesting ideas with and learn from.

22. My distinction between competitive and noncompetitive value is influenced by, yet differs from, Adam Smith's distinction in *Wealth of Nations* (I.iv.13) between "value in exchange" and "value in use." See Adam Smith, *An Inquiry into the Nature and Causes of the Wealth of Nations*, ed. R. H. Campbell, A. S. Skinner, and W. B. Todd (Oxford: Clarendon, 1976), 1:44–45.

imitations. Their competitive or market value, as that of gold, has to do with rareness.

Likewise, for humans, running very, very fast, which has a high competitive value in the Olympics, has a low noncompetitive value; it is not very useful in life except for those who need to run after buses about to leave the station or to escape from animals about to eat them. In fact, if medical claims about the damage that too-intensive training can cause to the body are correct, very fast running even has a negative noncompetitive value. Driving very fast to prove to others or oneself that one is a faster driver is another example of an act that has a competitive value but no, or even a negative, noncompetitive value. We could list many more things that have a high competitive value but a low noncompetitive one.

Some things, many of them easy to achieve or common, have a high noncompetitive value but a low competitive value. Healthy, nourishing foods are frequently not those that are the most expensive or hardest to come by. The best friends are frequently not those who are different from all the others, the most difficult to befriend, or those the relationship with whom is the most challenging and torturous. The most beautiful music need not be that which is most difficult to remember or to obtain as a recording. As was already noted, the value in the warm and supportive interaction between a parent and a child does not have to do with its rareness; if one has many such interactions, and if other people, too, have many such interactions, so much the better. The same is true of intellectual comprehension, deep aesthetic experiences, religious encounters, mystical insights, and courage in face of pain and difficulty. High noncompetitive value *may* be rare and difficult to achieve, but does not have to be so. Rareness and difficulty to achieve, then, are not good indicators of noncompetitive value, and we should not prefer what is difficult and rare just because it is so. Indeed, some of the things that are of the most noncompetitive worth in life are, for many people, rather easy to have. These are hearing music, appreciating natural and human-made beauty, enjoying oneself, talking with friends, having a good relationship with one's children, family, or community, and not being a nuisance to others and to oneself but, on the contrary, being a positive force in the lives of others and in one's own life. Unfortunately, some people hardly notice noncompetitive or noneconomic value.[23] Paradoxically, they are so caught up in the competitive paradigm that they appreciate the value in what is widespread and easy to achieve only when it becomes rare or endangered and, thus, unavailable to them.

Perfectionists, who are frequently hypercompetitive, tend to generalize from what is true of competitive settings, or of the marketplace, to all spheres of life.[24] They can perceive the worth of what is of noncompetitive value only when it also has high competitive value. This blinds them to noncompetitive value.[25] I suggest that

23. I am not at all sure that Oscar Wilde's claim, "Nowadays people know the price of everything, and the value of nothing" (*The Picture of Dorian Gray*, in *Complete Works of Oscar Wilde* [London: Collins, 1966], 48) was correct even in 1891, when the book came out, but many do seem not to notice sufficiently the distinction between price and noncompetitive value, often being overly sensitive to the former and insufficiently sensitive to the latter.

24. The pervasiveness of the competitive and economic paradigms can also be seen in common language. In English, the term "dear" means both "loved" and "expensive" (the same is true, to an extent, of "precious"). Likewise, terms such as "exceptional," "outstanding," "incomparable," and "extraordinary" are used synonymously with "excellent" or "superb," while "ordinary" and especially "common" are sometimes used synonymously with "inadequate" or "inferior."

25. It is surprising, for instance, to see how often people, when asked how good they are at something (say, playing the piano, painting, philosophizing), reply only in terms of competitive worth. They find it hard to think about (or even understand) the question "How good are you?" outside the competitive paradigm, without comparing themselves to others. They focus on the number or percentage of people who are better than they are, and if they find that many are better, they conclude that they are not good at (say) playing the piano, just because some other people are better. This leads to the odd fact that some people who are doing well and have something valuable are depressed just because other people are also doing well or better.

when we consider the meaning of life we should not see ourselves only as operating in the marketplace or as competing, and heed not only competitive value. Thus, the sixth consideration against perfectionism also has to do with the simple perception that many nonperfect things or achievements, or things or achievements that are common and easy to attain, are good, important, and worthy. Perfectionism, often excessively or exclusively immersed in the competitive paradigm, is insufficiently sensitive to noncompetitive value, and is thus blind to much that is of value in life.

Chapter 4

Anticipations of Nonperfectionism

1

The nonperfectionist position on the meaning of life, which suggests that meaningful lives can be realized in the nonperfect sphere as well, is not new. Various versions of this position already appear in the work of many different writers, even if the arguments for non-perfectionism I presented in the previous chapter differ from theirs.[1] Nonperfectionism about the meaning of life can also be seen as heavily influenced by nonperfectionist suggestions in other fields. For example, in their *In the Name of Love: Romantic Ideology and*

---

1. See, e.g., Ralph Waldo Emerson, "Experience," in *The Complete Essays and Other Writings of Ralph Waldo Emerson* (New York: Modern Library, 1950), 351; Aldous Huxley, "Swift," in *Do What You Will* (London: Watts, 1936), 79–80; Susan Wolf, "Happiness and Meaning: Two Aspects of the Good Life," *Social Philosophy and Policy* 14, no. 1 (1997): 224; Richard Taylor, "The Meaning of Life," in *The Meaning of Life*, ed. E. D. Klemke, 2nd ed. (New York: Oxford University Press, 2000), 174–175; Kurt Baier, "The Meaning of Life," in Klemke, *Meaning of Life*, 126–129; Paul Edwards, "The Meaning and Value of Life," in Klemke, *Meaning of Life*, 147–148; Brooke Alan Trisel, "Futility and the Meaning of Life Debate," *Sorites* 14 (2002): 75–80; Robert Audi, "Intrinsic Value and Meaningful Life," *Philosophical Papers* 34, no. 3 (2005): 335; Brad Hooker, "The Meaning of Life: Subjectivism, Objectivism, and Divine Support," in *The Moral Life: Essays in Honour of John Cottingham*, ed. Nafsika Athanassoulis and Samantha Vice (New York: Palgrave, 2008), 191; David Schmidtz, "The Meanings of Life," in *Life, Death, and Meaning*, ed. David Benatar, 2nd ed. (Lanham, MD: Rowman and Littlefield, 2010), 97; Thaddeus Metz, *Meaning in Life* (Oxford: Oxford University Press, 2013), 146–158.

Its Victims, Aaron Ben Ze'ev and Ruhama Goussinsky discuss what might be called perfectionist romantic ideology, according to which the only acceptable love is the perfect one.[2] In perfect love—which for perfectionists is the only type that should be called love—nothing else is needed: all difficulties in life are vanquished, the lovers are always on each other's mind, and they live in perfect union; the two hearts thump to exactly the same beat. In true love, lovers do not have to tell each other how they feel or what they want. They just know it. Needless to say, in true love there are also no disagreements and certainly no anger or even occasional quarrels. A relationship that does not measure up to these perfectionist criteria is not love at all and is better forsaken. Thus, people who commit themselves to nothing less than this impossible ideal cannot see the significant value that can be found in normal, realistic love with its ups and downs. They insist on having either all or nothing, and therefore they have nothing. Of course, those who criticize this perfectionist approach to love are not suggesting that any kind of loving relationship, no matter how deficient, is better than nothing—they have their standards, although less demanding. But they do think that many loves that are not perfect are good and worthwhile. Taking a nonperfectionist approach to thinking about meaning in life, as I argued that we ought to in the previous chapter, is, in some ways, an adaptation of the critique of perfectionist romantic ideology to the meaning of life.

The nonperfectionist approach to the meaning of life is also analogous to a proposal made in theory of knowledge. Through the generations, many philosophers have attempted to defeat

---

2. Aaron Ben Ze'ev and Ruhama Goussinsky, *In the Name of Love: Romantic Ideology and Its Victims* (Oxford: Oxford University Press, 2008), x–xvi, 1–38, 217–248. Ben Ze'ev and Goussinsky focus in their book on the relation between romantic ideology and murders in the family, a topic that is beyond the scope of the present book.

skepticism entirely and achieve completely certain knowledge. To be considered worthy of the name, knowledge had to measure up to this high (and unrealistic) standard. But their efforts were unsuccessful; the problem of skepticism prevailed. However, some philosophers, frequently referred to as "fallibilists," have suggested that this quest was wrongheaded; we can never reach absolutely certain knowledge, and it is foolish to waste so much effort and time in trying to achieve it and feel so frustrated for having failed to attain it.[3] Nor should all views that are less than absolutely certain be considered to be of similar, by and large worthless, value. Some of them are much more certain than others and are, moreover, satisfactory. Fallibilist theorists of knowledge (a category that includes most contemporary theorists of knowledge) hold that all that we believe to be knowledge might, in principle, be proven false one day. But views that have been sufficiently tested and argued for should be seen as highly corroborated and warranted. Although we can never be absolutely sure that they will not be proven wrong one day, we have good reasons to accept them and, moreover, to take them to be knowledge. It might be nice if there were absolutely certain knowledge, but there is none, and what we do have is of great value. The absolutist demand for knowledge gave rise to epistemically nihilistic views: since we cannot know anything with absolute certainty,

---

3. For some individual fallibilist accounts see, e.g., Charles Sanders Peirce, "Fallibilism, Continuity, and Evolution," in *Collected Papers*, ed. Charles Hartshorne and Paul Weiss (Cambridge, MA: Belknap Press of Harvard University Press, 1965), 1:58–72; Karl Popper, "Science: Conjectures and Refutations" and "Truth, Rationality, and the Growth of Scientific Knowledge," in *Conjectures and Refutations*, 2nd ed. (London: Routledge and Kegan Paul, 1965), 33–59, 215–250; Susan Haack, *Evidence and Inquiry: Towards Reconstruction in Epistemology* (Oxford: Blackwell, 1993). For some other discussions and defenses, see Stewart Cohen, "How to Be a Fallibilist," *Philosophical Perspectives* 2 (1988): 91–123; Baron Reed, "How to Think about Fallibilism," *Philosophical Studies* 107, no. 2 (2002): 143–157; and Stephen Hetherington, "Fallibilism and Knowing That One Is Not Dreaming," *Canadian Journal of Philosophy* 32, no. 1 (2002): 83–102.

we can know nothing, and anything goes. This is analogous to the situation of the person who holds that, because life is not perfectly meaningful, it is meaningless. The discussion here can be seen as reproducing the fallibilist move in the sphere of the meaning of life.[4] Many people have a fair degree of meaning in their lives. It is not perfect, and can usually be improved, but it is quite sufficient as a basis for taking their lives to be, on the whole, meaningful, if only they do not endorse the perfectionist supposition.

The analogy with fallibilism, like the earlier analogy with romantic love, should make it clear that I do not suggest that we should have no standards at all, that anything goes, or that people cannot have meaningless lives.[5] Rejecting the absolutist view of knowledge does not mean that every belief should be considered as knowledge: fallibilists distinguish between better and worse knowledge and work hard at improving the knowledge they have by enhancing its certainty and clarity. But they do not hamper their work by trying to achieve what is impossible, and they do not despair of having good, helpful knowledge just because absolute knowledge is unattainable. In other words, they do not feel that what they have is unworthy because it is not perfect.

The analogy is also meant to show that the rejection of perfectionism need not lead to the rejection of ideals. Ideals can be a positive force in life under certain conditions. They can be helpful even when they cannot be fulfilled since one can treat them as

---

4. However, the analogy between fallibilism and the nonperfectionist position does not hold fully, since fallibilism maintains that absolute certainty will never be achieved, while the nonperfectionist position is not committed to the view that no individuals can attain absolute meaning in life. Moreover, the criteria for epistemological success are clearer than the criteria for meaningful lives.

5. The claim that people can (and sometimes do) have meaningless lives is in tension with Viktor Frankl's view that "life is, and remains, meaningful in every case" and that "life is unconditionally meaningful" (*The Will to Meaning* [London: Souvenir, 1971], 69).

regulative ideals, that is, ideals toward which one directs oneself or makes slow progress without ever attaining them. They can serve as compasses or as norms to look up to. Under those circumstances, although we recognize that the ideal would be better than what we have, we can still appreciate what we have. In perfectionism, on the other hand, not only do I look up to an ideal, but I cannot live with anything short of it. We should also distinguish in this context between wishes or preferences, on the one hand, and anticipations or expectations, on the other. It is not at all unreasonable to have wishes along the lines of "It would be so nice if I were to attain this perfection." But that differs from expecting to attain the perfection and being unable to contain disappointment when the expectation is not fulfilled.

Note that nonperfectionism accepts that attaining perfections can make life meaningful. What nonperfectionism rejects is the view that *only* lives that attain perfection are meaningful. Nonperfectionism, then, is not symmetrically opposite to perfectionism, since perfectionism is exclusive, while nonperfectionism is inclusive. Perfectionism takes only what is perfect to be meaningful, while nonperfectionism takes both what is perfect and some of what is nonperfect to be meaningful.

2

I can only partly agree, then, with Voltaire's powerful and provocative saying that the best is the enemy of the good.[6] At first sight,

6. Voltaire, "La Bégueule," in *Les Oeuvres complètes de Voltaire*, vol. 74A: *Oeuvres de 1772* (I), ed. Nicholas Cronk and Hayden T. Mason (Oxford: Voltaire Foundation/Alden Press, 2006), 217.

of course, the saying appears to be completely incorrect: we expect that those who push themselves to achieve the best will either achieve it, which is good, or at least, if they fail to achieve it, are more likely to achieve something along the way to it, which is also good. Thus, the best would seem to be the friend, rather than the enemy, of the good. But there are also many cases in which setting one's mind on achieving the best, and nothing short of it, leads those who fail to achieve the best to complete despair and inactivity, and thus to refraining from the significant less-than-best that they could achieve. In yet other cases setting one's mind to achieving the best, and nothing short of it, leads people not to appreciate the good they already possess or that is all around them, or to sacrifice it in the effort to reach the best they can never attain.[7] It also happens that setting one's mind on achieving the best and nothing short of it results in the destruction of an existing good out of frustration and anger for not having attained the best ("If I can't have it all, or the best, I'll have nothing").[8]

But when the pursuit of the best is not perfectionist, that is, not exclusivist so that anything short of the best is rejected, the good can be highly valued (even if it is acknowledged that the best would have been better). There are cases in which pursuing the best does allow or motivate one to achieve the good; one can try to attain both of them. When this is the case, the best need not be the enemy of the good. Voltaire should have said, more accurately, "Do not allow the best to be the enemy of the good."

---

7. As in Shakespeare's "Striving to better, oft we mar what's well" (*King Lear*, I, 4).

8. A literary portrayal of such a move can be found in Camus's play *Caligula* (in *"Caligula" and "Cross Purpose"*, trans. Stuart Gilbert [Harmondsworth: Penguin, 1965], 27–98). Caligula destroys everything around him and then even himself, because life is not perfect. Those who, because of their perfectionism, take life to be meaningless and wish to commit suicide are making a similar move.

3

Nonperfectionism has also many cultural antecedents. Instances of the nonperfectionist tendency can be found, for example, in many religious practices and views. Some religions call on us to thank God for the *regular*, everyday things we have, so that we learn to appreciate them, too. For example, in many Christian communities it is customary, before eating dinner or going to bed, to thank God for a variety of things, including such seemingly trivial ones as the existence of food on the table or one's own and one's family's health (such thanks are not only said by people who are frequently hungry or sick). Likewise, in Judaism one thanks God every morning for having allowed one to wake up and be alive. We are called not to take for granted but, rather, to acknowledge the value of what we may, through time and routine, have become used to seeing as obvious: that is, to detrivialize the imperfect and common that has become invisible to us.

The intuition that there is much value in the common and easier to maintain is also evident in the religious notion of supererogation, that is, the sphere of actions that go *beyond* the call of duty, which legitimizes what is *within* duty.[9] The source of the notion is the Catholic distinction between commands or precepts, on the one hand, and counsels, on the other hand. If one fulfills one's duties, that is, the commands and precepts, one proves to be a good and worthy Christian whose salvation is guaranteed. But there are also the optional counsels, that is, religious standards (typically adopted by saints or members of monastic orders) that are *beyond* duty, such as renouncing carnal pleasures, pride, and

9. For a helpful discussion see David Heyd, *Supererogation: Its Status in Ethical Theory* (Cambridge: Cambridge University Press, 1982).

wealth. Meeting such standards confers excellence. Nevertheless, people are considered to be fulfilled in their religious status and guaranteed salvation even if they perform only the easier duties without committing themselves to the stricter, higher norms.[10] The latter are, indeed, better, but they are not necessary for a good and proper life. Religious laypersons who live good but ordinary religious lives should not think of themselves as insufficient, even if saints or clergy have done even better. Likewise, Islam distinguishes between, on the one hand, *fardh* and *wajib*, which are compulsory duties, and, on the other hand, *mandub, sunnah,* and *mustahabb,* which are optional behaviors one may take upon oneself although one is not required to do so. Performing the latter is praiseworthy, but refraining is in no way reproachable.[11] A similar insight appears in the core book of Habad Hassidism, *Likutei Amarim (Tanya),* whose subtitle is *A Book for Mediocre People,* where a distinction is made among the *tzaddikim* (the virtuous and saintly), the *benonim* (literally, those who are mediocre or intermediate), and the *resha'im* (those who are wicked).[12] The text is clear that although we should of course see to it that we do not fall to the status of the *resha'im,* most of us need not feel obligated to become *tzaddikim.* The status of *tzaddikim* is not mandatory, and encompasses only a few, exceptional people. Most of us should aim for the status of *benonim,* that is, those between the pole of the *tzaddikim* and the pole of *resha'im.* This text claims, then, that it is not only legitimate but in fact very good to be what the text sees as mediocre, a term that in modern English, perhaps because of the perfectionist ethos,

10. See, e.g., Thomas Aquinas, *Summa Theologica,* I, Q. 19 A. 12; I, II, Q. 108 A. 4; II, II, Q. 58 A. 3; II, II, Q. 147 A. 3; II, II, Q. 185 A. 6.

11. Joseph Schacht, *An Introduction to Islamic Law* (Oxford: Clarendon, 1964), 121.

12. Shneur Zalman of Liadi, *Likutei Amarim Tanya,* trans. Nissan Mindel (New York: Kehot, 1972).

has acquired connotations of being less than sufficient.[13] The non-perfectionist intuition can also be seen in the Talmudic principle that those who decide on religious law "may not impose a decree upon the public unless the majority of the public is able to comply with the decree."[14]

4

The nonperfectionist insight also appears in literature. By this I do not mean only that it appears as a central theme in some specific poems, such as William Carlos Williams's *The Red Wheelbarrow*, Frank O'Hara's *Having a Coke With You*, or Zbigniew Herbert's *Mr. Cogito Tells About the Temptation of Spinoza*,[15] but also that much poetry takes up common thoughts, feelings, and situations that are otherwise hardly noticed and considers them in a focused and slowed-down fashion. This closer, slower attention to some common phenomena shows how beautiful, interesting, or deep they are if we only take the time to pay heed to them. This is an indication that much of the ordinary world is, in fact, "poetic," moreover meaning-ful, if only we treat it as such rather than pass on in haste, as most of us usually do. Many poems affect us by detrivializing the seemingly trivial and focusing on the value and beauty in the commonplace.

13. It may be the same ethos that leads to the formulation "He is no Einstein" in English as another way of saying that he is quite stupid, or "She is no Perlman" as a way of saying that she plays the violin badly.

14. *Talmud Bavli (Babylonian Talmud) tractate Bava Batra*, ed. Hersh Goldwurm and Yosaif Asher Weiss, Schottenstein 1st ed. (New York: Mesorah, 1992), 60b.

15. William Carlos Williams, *The Collected Poems of William Carlos Williams*, ed. A. Walton Litz and Christopher MacGowan (New York: New Directions, 1986), 1: 224; Frank O'Hara, *The Collected Poems of Frank O'Hara*, ed. Donald Allen (New York: Knopf, 1972), 360; Zbigniew Herbert, *Selected Poems*, trans. John Carpenter and Bogdana Carpenter (Oxford: Oxford University Press, 1977), 51–53.

Much prose affects us in this way, too. But in some works, non-perfectionism is one of the main themes. Hemingway's "Big Two-Hearted River," for example, seems on first reading quite uneventful, even boring.[16] It describes how Nick Adams, a character who appears in several of Hemingway's other stories as well, goes fishing. Nick is back in the United States after fighting in the horrific and pointless First World War. Although Hemingway does not state this explicitly, his description suggests that Nick may well be suffering from shell shock or some other kind of traumatic despair. The story narrates, sometimes slowly and in detail, how Nick attentively builds a tent and cooks dinner. Then he goes to sleep, and when he wakes up in the morning we receive a description of how he catches some grasshoppers and prepares them as bait for the fish. Then we have some description of the fishing, and then the story ends. No drama, no achievement in the face of difficulty, no heroism, no excellence in the face of danger. Just fishing.

The first time I read this story I was certain that the copy I had borrowed from the library was damaged; someone must have torn off the end or perhaps the publisher by some mistake failed to print it. There seemed to be no plot. It took me some years to understand what it was about. One does not have to be a great hero, or even to have a "story," in order to find meaning. One does not have to excel or perform unusual feats. It is worthy, and hence meaningful, to do small things. You can find meaning in fishing if you do it in the right way; in the beauty and calm around you, in doing well what you do, and in the enjoyment of and the attentiveness to all of this. This can be a worthy and healing experience; this can make life meaningful.

---

16. Ernest Hemingway, "Big Two-Hearted River," in *In Our Time* (New York: Scribner, 1970), 133–156.

Hemingway also narrates how Nick catches a small fish but lets it go. It is too small; he wants larger ones. Then a very big fish takes the bait, but it is *too big* and breaks the rod. Although Nick would have very much liked to catch the big fish, and is frustrated at first, he quickly comes to accept it, and does not spoil the rest of his day, or just pack up and leave, because he did not get the big fish. Then he catches two medium-sized fish, and he is *happy* with them. In those circumstances, stubborn insistence on achieving the "best" and nothing short of it would have probably led to losing the "good." (But note that Nick did not settle for the fish that seemed too small to him.) Similarly, toward the end of the story, Nick deliberates whether to try to fish where the stream goes into a swamp. But he recognizes that there are many complications to fishing in the swamp, and Hemingway represents Nick as wisely, and contentedly, deciding not to go there at that time. It may be too much. Fishing in the swamp would be difficult, perhaps even dangerous, although the trout to be found there may be bigger. Sending Nick to the swamp might have been more interesting for the readers, and perhaps for Nick, since it might have involved danger, near escapes, overcoming difficulties, special achievements, and drama. But part of Hemingway's point is that there is no need for an uncommon, radical experience in order to have a meaningful story, a meaningful experience, or a meaningful life. It is also interesting to note that the story does not describe many of Nick's thoughts but mostly his deeds, and the few thoughts that are described are not deep or exceptional but have to do with some memories and some practical issues in which he is engaged. However, this does not (and is not meant to) convey to the reader that Nick is stupid, shallow, or acting mechanically; quite the contrary.

This intuition also appears in other works of fiction. Voltaire's *Candide* narrates the grotesque adventures of Candide and his friends.[17] They travel to exotic lands, are rescued from grave dangers, and suffer great hardship. One of them, Pangloss, keeps trying to make sense of what befalls them by presenting complicated (and in Voltaire's view silly) metaphysical explanations, mimicking aspects of Leibniz's philosophical theory. At the very end of the book, after all the characters have gone through extreme dangers and great dramas (and melodramas) of all types, Candide and his friends end up simply cultivating a garden. This is how the book ends. Here, too, some readers may wonder where the proper ending of the story is. But one way of understanding how the book concludes is that, after all the great adventures and pompous philosophizing, the good thing to do is simply to work in a garden. This ending conflicts with the typical ending of the adventure genre: we are used to tales that narrate how heroes and heroines enjoy an idealized life after withstanding grave dangers. But Voltaire is presenting, as the happy end, a simple life of working in the garden that has profited nothing from the complex adventures that preceded it. The great and exciting adventures, he is suggesting, are wholly unnecessary.

Likewise, Hermann Hesse's *Siddhartha* describes how a seeker finally finds the meaning of his life, his calling and solace, in working on a raft, listening to the river, and helping people cross it. Siddhartha arrives at this meaning after having tried some seemingly higher options for excellence, such as being a meditative, ascetic saint in the forest or a very rich merchant.[18] Tolstoy also advocates nonperfectionist meaning in his two great novels, *Anna Karenina* and *War and Peace*. Important characters in these novels, such as Levin and Kitty, and Pierre and Natasha, respectively, find a

17. Voltaire, *Candide*, in *"Candide", "Zadig", and Selected Stories*, trans. Donald M. Frame (New York: Signet, 1961), 15–101.

18. Hermann Hesse, *Siddhartha*, trans. Susan Bernofsky (New York: Random House, 2006).

meaningful life, toward the end of the novels, not in the uncommon and the difficult to attain but in the imperfect, unexciting, and good family life. Their love is strong, but is not of the "perfect," romanticized type in which lovers idealize and idolize each other.[19] Pierre learns much about meaning from Platon Karataev, a simple peasant who does not perform any great acts of heroism but, rather, views life with simplicity and acceptance. These are just a few of the many instances of nonperfectionism that appear in prose.[20]

The notion appears in film as well. For example, Ingmar Bergman's *The Seventh Seal* presents several ways of trying to cope with the perceived meaninglessness of life.[21] One character, the knight Antonius Block, approaches the meaninglessness of life intellectually: he cannot understand how the world can be meaningful in the midst of war, epidemics, superstition, and cruelty. Jöns, his squire, takes life to be meaningless but finds some value, in a Camusian manner, in defying this condition. Karin, Block's wife, retains her religious belief and loyalty to her husband. Skat, a performer of folk plays, fornicates and enjoys himself, while Raval, a former cleric, behaves immorally as a rapist and corpse robber. But it seems that Bergman, like his main character, Block, prefers the option presented in the characters of Jof and Mia, two other

19. Leo Tolstoy, *Anna Karenina*, trans. Richard Pevear and Larissa Volokhonsky (London: Penguin, 2000); *War and Peace*, trans. Richard Pevear and Larissa Volokhonsky (New York: Vintage, 2008). The concluding sentences of *Anna Karenina* describe how Levin realizes that although he will continue to lose his temper when dealing with Ivan the coachman, engage in irritating discussions, have misunderstandings with his wife Kitty and regret them, feel a wall between his innermost soul and other people, etc., his life has stopped being meaningless, as it used to be, and now has unquestionable meaning. This notion appears also in the first part of the epilogue to *War and Peace*.

20. See also, for example, Yoel Hoffmann's *The Heart is Katmandu*, trans. Peter Cole (New York: New Directions, 2001), and Avigdor Dagan's beautiful *Der Hahnenruf* (Frankfurt am Main: Ullstein, 1980).

21. Directed by Ingmar Bergman, produced by Allan Ekelund, distributed by AB Svensk Filmindustri, 1957.

performers of folk plays. Jof and Mia are simple people who love each other and their son, Michael. Their love is not tragic, dramatic, or overly romantic; it does not involve trumpets, drums, or stars falling from heaven. Bergman presents Jof not as a great artist or lover but, rather, as slightly silly. However, Mia, who recognizes this, loves him just the same, or even more, because he is so normal. After Mia has given him simple but fresh milk and common wild strawberries, Block looks at the family scene, the berries, the milk, and the meadow and says that he will try to retain all this; it will be a solace for him. Block understands that their life is the right one, and he does his best to save them from death. Likewise, in Wim Wenders's *Wings of Desire*, an angel relinquishes his immortality and ability to know people's thoughts for a simple, mortal, and vulnerable life in which he can sense common things physically and concretely and experience a romantic relationship.[22]

In Western visual art, too, there has been a shift from depicting grand religious, mythical, or historical characters and scenes to portraying simple people and mundane objects (typical of, for example, the golden age of Dutch art in the seventeenth century and of Impressionist and Postimpressionist art). As in poetry, the ordinary has come to be accepted as possibly beautiful, interesting, and worthwhile if only we agree to consider it in the right way, and to reject the inner censorship that forbids us to notice the great value that persists in the nonperfect and nonexceptional, thus blinding us to much that is of worth in human life.

Thus, alongside the perfectionist streak in Western culture and philosophy, there is also a powerful and interesting nonperfectionist streak. This book follows the latter streak, which finds great value in

22. Directed by Wim Wenders, produced by Wim Wenders and Anatole Dauman, distributed by Basis FilmVerleih, 1987.

ordinary things. As I see it, a person who is decent; who is a good family member, friend, or neighbor; who is curious; and who can enjoy the sight of the trees through the window of the bus on her way to work has already made it. She has a meaningful life. She has passed the threshold. Perhaps Mother Teresa or Bach had even more meaningful lives, but her life is already meaningful. Meaningfulness can be found in growing and enjoying geraniums on the balcony, not only orchids in the conservatory. Nonperfectionism as regards the meaning of life will reappear in many of the next chapters, which revolve around specific arguments that lead some people to see life as meaningless.

Chapter 5

Death and Annihilation I

1

The eventual annihilation of everything we achieve and do, as well as of our own selves through death, is a commonly raised theme in discussions of the meaning of life. But why should our eventual annihilation be taken to render life meaningless? One reply is that annihilation nullifies everything, making it into nothingness. And what is nothing has no value; it is meaningless. With time our body, our life, everything that we value and gain, will all be gone. All our achievements, whatever we are proud of, will evaporate. Their final stage is nullification, and that means—or seems to mean—that they all have no worth. True, they all persist for a while. But then they vanish. Hence, death and annihilation render what we do inconsequential and, thus, pointless. Consider a case in which we are sweeping the floor, and a minute after we clean it someone walks over it, leaving muddy footprints on the area we have just cleaned. Again we mop the floor, but again someone enters and dirties what we have just cleaned. We will feel that our activity is purposeless and worthless. What we do is in vain, since it leaves no results. In some cases, it takes a little longer till the floor is dirtied again, but dirty it eventually becomes. Similarly, it might be felt that, although some people live longer than others and some deeds have longer-lasting impact than others, in the end all is destroyed and vanishes. Hence, it is worthless and pointless. For example, we may have managed to acquire good artistic taste, acute understanding, wide knowledge, or a happy, loving relationship. But they will vanish when we die; they will perish when we perish. Likewise, we may have helped other people considerably by allowing them to live much-improved lives through our moral, medical, or scientific contributions. But they too will perish one day.

This is one way of understanding the story of Sisyphus as told by Cicero and Ovid, among others, and which later became a central theme in Albert Camus's famous *Myth of Sisyphus*.[1] According to the myth, Sisyphus had to push a heavy rock uphill. But whenever he reached the summit, the rock, rather than staying in position, would immediately roll downhill again, and Sisyphus would have to start his purposeless effort anew. Sisyphus's toil was pointless; he worked in vain. Like Sisyphus, whatever we do turns into nothingness at the end. Our work, too, eventually "slides back down the hill" and is, thus, useless.

Another way of expressing the same intuition is that death and annihilation render equal lives that we take to be of high value and lives that we take to be of low and insufficient value; whatever people do or do not do with their lives, they end up the same. Hence, it seems, what they do does not really matter. Annihilation, then, is the great equalizer. This intuition is expressed in Thackeray's *Barry Lyndon*: "It was in the reign of George II that the above-named personages lived and quarreled; good or bad, handsome or ugly, rich

---

1. Albert Camus, *The Myth of Sisyphus*, in *"The Myth of Sisyphus" and Other Essays*, trans. Justin O'Brien (New York: Vintage, 1991), 119–123.

or poor, they are all equal now."[2] They are all equal now, of course, because they are all now nothing. The same intuition appears in David Hume's remark that "death, though *perhaps* they receive him differently, yet treats alike the fool and the philosopher."[3] Both Thackeray and Hume are probably influenced by Ecclesiastes:

> Then I said to myself, "What befalls the fool will befall me also; why then have I been so very wise?" And I said to myself that this also is vanity. For of the wise man as of the fool there is no enduring remembrance, seeing that in the days to come all will have been long forgotten. How the wise man dies just like the fool![4]

Death is not only the great equalizer of people but also the great equalizer of all aspects of life. It makes our achievements and failures, our deepest and shallowest moments, our good and bad deeds, all equal, since they all end in the same way.

In his *Confession*, Tolstoy recounts how, at a certain point, he started experiencing his life as meaningless. One of the things that led him to this view was his growing awareness of his eventual death. He narrates a parable about a traveler who, wishing to escape from a wild beast, jumps into a dry well. However, the traveler finds that at the bottom of the well there is dragon waiting to devour him. So as not to fall to its jaws, the traveler grabs a twig that grows from a fissure in the well and hangs onto it. But when he looks up he sees

2. William Makepeace Thackeray, *The Luck of Barry Lyndon*, ed. Edgar F. Harden (Ann Arbor: University of Michigan Press, 1999), 6.

3. Hume's emphasis. David Hume, "The Sceptic," in *Essays, Moral, Political, and Literary*, ed. Eugene F. Miller (Indianapolis: Liberty Fund, 1987), 180. Hume seems to have had a rather high opinion of philosophers.

4. Ecclesiastes 2:15–16, Revised Standard Version. This is also one of the main themes in danse macabre paintings: they depict death taking away, together, both the most powerful members of late medieval society (emperors or popes) and the least powerful (peasants or children).

two mice, one white and one black, going round and round the stem of the twig while gnawing it. It is clear to the traveler that the twig will be torn off soon and that he will fall to his death at the jaws of the dragon. However, he also notices that there are some drops of honey on some of the twig's leaves, so he sticks out his tongue and licks the drops of honey. Tolstoy explains:

> Thus I cling to the branch of life, knowing that inevitably the dragon of death is waiting, ready to tear me to pieces; and I cannot understand why this torment has befallen me. I try to suck the honey that once consoled me, but the honey is no longer sweet. Day and night the black mouse and the white mouse gnaw at the branch to which I cling. I clearly see the dragon, and the honey has lost all its sweetness. I see only the inescapable dragon and the mice, and I cannot turn my eyes from them. This is no fairy tale but truth, irrefutable and understood by all.
>
> The former delusion of the happiness of life that had concealed from me the horror of the dragon no longer deceives me.[5]

Tolstoy describes the human condition, then, as similar to that of the traveler hanging onto the twig. The passing days and nights, represented by the white and black mice that gnaw the twig, bring people closer to their certain eventual death. Many people do not think about this end because they are distracted by the pleasures of life, represented by the few drops of honey that the traveler licks, animal-like, off the leaves of the twig. But Tolstoy tells us that he could not continue to be distracted and deluded. The truth of his eventual death was very clear to him, and thus what had seemed pleasant or valuable in his life lost its worth for him.

5. Leo Tolstoy, *Confession*, trans. David Patterson (New York: Norton, 1983), 31.

Note that the arguments suggesting that death renders life meaningless, like many of the other arguments for the meaninglessness of life that will be discussed in the next chapters, conclude that not only are your life and my life meaningless, but that so too are the lives of people such as Mother Teresa, Einstein, Mozart, and Gandhi. Furthermore, nothing can be done to correct this predicament. No one has, or could have, a meaningful life, no matter what she does or achieves in her life.

Of course, in some religious views, we and what we do remain and matter forever; life does not, in fact, end in death, but continues (e.g., through reincarnation, resurrection, or heaven or hell), even if in a different form. Death is transformation rather than annihilation. Nor do our achievements fade into nothingness. They matter forever since they affect our afterlife for all eternity or are known to God and please or displease him forever. For those who believe in the afterlife such suggestions may help solve the concerns raised above.[6] But they will not help those who hold that death ends not

---

6. Such theories, however, also carry some difficulties. According to reincarnation theories, our personality, as we know it, vanishes, and another person, with a different biography, is born. (In some theories of reincarnation people are sometimes even incarnated into other species.) Thus, reincarnation theory does not, in fact, suggest a continuation of our self as we usually understand this term; it is annihilated at death. Perhaps our sins or virtues do affect the poor or lucky creature who is born after we die, but it is a different creature.

Things are also difficult with theories of heaven and hell. If I have no body, since only the soul continues but the body does not, then my identity will change significantly; much of what is "me" has to do with my body. For example, those who enjoy physical activities such as running, dancing, or having sexual relations will not be able to do so. To maintain heavenly bliss they will probably have other, nonbodily preferences satisfied. But that means that their personalities will be radically different from what they are now; their old selves will be eradicated.

Some views of resurrection presume not only the soul but also the flesh to return to life. This solves some problems but may create others. In such a resurrection our personal interactions with other people, which are very important to many, will also change considerably. Some people are widowed and then remarry. When they and their spouses rise in the resurrection, with whom will they spend their time? According to the New Testament (Matthew 22:30) there will be no husbands and wives in the resurrected state; people will live like

only our physical existence but also our mental or psychological one. In what follows I examine whether, under the supposition that there is no afterlife, our eventual death and annihilation indeed render life meaningless. This chapter presents several arguments that, I believe, fail to show that life can remain meaningful in spite of death; the next chapter will proceed to present an argument that, in my view, does succeed in doing so.

2

To challenge the claim that death renders life meaningless one could argue that, even if there is no afterlife, we and our achievements do not completely wither away. For example, people who hold us dear will continue to remember us fondly for many years to come. Moreover, some of our creations, such as books we may have written, or things we may have built, remain after us. If we have

angels in heaven. But many couples would not want to live separately in the next world, and would like their relationship to continue. Or perhaps, being like angels, they would not want that. In that case, again, they would have a different personality. Somewhat similar questions arise concerning parents who died at an early age, leaving children who, eventually, die at older ages than their parents did. The child may be seventy-five years old and the parent only twenty-five. What will their relationship be in the afterlife? Maybe ages also have no relevance in heaven, or when all are resurrected. But ageless persons, too, are very different from persons as we know them.

It is also unclear what will happen to our interests, hobbies, careers, and other occupations when we are in heaven or are resurrected in the latter days. It may be that we are passionate about our work, bingo, coin collecting, reading romantic novels, or watching football games. It is not clear whether, and if so how, we will be able to indulge in these things in the afterlife. Perhaps in the afterlife we will not want to do all these things, experiencing bliss in other activities or forms of being. But that, again, suggests that our personalities will be significantly transformed, and it is not clear that we would be "ourselves" any longer. The very notion that those creatures in the afterlife will experience continuous bliss suggests that they may have become different creatures from us, since most people's personality is characterized by some ambivalence and tension as a deep, essential aspect of who they are.

offspring, then part of our genetic pool endures in each of them and is transferred to future generations.

However, these claims are problematic. When dear ones die we are certain that we will remember them. Sometimes we also vow, strongly and emotionally, that we will remember them *forever*. The vows are sincere at the time they are made, but with time, most of us think about the dead less and less and remember them only occasionally. Even if that were not so, when *we* die the memory of those we vowed to remember would definitely be lost. With time, what remains of each of us will, at best, be some pictures at which our great-grandchildren will look with a combination of curiosity and estrangement, maybe reading our name, occupation, and our dates of birth, marriage, and death but without being able to decipher the person behind the pictures and information. After a few more generations, this too disappears. What happened to our predecessors will surely happen to us. We, too, *will* be forgotten and sink into oblivion.

Although some of us do leave a distinctive heritage, even this eventually perishes, and much of what remains, such as the pyramids, carries no remnants of our personal identity. Even where the name of a person endures, the memory of the actual living person is lost. Suppose that some inscription teaches us that a certain pyramid was built on a certain pharaoh's orders, or suppose that some document shows that a certain Jacques, a carpenter, lived in a small village in France in the sixteenth century, and that he was tried for theft. It is not the *individual* who remains, but some impersonal citation. Some facts about people remain, but the people themselves are gone.

Admittedly, a few works of art, for example, great works of literature, both endure over the years and bear elements of their author's personality. But Homer's works (assuming that there was indeed such a person and that he was their real author) have now endured for only about two thousand and eight hundred years, which is far from eternity, but longer than most authors can ever hope to be remembered. Shakespeare's works have endured for a little over four hundred years. A few thousand years from now, even if humankind has not been destroyed through nuclear warfare or natural calamities, their works may or may not still be read and remembered. But even if they are, astrophysicists suggest that sometime in the distant future, the sun will turn into a red giant and expand explosively, destroying the solar system, or the universe will contract, and our solar system, galaxy, or the whole universe will perish. True, before that happens we will have been able to produce quite a few great-grandchildren; these astrophysical events are not an immediate danger. But they are certain to happen one day. Thus, even if the works of Homer and Shakespeare were to endure for many thousands of years, sometime in the future they too will vanish.

Robert Audi has argued that although people are mortal, institutions are not. If I am part of an institution (such as a state, a nation, or a social movement), my impact, and thus in a way I myself, survive indefinitely.[7] But that seems incorrect. The life of an institution, too, is limited, even if it is sometimes longer than that of a person. Institutions, too, perish sooner or later; if not in several dozens or hundreds of years, then when the sun, the galaxy, or the universe dissolves. Nor do we endure through our genetic legacy. Although our children carry a part of us within them, our genetic material is diluted by 50 percent in each generation; each of our great-grandchildren carries only one-eighth of our genetic pool. Even if all that were not the case, and we could largely replicate ourselves

---

7. Robert Audi, "Intrinsic Value and Meaningful Life," *Philosophical Papers* 34, no. 3 (2005): 354–355.

through the generations, those close replicas, too, would certainly cease to exist some far-off day because of astrophysical catastrophes. Thus, everything that makes us up, including everything we do and achieve, will certainly vanish one day. For some it will happen sooner, and for others later, but at a certain point it will happen to us all.

3

Thomas Nagel presents some arguments that question the claim that death renders life meaningless, noting:

> It is often remarked that nothing we do now will matter in a million years. But if that is true, then by the same token, nothing that will be the case in a million years matters now. In particular, it does not matter now that in a million years nothing we do now will matter.[8]

But mattering need not be symmetrical. It may well be that John matters to me, while I do not matter to John. This is true temporally, as well: it may well be that at twenty it did not matter to me what would happen when I was sixty (and that I therefore behaved in ways that ruined my health at a later age), but that at sixty it matters to me very much how I behaved at twenty. Or, to take another temporal example closer to Nagel's claim, suppose that I am a singer and that my stage persona and the hits I record are very popular today, but I know that no one will care for them or for me in five years;

---

8. Thomas Nagel, "The Absurd," in *Mortal Questions* (Cambridge: Cambridge University Press, 1979), 11.

they matter now, but will not matter then. Their impermanence may well disturb me. It would be wrong to say that since the hits I sing now are not going to matter in five years, then what happens in five years should not matter to me now, or in particular that it should not matter to me now that my songs will not matter in five years. In most cases, if something matters to me, it also matters to me that it will matter in the future. In most circumstances, it would affect my love, religious beliefs, or commitment to moral ideals now to know that in five years they would stop mattering at all to me or to other people.

Nagel also presents another argument that questions the claim that death renders life meaningless:

> Even if what we did now *were* going to matter in a million years, how could that keep our present concerns from being absurd? If their mattering now is not enough to accomplish that, how would it help if they mattered a million years from now?[9]

However, this misrepresents many people's reason for taking their eventual annihilation to make their life meaningless. As Nagel presents it, I am feeling that what I do is meaningless, and yet I am sorry that in a million years this meaninglessness will not continue. When presented that way, the sorrow is indeed odd: if my life is meaningless anyway, then prolonging it would not make it less meaningless, but perhaps, on the contrary, more meaningless. However, those who feel that annihilation makes life meaningless are ready to grant that life could have sufficient worth if it were not going to be destroyed, and see its eventual destruction as taking away that worth for the reasons presented at the beginning of this

9. Nagel, "The Absurd," 11.

chapter: what we do, even if worthwhile now, eventually becomes inconsequential (like sweeping a floor that a minute later becomes dirty); and death makes everything equal. For such people, if worthwhile elements in life were going to persist rather than to be annihilated, life would be meaningful. For them, a meaningful life has to both include various valuable elements *and* carry them on infinitely. If either of these two conditions is absent, life is not meaningful. Nagel discusses a case in which the first condition is not fulfilled and the second is, and is correct to point out that such a life would indeed be meaningless. But those who think that annihilation renders life meaningless are discussing the opposite scenario: they take the first condition to be fulfilled, and complain that the second is not, because the presently valuable aspects of life will perish. As Thaddeus Metz argues, they take persistence through time to be a necessary, but not sufficient, condition for a meaningful life.[10]

4

Epicurus presents several arguments that aim to show that we should not fear death. In one of them, he explains that we should not fear death because it cannot harm us: when we are alive, we are not dead, so death does not harm us. And when we are dead, we no longer exist, and hence again no harm comes to us; we are not there to suffer from it. When we are here, death is not, and when death is here, we are not. Either way, we are not harmed.[11]

---

10. Thaddeus Metz, "Recent Work on the Meaning of Life," *Ethics* 112, no. 4 (2002): 790.
11. Epicurus, *Letter to Menoeceus* 124–125.

In reply, Nagel has argued that death, even if not harmful in itself, is harmful because it impedes the continuation of something good, namely the pleasures of life. Death is bad because it deprives us of something good; it terminates something that we enjoy and could have had more of if death had not stopped it. We are harmed by death in the same way that we would be harmed if someone snatched us away in the middle of a pleasant party that we could have continued to enjoy.[12] Many philosophers have found this reply to Epicurus to be satisfying. However, following the theme of this chapter, I suggest also another possible reply to Epicurus's challenge: death is harmful because, as argued in section 1 above, it undermines the meaning of life. If death and annihilation turn whatever we do into naught, thus making whatever we do or fail to do, along with ourselves, equal and equally pointless, they do harm us, since they make our lives meaningless and thus undercut an important interest of ours. Epicurus would be right to point out that, while we are alive, we and our achievements have not yet evaporated, and when they do evaporate we will not be here to know it. But we do know now that we and everything we do will eventually come to naught, and that may well lead us to the conclusion that we and everything we do are worthless. The fact that when we come to naught we will not know it does not answer this concern. Perhaps our eventual annihilation, and the damaging effect it is claimed to have on the meaningfulness of our lives, is no reason to *fear* death, but it certainly seems a reason to be sorry for it. Thus, Epicurus's argument does not answer the concerns presented in section 1 above.

---

12. Thomas Nagel, "Death," in *Mortal Questions* (Cambridge: Cambridge University Press, 1979), 4–7.

Another argument, by Lucretius, points out that it is inconsistent to feel sad or angry that we will not exist in the future, after we die, but not to feel sad or angry that we did not exist in the past, before we were born. He calls on us to adopt the same attitude toward the future that we have toward the past.[13] My reply, however, is that this does not solve the issue presented at the beginning of this chapter either. Death and annihilation perturb us because they are claimed to render what we do ineffectual over time and thus worthless or meaningless. The fact that sometime in the future, after we achieve something, it will come to naught seems to make the effort pointless and the achievement inconsequential. But we do not feel that the effort is pointless and the achievement is inconsequential because what we achieved did not exist in the past, *before* we achieved it. To use again the analogy of sweeping: we do not think that sweeping the floor is futile or worthless because the floor was dirty *before* we swept it, but only because it becomes dirty soon *after* we sweep it. We have reason, then, to think that our and our achievements' future nonexistence makes our lives meaningless without also thinking that our past nonexistence, before we were born, or the nonexistence of what we achieve *before* we have achieved it, makes our lives meaningless.[14]

---

13. *On the Nature of Things* III, 829–839, 969–974.

14. There are also some other, more general replies to Lucretius's argument in the literature. Nagel ("Death," 7–8) points out that we are not sorry that we were not born years earlier because when we imagine ourselves in that condition we do not think that the person born then would have been *us*. Had we been born five or twenty years earlier, we would have had a somewhat different genetic makeup, been educated by different teachers, socialized with different friends, grown up in somewhat different historical circumstances, etc. That person born earlier would have been someone else: perhaps our older sibling, but not us. On the other hand, when we think of ourselves as passing away later than we actually will, we think of *ourselves* as enjoying that longer life. Derek Parfit (*Reasons and Persons* [Oxford: Clarendon, 1984], 165–170) presents interesting thought experiments that suggest that in general we mind what is going to happen or fail to happen in the future more than what has happened or failed to happen in the past.

5

Those who claim that death and annihilation do not make life meaningless may also argue that, in fact, many people prefer to die rather
than to live. This may seem an odd claim, since most people will tell
us that death is one of the things that they fear most and are ready to
do nearly anything in order to delay or prevent it. But consider the
following thought experiment: suppose that a scientist or a wizard
gave you a pill that would make you live forever. Would you take it?
Before you reply, I should like to make the option of immortality
as tempting as possible. This will not be an immortality of senile
dementia, extreme pain, or frailty. Rather, you will live forever with
the same physical and mental capacities you have now. Taking the
pill will "freeze" you as you are now. If you are thirty when you take
it, you will remain thirty, and if fifty, then fifty it is. This does not,
however, mean that you will not be able to learn new things, master
new skills, or develop in other ways. You can, if you so wish, read
more books, travel to new places, learn a foreign language, meet new
people, improve your musical taste, or continue to develop your
stamina in long-distance running. But the general, natural deteriora-
tion of your physical and mental capacities will be stopped. Suppose
also that this wizard can guarantee that you will not experience an
accident or malady that could leave you incapacitated or in pain.
Another condition of this thought experiment is that you will live in
a more or less agreeable social and physical environment. You will
live, say, in some kind of liberal Western society and will not find
yourself after a generation or two stuck forever in a kind of a Nazi or
Stalinist regime. Nor will you find yourself living forever in a nuclear
desert, or a world that has undergone an ecological catastrophe. You
will be similarly protected from other calamities. And if one of the
reasons for your hesitation to take the pill is that you do not want

your family to perish while you live on, you may receive a supply of fifty or a hundred pills to allocate to them as well.

There are various versions of this thought experiment. In one, the step is irreversible. If you take it, you will indeed live forever, no matter what. In a second version, presented by Bernard Williams following a play by Karel Čapek, you will have the choice every, say, forty years to cease living.[15] In yet another version you can cease living whenever you want to (in effect, this last version does not really ask you whether you want to live forever, but rather whether you want to live for as long as you want). Various versions of the thought experiment may also present different life spans. Eternity is a rather long stretch of time; we could instead choose a shorter, more compact time unit, such as two hundred million years, twenty million years, two million years, or even two thousand or two hundred years.

Suppose you had the choice to take one of these pills. Would you? I have no reliable statistics, which would have to be based on proper samples. But most people to whom I have posed this question (a few hundred people in all, about half of them students of mine) have not opted for the pill, and certainly not in the first version of the thought experiment. It seems that many do not want to die, but nor do they want to live forever. Many do not even want to live for the shorter time period of a mere two hundred million years. Nor does shortening the period to twenty million, two million, or even to two hundred thousand or twenty thousand years change the reaction much. A few more people are willing to change their votes when the time decreases to two thousand or

15. Bernard Williams, "The Makropulos Case: Reflections on the Tedium of Immortality," in *Problems of the Self* (Cambridge: Cambridge University Press, 1973), 82–100; Karel Čapek, "The Makropulos Case," in *Four Plays*, trans. Peter Majer and Cathy Porter (London: Methuen, 1999), 165–259.

two hundred years, but not all even accept that last option. Given the version of the thought experiment in which they can live indefinitely but can also choose at any moment to end their lives, many (but not all) say that they would choose this option, but think that they will indeed end their lives one day, and probably not too far in the future.[16] Thus, some, but not all, choose a longer life, but very few choose immortality.[17] We seem, then, to be very hard to please: we do not want to die, but we also do not want *not* to die. Like the stereotypical teenager, we complain about whatever is offered to us.

It might be argued that if so many people, upon reflection, want death to come at some point and see it as a positive phenomenon, then death should not be understood to make life meaningless. But I do not think that this is a good reply to the concerns raised at the beginning of this chapter about the ways in which death and annihilation render life meaningless. For one thing, I belong to the group of people who, even in the first version of the thought experiment, in which life goes on forever, would take the pill. Williams argues that an everlasting life would be boring.[18] Following John Martin

16. I find it interesting that many admit, when asked, that other people's life expectancies considerably affect their own desires. If everyone else is going to live to the age of ninety, they too wish to live to about that age and not to seventy or a hundred and thirty. But if everyone else is going to live to a hundred and thirty, they do not want to live only to ninety (or live to a hundred and eighty); they want to live for about a hundred and thirty years too. It seems, then, that people's wish to be like others very strongly affects their choices about continuing to live. Put more provocatively, for many people, the wish to be conventional is stronger than their wish to live or their fear of death.

17. This decision also has some implications for the discussions of the afterlife mentioned at the beginning of this chapter (and see note 6). One of the reasons why the afterlife that comes after the resurrection on Judgment Day, or in heaven, is seen in a positive light is that it is endless. But it is quite possible that many people might not desire this kind of endlessness. Perhaps, then, the option of an immortal afterlife is not that attractive after all. Interestingly, in Theravada Buddhism the ultimate goal, or blessed condition, is that in which one's chain of rebirths finally *ends*, so that one is annihilated.

18. Williams, "The Makropulos Case," 94–98.

Fischer, however, I disagree.[19] If I could retain my physical and mental abilities, I do not think that I would be bored (under the favorable life conditions outlined above). Let us limit the discussion to one narrow sphere of cultural life: books. Even if I were to finish all the (good and interesting) books ever written, I could very well start reading them again and continue to enjoy myself, either because I had forgotten them or because second and third readings reveal so much more and allow so many new reflections and, even if that is not the case, they are often simply just enjoyable to reread. But I would of course not be limited to the books of the past: the world will go on and more new and interesting books will be written. The same would be true for other spheres of cultural life, such as, say, music. One would not want to hear the same piece of music incessantly, over and over again; that would indeed be torturous. But if we hear the same musical piece again after some time has passed, we enjoy it again, even if we have heard it before. And of course, the joys of life are not limited to culture. The delight in, say, a hug with someone we love can be relived again with each new hug. As Fischer points out, the same is true for tasty food. The gastronomic enjoyment to be had at different times may not be that different, but it is still very pleasing every time. Even the same, simple food (say, pasta) can be pleasing in the same way, again and again, if only there are sufficiently long intervals in between. True, I might find myself tired, after many, many years stuck in life, of the very experience of living; I might then feel very sorry for having taken the pill and for remaining alive. There is a danger in taking the pill—in the first version of the thought experiment—because the outcome is irreversible. But death, too, is irreversible. And I believe that my life will be

19. John Martin Fischer, "Why Immortality Is Not So Bad," *International Journal of Philosophical Studies* 2, no. 2 (1994): 257–270.

good: that I will not experience it as tedious but will enjoy the hugs, the friendships, the food, the love, the beauty of the scenery, the music, and the books.

But let us for the sake of argument assume that I am wrong, and grant that immortal life must be meaningless. I suggest that this does not answer the arguments for the claim that mortal life must be meaningless presented at the beginning of this chapter. The meaninglessness of immortal life does not entail the meaningfulness of mortal life; it may well be that immortal life is meaningless, for some reasons, *and* that mortal life is also meaningless, for *other* reasons (such as those presented at the beginning of this chapter about how death makes everything we achieve inconsequential and how death renders us all equal in the end). The claim that immortality makes life meaningless and the claim that mortality makes life meaningless do not conflict with each other. Thus, people's unwillingness to live forever (if indeed there is such unwillingness) is unhelpful for coping with the view that our eventual death makes our lives meaningless.

6

Another, more robust way of trying to answer the claim that annihilation makes life meaningless, somewhat similar to the previous argument, is to claim not only that we would renounce immortality if it were offered to us but that annihilation is *necessary* for meaning in life. It might be argued that only if life's span is limited can one waste it, and that what cannot be wasted cannot be of value. Further, if life were limitless and we did not have to get anything done by a certain date, there would be no reason to try to do anything meaningful, since we could always do it later; we would not feel the need to make good use of the time we have. Another argument may employ the notion of supply and demand: as already mentioned in chapter 3, limited supply is a necessary condition for economic value; no one would want to buy what is of limitless availability. Similarly, the argument may go, we take life to be of worth only because it is in limited supply. If it were unlimited, it would have no worth for us.[20] We are lucky, then, to have death; death is what allows life to be meaningful.

But the claim that immortal existence could not possibly be valuable or meaningful seems incorrect. According to many understandings, God's existence is eternal and yet also worthwhile. One does not have to believe in God in order to see from this example that there is nothing conceptually impossible in the notion of a person having an eternal existence that is meaningful or worthwhile. Nor is it true that it is impossible to waste an immortal life. An immortal person who spent his eternal life eating potato chips in front of a television set, watching the same 1950s soap operas over and over again, could well be said to have wasted that life, while an immortal person who spent his eternal life looking at objects of beauty, studying, meditating, and decreasing pain in the world could be said not to have wasted it. The former could be said to have had a meaningless eternal life while the latter to have had a meaningful eternal one.

I suggest that the supposition that immortal persons will not choose to do what is meaningful because they will always be able to do so later is also wrong. It might be true for some immortal persons, but need not be so for all. I think that if I had an endless life I would still choose to do worthwhile rather than unworthwhile things, for the same reason that I would choose, in an eternal life, to do pleasant rather than painful things: the former are better. If we find what

---

20. See James Lenman, "Immortality: A Letter," *Cogito* 9 (1995): 168.

is meaningful to be of value, and we want value, we will opt for it even in an eternal life, simply because it is valuable. To many, value has its own motivating force: it is attractive. Furthermore, as already suggested in chapter 3, the economic model is insufficient for discussing issues of meaning of life. The worth of things is determined not only by supply and demand; things also have noncompetitive worth, although we sometimes ignore it. And if we see minutes as containers of possible worth, then in a longer life there would be more containers, which could include more units of worth. Extending this further, an eternal life would have the most such containers and units of worth. I disagree, therefore, with the claim that an eternal life must be meaningless.[21]

Suppose, however, that all of what I have just said is not true, and grant, for the sake of argument, that our future annihilation is indeed necessary for life to be meaningful. As argued in the previous section, this does not conflict with the claim that annihilation makes life meaningless. It may well be the case that our life is meaningless because it is finite, and that it would also be meaningless, for different reasons, if it were infinite. Since it is possible for life to be meaningless in both cases, showing that an infinite life would be meaningless does not prove that a finite life is meaningful.

In this chapter, I have examined several arguments that, I suggest, fail to show that life can remain meaningful in spite of death. In the next chapter I proceed to present an argument that, in my view, does succeed in doing so.

---

21. Moreover, an unlimited life would not necessarily be one in which valued things (such as good books, good artworks, or good friendships) come in unlimited supply. Thus, even if we accepted the supply-and-demand model for an eternal life, we might see that life as meaningful because it achieves things that are of limited supply.

Chapter 6

Death and Annihilation II

1

I think that death and annihilation do *diminish* the meaning of life.
When life is good and worthwhile—and I believe that many lives
are so, and that many others that are not could become so—death
and annihilation are indeed negative, meaning-diminishing phenomena. It is a pity that this is the nature of life. Infinite life would
be much more meaningful, in my view; as mentioned in the previous chapter, if I had the chance, I would take the immortality pill.
Thus, I partly agree with the claims presented at the beginning of the
previous chapter. Death and annihilation do decrease the meaning
of life.

But this does not mean that they make life completely meaningless. First, even if a relationship, deed, day, or a life is temporal, the
fact of its worth at a certain point in time has eternal status. For example, it will always be true that you had a close, trustful, and blissful
moment with a family member; or that you felt some exhilaration in
reading a poem or looking at the sea; or that you were a decent person; or that you had a very good year. Even when the moment or year
is finished and gone, and no one remembers it (perhaps because, in
the distant future, there is no one left to remember it), it will remain

forever a fact that at a certain date (even if different calendars are used, or there are no calendars at all and no one to look at them), you or I behaved in fine ways and had fine achievements and experiences. That cannot be changed.

But second, even if we ignore this, and just see an achievement or state of affairs as passing and transient, this does not mean that they were worthless. Saying that death diminishes worth and, thus, that infinite life would have had more worth does not mean that a finite life has no worth at all, unless one is a perfectionist. A finite life may have a value that is not absolute, yet nevertheless substantial and sufficient, because things can be temporal *and* valuable. Even if finitude diminishes value, it does not remove it. In my view, a finite, meaningful life could be a life in which, for example, one was decent and truthful to oneself and others most of the time and had a close and warm relationship with one or two people; or managed, through effort, wisdom, patience, and luck, to create a loving relationship with one's spouse; or brought up one's children to be happy, decent, and productive people; or read a lot of beautiful poetry; or knew how to enjoy the great beauty of the trees growing on the sides of the street; or helped other people. There are many other ways in which one can lead a meaningful life. True, the decency, truthfulness, warm relationships, joy, helpfulness, and so on will eventually pass away. One day they will no longer exist. They are temporal rather than eternal. But that does not make them worthless. Thus, I can see my life, or aspects of it, as having great value although I know that that worthwhile life, or aspects of it, will pass away.[1]

I find odd the claim (presented at the beginning of the previous chapter) that, because of their transience, all experiences and lives

---

1. See John Cottingham, *On the Meaning of Life* (London: Routledge, 2003), 68.

are equal. Consider a case in which one person who was knowledge-
able and active all her life now suffers from severe cognitive limitations, while another person has suffered from such severe cognitive
limitations all her life. They are similar *now*. But we would not say
that their lives were the same. Of course, if we examine only the
aspects in which these two people are similar, completely disregarding those aspects in which they differ, the two appear the same. But
it is unclear why we should disregard all those aspects in which they
differ and focus exclusively on the aspects they share. This is true
also of cases in which their lives are over and the people are equal
now in being dead: although both Martin Luther King Jr. and Jack
the Ripper are now dead, it would be odd to consider their lives as
similar in meaning.[2] We would not usually think that because both
are now dead it does not really matter how they lived their lives.
This is true even if Martin Luther King Jr. and Jack the Ripper were
one day to be completely forgotten, or there were no person or conscious creature left to remember them.

When burying people we love, we frequently console ourselves
partly by noting that the departed had meaningful lives. It is indeed
sad that they died. But we find significant solace if we know that the
time that they had was used wisely. They did not waste their lives.
When I am about to die, if death is not abrupt and surprising, and if
I am not too senile or drugged to be conscious, I believe that I too
will be able to find some solace in the fact that I had a meaningful life. I will be sad to die, but the knowledge that my life was not
wasted, that what I had was used, by and large, well—that there was

---

2. Note also that this argument from equality of everyone in death assumes not only that all
lives are alike but also that all lives are alike *in being meaningless*. But this assumption is not
warranted, as it may be that all have the same value, and that value is high. If we take the lives
of Gandhi and of a beach bum to be of the same value, it is as plausible to claim that their
value is that of Gandhi's life as it is to claim that their value is that of the beach bum's.

much value in it—will be a real comfort.[3] It is a great boon, and a great consolation, to have had a meaningful life.[4]

2

The previous chapter presented various parables that aim to show how death and annihilation render our lives meaningless. But I do not think that they succeed in doing so. The analogy to floor sweeping, which aims to show how death or annihilation renders life meaningless, seems to me to substantiate the opposite claim: that death and annihilation, although diminishing the meaning of life, need not demolish it. Suppose, again, that immediately after we finish sweeping the floor someone steps on the part of the floor we have cleaned and dirties it, so that we have to do it all over again. This of course gives us the feeling that we are working in vain and that our effort is pointless—we may as well not bother at all. However, we do not normally feel this way when the floor we have cleaned becomes dirty after a couple of days. We enjoy the cleanliness of the floor for

---

3. Some people think that just as "All's well that ends well," so too "All's unwell that ends unwell." Hence, because death comes (of course) at the end of life, sometimes with pains and senility, they take it to undermine the worth of everything that preceded it. But in real life, unlike in films and plays, many events that ended well were not themselves good, and we would have been very glad if they had not occurred at all or had happened differently. Likewise, what has a bad end may still have been very worthwhile in many of its parts and very valuable overall, and we may be very glad that it happened. When we appraise the overall meaning of a life, the low degree of meaningfulness in later or final events should not be taken to undermine the high degree of meaningfulness of earlier events.

4. This is probably the insight behind the saying one sometimes hears from people after they have achieved something of great importance to them, "Now I can die happy." The saying seems to me exaggerated; they will probably not die happy, but will be somewhat sad to die, in spite of that achievement of considerable worth. But there is a feeling that achieving worth can make death easier. Death is sad, but it is a significant consolation to know that life was worthwhile.

several days; it has worth for us. Perhaps we would have liked it even better had the floor remained clean for a few days longer or even for weeks, months, or forever. But we accept that we have to sweep the floor every few days and, enjoying its cleanliness for those days, do not think that our work and activity were meaningless because their consequence was not eternal. The example of the swept floor, then, does not support the view that death destroys all meaning in life but, on the contrary, shows that, although death and annihilation diminish worth, they do not destroy it completely. What is transient is not of *perfect* value. But it is of *some* value, and that may well be very much. What is true for floor sweeping is also true for most of our other activities. We do not think that eating, washing dishes, sleeping, and making our bed in the morning are meaningless activities, although their results are not eternal and we have to do them over again periodically. If we thought that, we would not bother eating or washing dishes. Much of what we find to be worthwhile is transient, and this transience does not make it worthless.

I suggest that the myth of Sisyphus also does not serve as the apt parable of the human condition that many have found it to be; there are too many differences between Sisyphus's condition and ours. Sisyphus always fails. Even if he were to succeed, his task— putting a stone on a top of a hill—is stupid and unrewarding. The activity he performs is both endlessly repetitive and painful. He does not choose or want to do what he does, but is forced to do it. But unlike him, we sometimes do succeed in our endeavors, and many of them are not as stupid and unrewarding as just putting a stone on a top of a hill. Again unlike Sisyphus, we do not perform a single activity repetitively and painfully, and often we choose to do whatever we do freely.[5] Hence, our lives are often quite different

5. Assuming that we have free will. See chapter 8.

from and certainly not as meaningless as his. To represent the myth as an accurate depiction of all human life, as Camus does, is misleading. Unfortunately, Camus's literary ability and rhetorical power are so great that some people are convinced and come to see their lives as his parable describes them.[6]

Tolstoy's parable, too, is an inaccurate portrayal of the human condition. Most people's lives differ greatly from that of the traveler while he is hanging on the twig in the well. Of course, our lives, like his, will end. The black and white mice that gnaw at the base of the twig, representing the passing days and nights that bring us toward our eventual death, shorten both the traveler's life and ours. But what makes his experience meaningless is not his imminent death but rather the meaningless activity in which he is engaged: he is hanging from a branch while sticking out his tongue to lick some drops of honey off a twig. Consider another, slightly different parable, telling of a traveler who did something extremely meaningful or who had some extremely meaningful experiences such as rescuing someone, attaining some deep mystical enlightenment, or achieving some profound understanding of something about the world or herself, before falling into the dragon's jaws. Or imagine that the traveler chose to die in order to save the lives of a group of children. We would then probably not think that the traveler's death makes the previous achievements and experiences meaningless. We may well think, on the contrary, that her life was meaningful. Thus, unlike what Tolstoy would have us believe, finitude does not, in fact,

6. The Sisyphus story is not only a wrong depiction of many people's meaningful lives, but also of numerous people's meaningless ones. Some people take their lives to be meaningless because of death, but death does not affect Sisyphus at all. Some people consider their lives as meaningless because they have failed in something they see as valuable and want to succeed in while Sisyphus fails in what he does not see as valuable and has no interest in. The Sisyphus myth, then, is a bad parable even for people's meaningless lives.

cancel the meaning of life. The determining factor, on the contrary, is the value of the acts and experiences one has in that finite life, so that a life in which there are many sufficiently meaningful acts and experiences can be meaningful in spite of its finitude. Put differently, Tolstoy's story involves two factors that can make a life meaningless—the finitude of that life and the meaninglessness of the activities one engages in within that life. (Nagel, as we saw in the previous chapter, does not distinguish carefully enough between these two factors of the meaning of life either.) Tolstoy does not distinguish between the two factors, and employs the meaninglessness in the latter to argue for the meaninglessness in the former. But that is a problematic move. The parable does not show that death makes life meaningless but only that meaningless activities make life meaningless.

Arguments from parables should be approached with caution, since parables often include elements that do not in fact appear in what the parables are likened to, and often preclude relevant elements that do appear in what the parables are likened to. Keeping that in mind, I would like to present here my own parable of what are (or could be, with some work) many people's finite lives. Once there was a seed that grew up into a sprout, and then a shoot, and then developed into a big tree. In the hot summer its branches and foliage provided pleasant shade under which travelers and animals used to rest and rejuvenate. In the winter travelers and animals took shelter from the rain under its foliage. They would lean against its fine trunk and rest, and they enjoyed its beauty. Between its twigs birds and small animals lived and thrived. When the wind rustled through its leaves, the sound was pleasant to hear and the movement pleasant to see. It had fruits that nourished animals and people, and some of its seeds developed into other, younger trees. Although some bad people cut some of its branches, and in years of drought some of its boughs withered, it had a life that was beautiful and a blessing to itself and to others. Then, at a certain age, like all living things, it died.

My parable, too, should be used with caution. But unlike Tolstoy and Camus, I do not claim that it provides a correct description of the way *all* lives in fact unfold. While some people's lives are more similar to what Tolstoy and Camus recount, many others are more like what I have just presented here. I will argue in chapters 15 through 17 that we can also often affect how our lives unfold (to a large degree, although not completely) and increase their meaning-fulness. It is often possible for us to live a life like that of the tree and not like that of Sisyphus (after he began to be punished) or like the last hours of the traveler's life, even though we know that at the end we will die. Death and annihilation do not make all our activities as grotesque as repetitively pushing a rock uphill while knowing that it will never remain there, or licking drops of honey off a leaf while clinging to a branch. Consciousness of the death that will come in the end is consistent with bearing fruit, giving shade, and having one's foliage rustle in the wind.

Life has both terrible and wonderful aspects. Neither should be denied. I take death and annihilation to be part of what is terrible about life; they are very unfortunate. They do take away some of the meaning of life, and it would be better, in my view, if we could have eternal life. But that does not mean that life is not also wonder-ful, or that death and annihilation take away all meaning from life. Death is a significant disadvantage about which it is reasonable to be sorry, but—unless we are perfectionists—it does not destroy life's meaning.

Chapter 7

Life in the Context of the Whole Universe

1

Some people take their lives to have sufficient value, and thus be meaningful, only if considered in the context of the here and now. They argue that when they examine life in the context of the cosmos, its value emerges as tiny, ineffectual, and hence insufficient. When seen against the background of the universe, whatever we do is negligible and hence meaningless. Thus Simon Blackburn, for example, claims that "to a witness with the whole of space and time in its view, nothing on the human scale will have meaning."[1] Thomas Nagel distinguishes between the cosmic perspective, to which he refers as general, external, objective, detached, impersonal, and as examining life *sub specie aeternitatis*, and another perspective, to which he refers as internal, subjective, engaged, and personal (or first-personal), which can be called *sub specie humanitatis*. He argues that "when we look at the world from a general vantage point it seems not to matter

---

1. Simon Blackburn, *Being Good* (Oxford: Oxford University Press, 2001), 79.

who exists."[2] This is true even for people such as Mozart or Einstein.[3] Some of those who bring up this argument for the meaninglessness of life suggest that to cope with it we should pretend to ourselves that we are not part of the universe and repress our knowledge of its vastness. Blackburn, for example, writes that if we avoid the perspective that considers the meaning of life in the wider context, the thought of life's meaninglessness does not arise. Hence, he suggests, we should adopt a narrower perspective that examines life only in the context of the here and now, shunning the point of view of the whole of space and time. Blackburn quotes Frank Ramsey as presenting a somewhat similar view and preferring the perspective of the here and now: "My picture of the world is drawn in perspective, and not like a model to scale. The foreground is occupied by human beings, and the stars are all as small as threepenny bits."[4] Nagel, too, holds that when we examine our lives from the narrow *sub specie humanitatis* perspective of the here and now, we again seem to matter. But unlike Blackburn and Ramsey, he believes that we can never completely disregard the cosmic, objective perspective: "The objective standpoint, even at its limit, is too essential a part of us to be suppressed without dishonesty."[5] According to Nagel, then, we cannot but continue to cope with the conflict between the two perspectives, and with the fact that, from the cosmic perspective, we do not really matter.

I will argue here that our lives can be seen as meaningful also from the wide, cosmic perspective that considers whatever we do within the context of the whole cosmos. There is no need to try to

---

2. Thomas Nagel, "Birth, Death, and the Meaning of Life," in *The View from Nowhere* (New York: Oxford University Press, 1986), 213.

3. Nagel, "Birth," 213.

4. Blackburn, *Being Good*, 79.

5. Nagel, "Birth," 210.

disregard the cosmic perspective or to pretend to ourselves that we are not part of a huge universe.

2

Why should life seem at all meaningless from the wide perspective? One may take one's life to be so because, when seen in a very large context, it becomes clear that most of the cosmos is not affected at all by our existence or our actions. Had we behaved differently, or not existed at all, most of the cosmos would not have been affected. Whatever we do may have some effect on our immediate environment, but it has absolutely no impact on, for example, a crater on the planet Neptune, a fortiori on some rocks on a distant star in another galaxy.

But this argument supposes that only a life that affects the whole universe can be considered meaningful. I see no reason, however, to accept this highly perfectionist supposition. I suggest that we should distinguish sharply between *perspectives*, on the one hand, and *standards for meaningfulness* on the other hand. We can have an expansive perspective that reflects on a certain life *in the context* of all other things, while at the same time holding standards of meaningfulness that do not require a life to *affect* all other things in order to be considered meaningful. Authors such as Blackburn and Nagel not only inspect a person's life in the context of the whole cosmos but also endorse a (perfectionist) threshold of meaningfulness that has to do with a life's effect on the whole cosmos. But it is possible to inspect one's life in the context of the whole cosmos while using standards of meaningfulness that do *not* have to do with the effect of that life on the whole cosmos. A cosmic perspective may endorse noncosmic, but rather much more moderate, standards of meaningfulness, and consider many people to have satisfied those standards. For example, many parents who see their children flourishing thanks to their parenting consider their lives meaningful even if they fully recognize that their efforts have not affected the cosmos at large. Standards of meaningfulness may have to do not only with a moderate effect, but even with no *effect* at all; they may have to do, for example, with courage in the face of pain, failure, and disappointment, or with reaching a certain degree of wisdom, or happiness, or aesthetic fulfillment in one's life, even if such achievements did not affect anyone else. And all of that can also be seen from the wide, cosmic perspective.

The distinction can perhaps be understood better if we recall that, in some theistic traditions, God knows everything, including whether a particular sparrow has fluttered its wings. Of course, God also knows that I am alive and whether I committed a small sin or a small virtuous act yesterday (for example, when a coworker failed at something, whether I looked at him either disdainfully, making him feel even worse, or encouragingly, making him feel better). According to such theistic traditions, God knows of each act and event in the context of all the many acts performed by each of the many people who ever lived and will live, and of course realizes that what I did yesterday does not affect many people in the world and would not affect anything five hundred years from now. Yet God may still evaluate what I did and judge it to be worthy or unworthy. Seeing an action in a large context and acknowledging that it has only a very limited effect, then, does not mean that God will not consider the act to be of worth; a cosmic perspective does not entail cosmic thresholds of meaningfulness. Indeed, according to some theistic notions, this is precisely what happens: God knows things from the wide perspective, *sub specie aeternitatis*, yet takes our lives, even our deeds, to be very meaningful.

One need not be a theist to accept this point; I gave the example of God just as an illustration of a possible position that examines lives from the cosmic perspective, noting our place in the context of all other events, yet does not infer from that that the value of what we have is insufficient or meaningless. We can replace the notion of God in the example above with that of another external observer (such as Blackburn's "witness"): the observer might be a creature from another planet, or even you or me when we think about our lives in the context of the cosmos at large. The point is that it is possible to accept a cosmic perspective without adopting extremely challenging standards of meaningfulness that require one's life to affect the whole universe forever. More generally, the standards of evaluation are largely independent of the size of the framework in which a certain issue is evaluated. When the latter grows, the former may, but need not, become more demanding. Of course, the two are not *completely* independent. If one employs only a limited framework, one cannot endorse all-encompassing standards of evaluation, since all-encompassing standards—such as influencing the whole cosmos—require a wide framework that enables one to notice the cosmos. But this does not imply the reverse: a wide framework does not necessitate all-encompassing standards. The wide framework allows both all-encompassing standards and much more moderate ones. And moderate standards can be adopted within both a limited framework and a wide one.

Blackburn argues that "when we ask if life has meaning, the first question has to be, to whom? To a witness with the whole of space and time in its view, nothing on a human scale will have meaning (it is hard to imagine how it could be visible at all—there is an awful *lot* of space and time out there)."[6] But this argument takes the visual

6. Blackburn, *Being Good*, 79.

metaphor too literally. True, it is visually or optically difficult to notice a small item against an immense background, but that does not mean that we cannot intellectually conceive of, or evaluate, the worth of such an item while acknowledging its place in a larger, and even infinite, context. Note also that discerning the difference between two things does not mean that we have to judge one of them relative to the other. It may be that in *comparison* to cosmological events, whatever happens in our lives is tiny, but in itself it is sufficient to reach the threshold of meaningfulness.

I suggest, then, that the cosmic perspective does not necessitate the adoption of perfectionist standards of meaningfulness. We may consider our lives from the cosmic perspective; we may also adopt godlike, perfectionist standards that require affecting the whole cosmos; but we need not adopt the latter *because* of the former. And if we do not commit ourselves to godlike, perfectionist standards of meaningfulness, our lack of effect on most of the cosmos need not lead us to see our lives as meaningless. Perhaps affecting most or the whole of the cosmos would have been grander; but affecting what we do here and now is often sufficient and meaningful as well.[7]

3

The previous section argued that even those who would have liked to affect the whole cosmos can, if they are not perfectionist, consider also lives with much more modest effects to be meaningful. But note that some people would not even want to affect the whole cosmos. I, for one, have no such interest, because almost all of the cosmos,

---

7. For a more elaborate discussion of these claims see my "The Meaning of Life *Sub Specie Aeternitatis*," *Australasian Journal of Philosophy* 89, no. 4 (2011): 727–734.

being nothing more than an enormous quantity of utterly dead matter, seems to me to be completely irrelevant to the meaning of my life. I have no interest in affecting craters on Neptune or rocks on faraway planets in other galaxies. Some thought experiments could be helpful here. If Earth and its inhabitants miraculously became a million times larger while the rest of the cosmos remained as it was, or if everything else in the cosmos became a million times smaller while Earth and its inhabitants remained the same size, I would not feel that my life had therefore become a million times more meaningful, or in fact any more meaningful at all. Nor would I feel that my life had become more meaningful if nine-tenths of the cosmos suddenly vanished.

I, for one, am also not troubled even by my lack of effect even on many occurrences on Earth. For example, I am not troubled by the fact that, being now in Haifa, Israel, I have absolutely no impact on how a certain family lives its life in Toulouse, France, or in Perth, Australia. This is because I neither have the desire nor the expectation to influence everyone everywhere. I feel no urge to affect these people, nor do I see why I should do so. As far as I am concerned, it is fine that they continue to live their lives happily and peacefully without being affected by me in any way. True, I do wish to affect people's lives when I hear about desolation (for example, starvation in Africa), since I very much want this suffering to cease. But my desire is for the suffering to stop, not that I should affect those who suffer. If the suffering ended in the right way at the hands of other agents (including the hands of the suffering themselves), or by itself, I would be just as content.

Chapter 8

Determinism and Contingency

1

Another challenge to the meaning of life comes from the view that we do not, in fact, ever choose freely to do what we do. Our will is not free; we are forced to will whatever we do by causes of which we may well not be aware. It does feel to us as though we are freely deliberating and choosing, but that is an illusion.

To many, the view that our will is not free seems incorrect. But one way to try to substantiate it is to rely on a presupposition that many of us share: that everything that happens has a cause, or a group of causes, that determines that it be the way it is. For example, the pen falling from my hand to the table falls precisely the way it does because various causes affect it, making it do so. One of these forces is gravity. Others have to do with the wind in the room, the temperature, the humidity, and the density of the air. There may be other causes at work as well, even if we are not aware of them. But we suppose that the pen fell precisely as it did (including its bouncing on the table three times exactly in the way it did before it came to rest) because of the various causes that affected it. If the causes were different, it would fall and bounce differently. We may not know what these causes are, but they are surely there.

This is true not only of movements or changes, as with the pen falling; when the pen rests on the table without moving, we also suppose that it stays there because of various causes that affect it so that it does not move. For example, the air pressure on the right side of the pen is as strong as that on its left, so the pen does not roll or move sideways. If the equilibrium of forces keeping it at rest were to change, the pen would move. Whatever happens to the pen, we suppose, does not just happen; it happens because various factors cause it to happen.

Our presupposition that things do not just happen, but are always caused (even when we may not recognize the causes), is so strongly held that it leads us to treat suggestions that events do not have causes as nonsense. To take an example commonly used in such discussions, suppose that our computer stops working. Suppose as well that the computer technician tells us that there is no cause for this malfunctioning; it just happened. And since there is no cause for the computer's malfunctioning, it cannot be fixed. The technician agrees that events usually do have causes, but insists that some do not, and that the computer's malfunctioning is one of these latter cases. We would find this suggestion so odd that we would assume we had not really understood the technician correctly. We might then ask if perhaps there is something wrong with the electronic connections inside the computer. But the technician patiently replies that it cannot be the electronic connections. If the problem had to do with the electronic connections, there would be a cause for this malfunctioning, and then it could be fixed. However, as he already explained, in this case there is no cause. We may still be perplexed and ask whether the problem might have to do with the power switch. But the answer again is that if that were the problem there would be a cause, and then the cause could be manipulated and the computer fixed. The computer worked until 5:36 yesterday afternoon and then stopped working for no cause at all, and therefore nothing can be done about it. Surely, we would switch computer technicians. We might accept the reply, "We haven't found the cause," but not "There is no cause," because we are certain that there are always causes that cause things to be precisely as they are, even if we sometimes do not know the causes. It is for this reason that in science, medicine, and all other spheres, even if long and thorough research into the causes of various events has not yielded results, we continue to suppose that the causes exist and that we have not found them, rather than that the causes are absent. We suppose that everything that happens or does not happen does so because there are some causes that cause it to be exactly the way it is and not otherwise.

Causes, however, are also events, and according to the supposition above they, too, cannot just happen, but must have their causes. And those causes must have their own causes in turn. Thus, *everything* is, was, and will be caused, that is, determined by causes that affect it to be exactly the way it is. But this implies that not only pens, computers, and illnesses have causes that determine precisely how they are (even if we cannot always identify the causes), but also that our choices and decisions are caused in the same way. We may not always know what exactly causes us to choose the way we do, but our will, or our choices, must also be determined by various causes, which, in turn, are determined by even earlier causes, and so on. There is no freedom of will; like everything else, the will too is fully determined, so that we do not really choose anything freely. For example, I may have had the feeling that I freely decided whether to have soup or a sandwich for lunch, but in fact I did not have that free choice; it was necessary that I choose the sandwich, even if I do not recognize the causes that operated on my will. Likewise, I did not really have a free choice (in the sense of being able to do things differently) to marry when I did, or to marry the person I did. Unbeknownst to me, various internal and external causes made me marry the person I did when I did, and I had no free choice about it. Spinoza, an important determinist, suggests that if a stone that has been thrown could think, it too would be convinced that it had freely chosen to be in motion.[1] What has been said here of the past is also true of the future: I may well believe that I am free to act morally or immorally tomorrow afternoon, but in fact I do not have this freedom; I may not *know* the causes and thus may entertain the illusion of choosing freely. But the causes, and their causes, and so on, are there, and a mind that is intelligent enough to know all of them (say, God) could already tell now what I am going to do tomorrow afternoon. Of course, my sensation that I am choosing freely and my belief that my will is (at least partly) free are also causally determined, and the same is true for your reading and thinking now about free will.

But the denial of our ability to choose freely can be seen as undermining the meaning of life. Many of us attach great value to our ability to choose freely. It is something that we are proud of and want to preserve. We also see it as distinguishing us from entities that we usually value less than ourselves, such as animals, plants, or machines. But if we do not have any free choice when we act, say, cowardly or courageously, we do not seem to differ from animals, plants, or a machine that dispenses popsicles when we insert coins and press a button. The only difference between popsicle dispensers and us is that the causal chains that move popsicle dispensers are short, simple, and clear, while the causal chains that move us are long, more complicated, and as yet unclear. Perhaps one day, if

---

1. Letter 58 to Schuller, in Baruch Spinoza, *Complete Works*, ed. Michael L. Morgan, trans. Samuel Shirley (Indianapolis: Hackett, 2002), 909.

research advances sufficiently, we will also know everything about the causes that lead us to, say, courageous decisions.

The view that our will is not free also renders our notions of moral responsibility and of being deserving highly problematic. If various causes force us to will whatever we do and, thus, never choose freely, we do not deserve admiration for our charity, courage, artistic achievement, or diligence. The same is true for reproach or shame. We morally reproach murderers, not knives, since we do not think that knives freely choose to murder. We take humans to be morally blameworthy, however, since they do choose freely between options. But if murderers could have not chosen otherwise, they should not be seen as being any freer or any more blameworthy than knives. Likewise, the person who cheated and the person who behaved honestly, or the person who succumbed to laziness and the person who overcame it, are equal in not having freely chosen to be one way or the other; various forces made them be as they are and do what they did, and they had no choice about it. Our way of explaining to ourselves why we punish some people and reward others would also have to change if we accepted the notion that the will is not free. Denying the freedom of the will, then, can be seen as obliterating significant aspects of what we take to be valuable, and thus meaningful, in our lives.

I have focused here on a secular rendition of the argument, but it is noteworthy that it can also arise in a religious context. If God knows everything, God also knows what my moral decision tomorrow afternoon will be. But that means that I am not really free (in the sense that I can do things differently) to choose whether to act morally or immorally tomorrow; it is already determined—that is, it must be the case—that I will choose tomorrow afternoon to act (say) morally. I may well have the *sensation* that I decide freely, and I may go through inner deliberations, qualms, and psychological processes, but I am not really free to decide one way or the other. I *must* end up with a particular decision that is already established. But if I cannot really choose freely between one option and another, then it is unclear why I should be considered praiseworthy or blameworthy for what I choose. Nor is it clear that it would be just, in such circumstances, to reward or punish me, in this world or the next, for those unfree decisions.

2

There are several ways to argue against the view that we have no free will and that, therefore, life has no meaning. An obvious way is to defend the view that our will is at least somewhat free (call this view *metaphysical libertarianism*). I do not have the space here to discuss the vast and intricate literature that debates metaphysical libertarianism versus determinism, and will therefore only mention that it is not at all clear that we have no free will. Both historically and today, important participants in the debate have presented interesting and strong arguments to show that we are free in significant aspects of our lives or that the existence of free will has yet to be disproven.[2] Note that, in one respect, metaphysical libertarianism is easier to defend than determinism, since it is less total and less radical: whereas determinists hold that everything is determined, metaphysical libertarians do not hold that *nothing* is determined. They claim that much is determined: for example, my moral choice tomorrow afternoon will be affected by (among other things) my

2. For some such accounts see, e.g., Robert Nozick, *Philosophical Explanations* (Cambridge, MA: Belknap Press of Harvard University Press, 1981), 294–309; Robert Kane, *The Significance of Free Will* (New York: Oxford University Press, 1996); Mark Balaguer, *Free Will as an Open Scientific Problem* (Cambridge, MA: MIT Press, 2010).

genetic makeup, early education, peer pressure, and past experiences. A libertarian need not deny such factors. But she will hold that, at least in some cases, my will is not completely determined, and my choice is free to a significant extent, since I have some ability to choose between alternative courses of action.

This is not the only way to challenge the argument that because everything happens necessarily, life lacks meaning. Some grant that causes determine the will and that people could have never chosen differently than they did, but argue that, at least in one sense, people could still be seen as free and as responsible for what they do if they realize their *own* wills and choose consciously without being compelled or obstructed by external forces. (Call this position *soft determinism* or *compatibilism*.) Again, I do not have the space to explore the literature for and against the many versions of this position, and will just note that many in the modern era have defended it.[3]

Grant for the sake of argument, however, that both metaphysical liberalism and compatibilism are wrong, so that there is no free will and people cannot be seen as free and as responsible for what they do. (Call this third position *hard determinism*.) Could life still be seen as meaningful? A third route for those who want to defend the view that life can be meaningful, following the work of, among others, Michael Slote and Derk Pereboom, argues that hard determinism need not render life meaningless.[4] Although hard determinism does eradicate some aspects of value from our lives, it does not

---

3. For some compatibilist accounts see, e.g., Harry Frankfurt, "Freedom of the Will and the Concept of a Person," *Journal of Philosophy* 68 (1971): 5–20; John Martin Fischer, *The Metaphysics of Free Will* (Oxford: Blackwell, 1994); Michael Fara, "Masked Abilities and Compatibilism," *Mind* 117 (2008): 843–865.

4. See Michael Slote, "Ethics without Free Will," *Social Theory and Practice* 16 (1990): 369–383; Derk Pereboom, *Living without Free Will* (Cambridge: Cambridge University Press, 2001); Pereboom, "Free Will Skepticism and Meaning in Life," in *The Oxford Handbook of Free Will*, ed. Robert Kane, 2nd ed. (Oxford: Oxford University Press, 2011), 407–423.

eliminate all value; and what is left is quite sufficient for us to regard our lives as meaningful, even if somewhat differently than we would otherwise.

True, it is easier to differentiate between animals, plants, and machines, on the one hand, and ourselves, on the other hand, if there is free will. But even if we do not have free will to set us apart, we still differ from them in being conscious creatures. Machines, plants, and many animals are not conscious at all. Some animals are conscious, but our consciousness is much richer, more multilayered, subtler, and more rational and creative than theirs. We are able to undergo deep aesthetic, spiritual, and intellectual experiences, to be self-aware, to hope, and to experience various moods and feelings. This does not mean, of course, that nothing is lost if our will is not free. But not everything is lost, and perhaps what is lost is not too much. We are still quite different, in an important way, from vending machines, cacti, worms, and even dogs.

Moreover, much of what we find worthy in our lives does not, in fact, presuppose freedom of will. Take bodily beauty, for example. Most of us appreciate beauty although we know that, to a large degree, it is not achieved by free will. Most of us even appreciate natural beauty *more* than beauty achieved through the operation of free will, such as with cosmetics or plastic surgery. Or consider sports. Some people treat elite sportsmen and sportswomen with great respect. Here too, however, learning that a certain sportsperson had excellent genetic conditions for being a good runner or for playing tennis does not decrease the respect of the fans. Of course, we also appreciate the effort that went into their training. Effort does not testify to freedom, however; a person can invest extreme effort because she was pressured by a demanding parent who instilled in a young mind, before it could choose, the expectation to excel. But learning such a fact about the early education (or conditioning) of a champion does not usually lead fans to respect that champion's achievements any less. When we think of achievements in sports, it is not the freedom of choice that we respect most. Even if we value it to a certain extent, that is not what we value primarily.

The same is by and large true also of other, more intellectual or artistic achievements. Take, for example, Michelangelo, Kant, Bach, or Shakespeare. Much of what we admire in them has to do with the rare gifts they had, and we sometimes say approvingly of them and of other geniuses that they are "naturals," that is, that the high quality of what they produced was in large part due to a natural gift and disposition. But this gift, or natural disposition, was not freely chosen. Other factors that affected their achievements have to do with the environment in which they grew and created. For example, their upbringing and education at an early age, including that which determined their technical ability, their capacity to focus, their ambition, self-confidence, diligence, determination, and so on, also helped them develop their abilities and, thus, produce splendid works. But that was not freely chosen either. We do not think poorly of famous composers, writers, or mathematicians whom we know to have inherited their natural gifts from parents and to have been educated from a very early age to excel in and love their respective fields. We may accept that they have internalized parental guidance and perhaps natural inclinations to the extent that they now feel a strong drive to create in their respective areas. It is not clear that they do what they do out of free choice. Some artists indeed report that they feel they "must" do what they do, that they have a strong passion, that they feel that a muse or inspiration works through them so that they are just its vehicle, or that they find it problematic, even psychologically painful, not to create. But that does not lead us to think any less of them.

Suppose that we grant, with the metaphysical libertarians, that Michelangelo, Kant, Bach, and Shakespeare had free will and exercised it when they created. It does not seem that that freedom is what we primarily value about them. Assume that in Shakespeare's time there had lived another person, let us call him Shakespeare*, who made roughly the same free decisions that Shakespeare did. However, because Shakespeare* lacked Shakespeare's genetically or environmentally endowed gifts and characteristics, Shakespeare* did not produce works of the same quality as Shakespeare's; in fact, Shakespeare* produced very bad plays and sonnets. If free choice mattered to us very much in our evaluation of Shakespeare or of Shakespearean drama, we would admire, or envy, Shakespeare and Shakespeare* to more or less the same degree. However, most of us would value Shakespeare much more highly than Shakespeare*; most would value Shakespeare over Shakespeare* even if we believed that Shakespeare* was much freer than Shakespeare.

Free will, then, is of value to us, but we also find many other aspects of life worthy. If science were to progress to the point that we could know all the causes—neuronal, psychodynamic, genetic, environmental, and so on—that necessarily made Beethoven create the Ninth Symphony, most of us would continue to appreciate both the Ninth and the greatness of Beethoven, the person who could create the Ninth, although we knew that he did not freely choose to compose it. The value of the *activities* or *products* at issue makes a great difference to us: our evaluation of the life of an obsessive towel collector would change if his obsession were somehow transformed and he became an obsessive great pianist or mathematician. Likewise, many of us enjoy and want to befriend constructive, pleasant, interesting, or good people and try to avoid the company of destructive, unpleasant, boring, or bad people even when we learn that the former grew up in a nurturing environment and the latter in a terrible one. Our understanding that, at least in some ways, "it is not up to them" does not much change our attraction to and appreciation of the former or the repulsion and disrespect we feel toward the latter.

I have discussed the issue up to now in a secular context, but the same would also be true in many theistic ones. Many religions hold that people do have freedom of choice. But suppose that this is denied, so that God determines everything one does. It is still plausible to see many activities and people as worthy in such a framework. Those people who have been blessed by God and who do what God has ordained to be good and worthy (even if not through their free decision) are the worthy ones. People through whom God speaks, even if that was not their choice, are also worthy.

As Pereboom, Slote, and others argue, then, although freedom of will is worthy, it is not the only worthy thing in our lives. A determined world, although lacking an important dimension, need not be meaningless; it may well have value in many other dimensions. It would be difficult, in some ways, for us to understand it, at least in the beginning. But it could still be a world in which people's lives are meaningful, even if in a somewhat different manner than that we are used to. There is no need to feel, then, that life is meaningless because of hard determinism. It is not at all clear that hard determinism holds, but even if it does, although it may in some respects change the meaning of our life, it need not eradicate it.

3

Other possible arguments for the meaninglessness of life are based on a view that is roughly the *opposite* of the one above: namely, that much in our lives is not necessary but, rather, contingent or arbitrary.[5] Much could have happened differently than it did or could have not happened at all, as blind chance plays an important role in our lives. Indeed, if one does not endorse determinism, it seems that the most basic aspects of our identity and existence are contingent. As Thomas Nagel points out, chance and contingency affect the very people we are. If our parents, or our parents' parents, and so on, had not met we would not have been here at all.[6] If on the night of our conception the telephone had rung, a different sperm cell might well have fertilized the egg, resulting in an embryo, and then a person, of a different genetic makeup. Someone else, not us, would have been born. Many things in our lives, including various incidents in our early formative years, significant meetings with people who affected us, the people we marry, the books that influence us, and the accidents we do or do not manage to avoid have to do with chance. What has happened could have happened differently, and that affects the meaning of our lives.

However, it is unclear why this shows that contingency undermines meaning. True, I might well not have been here at all; but now that I am here, my life may be of sufficient worth, that is, meaningful. True, many meaningful aspects of my life need not have come about. For example, my interest in philosophy—a major source of meaningfulness for me—was excited by a high school teacher who might well have taught another class. Without this teacher I might have discovered philosophy at a later stage in my life, or I might never have discovered philosophy but found another source of meaning, or I might never have found a source of meaning in life. At least for the sake of argument, let us suppose that my meeting with that

---

5. However, the concern in the basis of the two views seems to be broadly the same, namely, that we are not masters of our fate.
6. Thomas Nagel, "Birth, Death, and the Meaning of Life," in *The View from Nowhere* (New York: Oxford University Press, 1986), 211.

teacher changed my life in a way that increased its meaningfulness considerably and that without that meeting my life would have been far less meaningful. The degree of meaning I have in my life, then, is contingent, and could have easily not been what it is. Still, even if all that is true, I do not see why, now that I do what I do and find meaning it, my life should be counted as meaningless just because what has happened could have also not happened. Contingency does not undermine meaning; it only makes meaning contingent.

Evolutionary theory may be used to present a somewhat similar reason for thinking that our existence is arbitrary.[7] Just as we, as individuals, would not have come to be if not for specific contingent occurrences, so the human species that we are part of would have not come to be if not for specific contingent evolutionary events. We came to be human only thanks to a series of arbitrary mutations that happened, by chance, in the chromosomes of many different creatures through the ages. There were many, many intersections at which the mutations could have been different or could have not occurred at all. There were also many mutations that persisted, especially when there were few exemplars of them, largely thanks to chance; they could easily have been lost. Thus, the existence of the human race, with its consciousness, knowledge, morality, and art, is a result of blind chance. The processes that led us to be what we are now were blind, mechanical, and senseless, largely based on pure chance. And that, it might be argued, makes our existence meaningless or unworthy.

However, a blind, mechanical, and senseless process need not bring about a blind, mechanical, and senseless product. Although, according to evolutionary theory, our mind has developed thanks to

7. See, e.g., William Lane Craig, "The Absurdity of Life without God," in *The Meaning of Life*, ed. E. D. Klemke, 2nd ed. (New York: Oxford University Press, 2000), 45.

blind chance, now it operates not by blind chance but by thought, intention, and decision. The brutish and mindless process brought about a result that is mindful and capable of sophisticated reflection and self-reflection; resolved courage in the face of failure, disappointment, and pain; deep aesthetic experiences; warm, rewarding personal interactions; love; serenity; and mystical insights. And in all these there is much value and meaning. The arbitrariness in the evolutionary process, then, need not be seen as rendering our lives meaningless.[8]

4

Chance can also be understood as making our lives meaningless because of how it sometimes undermines all our plans and efforts. Planning, efforts, and precautions can diminish the role of chance in our lives but can never overcome it completely. Although we may have taken every precaution, done all the right things, and have no reason to expect an illness, accident, natural catastrophe, economic crisis, or war, any of those could still happen and upset all our plans. Our job may be terminated, health destroyed, family dissolved, or children die from one second to the next through forces over which

---

8. Evolutionary theory can be taken to render our lives meaningless also in another way that does not have to do with arbitrariness or chance: the theory suggests that our ancestors were amoebas, worms, reptiles, and apes, and this pedigree may be claimed to render our lives, even today as humans, insufficiently worthy. However, even though our ancestors were amoebas, etc., we have evolved. Today we are neither amoebas nor worms but humans, a different type of organism and a definite species quite different from those beings. There is no reason to shudder at the fact that we have evolved from amoeba-like creatures. This would also be true even if amoebas, reptiles, or apes were our immediate ancestors. The meaning in one's life has to do with the worth in one's own life, not the lives of one's ancestors. A person may have a meaningless life even if her parents had meaningful ones, and a meaningful life even if her parents had very meaningless ones.

we have no control. We may take this to diminish worth and meaning in life. Chance takes the control of our lives—something we value and count on—away from us, and when unexpected things happen by chance and prevent us from achieving ends toward which we have been working, we may feel that our efforts have been worthless.

But chance and lack of control are not always bad. We also find value in spontaneity, surprises, and whimsical and uncontrolled (or not completely controlled) activities. Chance can topple our plans, but it also sometimes opens new and unexpected opportunities. Assume, however, that this is incorrect, and that chance and lack of control are solely negative forces in life. It is still unclear why a lack of absolute control need make life meaningless (unless, again, one endorses perfectionism). Perhaps life would be more meaningful if we had fuller control over it, but many people's lives still include a sufficient degree of control. Of course, sometimes arbitrary occurrences upset important aspects of a person's life. Some people who go through such experiences say, sometimes while in shock, that therefore everything in life is completely arbitrary. But that is incorrect. In most cases, what happens to us is affected by both luck and our actions, and what we do (or fail to do) has a significant effect on our life. Much of what happens to us, externally as well as internally (that is, in our feelings and thoughts), although it is not completely controllable, is still somewhat controllable and frequently significantly so.

Moreover, even situations that are highly arbitrary or uncontrolled need not be meaningless. Consider a patient who does not know whether the pills he has been given are the new experimental medicine, which may cure the terminal illness he suffers from, or the placebo being given to the control group. He may well find worth in the chance that he has been given the experimental medicine and that it will turn out to be effective. And his life may also include other, sufficiently worthy aspects, such as those having to do with understanding, love, aesthetic experiences, happiness, or courage. Likewise, the concentration camp inmates Frankl discusses retained meaning in their lives although they had very little control over what happened to them.

There is a Western tradition that takes necessity to be of higher value than contingency. For example, in Monotheist theology, God is considered to have extreme value because (among other reasons) he is believed to exist necessarily, whereas our own lesser—even if still considerable—value has to do with our contingency. I am not sure that I accept this tradition, but there is no need for me to enter into the issue here. For my purposes, I may well accept that necessity is of higher value than contingency, but point out that there is still much value in contingent things as well (this is a view also held by many theistic systems). The expectation that our being and our deeds should be of a nature similar to that which in Western theology is ascribed only to God seems overly ambitious.

Now that we have looked at several of them, we can see a pattern in how some arguments for the meaninglessness of life work. They identify a certain aspect of life that endows it with some worth, such as freedom, necessity, or control, and suggest that because that aspect is not fully present or is absent, life is meaningless. But an aspect of worth may make life meaningful even when it is not fully present. Moreover, there are many aspects of life that endow it with worth. Even if one of them is completely absent, the robust value in other aspects of life is frequently sufficient, if one is not a perfectionist, to render life meaningful.

Chapter 9

Skepticism and Relativism

1

We may be wrong about what we take to be of value. Some of us have been wrong to love someone who turned out not to deserve it. Or we may have acted in ways that we later realized to be morally wrong. We know that we made some mistakes in the past, and that it is possible that in the future this is also how we will see what we judge to be of value now. Chapter 15 describes some methods we may use in order to identify what is meaningful for us, but none of them provide certainty. We can never know anything with certainty even in the exact sciences, all the more so when it comes to values. This may suggest that all our views about the meaning or meaninglessness of our lives, about what would make our lives more meaningful, and about the arguments presented in this book, are unreliable. We live in a complete evaluative chaos, cannot know that any experience, decision, or behavior is worthy, and hence can never take our lives to be meaningful.

However, the insistence on nothing less than absolute certainty and the rejection as insufficient of what is not known with absolute certainty is again perfectionist. As fallibilism (discussed in chapter 4) points out, precisely because we cannot, and never will be able to, achieve complete certainty—knowledge is always tentative and could be proven wrong one day—we should not aim at absolutely certain knowledge, nor consider everything short of certain knowledge as worthless. According to fallibilism, the views that emerge as the most plausible after sufficient consideration and testing should be seen as knowledge and, for those who are not perfectionists, are sufficient and satisfying. Thus, it is wrong that, because of susceptibility to doubt, we cannot take anything to be worthy; that any one behavior or way of life is as plausible as any other; and that we should accept that we live in a complete evaluative chaos. Of course, we may be, and sometimes are, wrong. Because our knowledge, decisions, and values are not foolproof, we should periodically reexamine what we value, thus diminishing the likelihood of making mistakes. But we can frequently rely on our considerations rather than completely despair of being able to make choices regarding what is valuable and meaningful in our lives. Moreover, in some cases we are almost certainly not far off the mark. A claim that suggests that Martin Luther King Jr.'s actions have decreased justice in American public life is surely wrong, as is the claim that the lives of Jack the Ripper and Mother Teresa had the same value.[1]

2

Yet another argument may rely on relativist claims. There are many different types of relativism. I will focus here on two, cultural relativism and individual relativism, but much of what will be said of them

---

1. Discussions with some of those who claim to be radical skeptics reveal that they sometimes do not actually believe what they say. They occasionally like to play games or tease, sometimes also themselves, but when asked whether they *really* accept claims such as those about Jack the Ripper and Mother Teresa, they almost always reply that, if they are being serious, they do not. Sometimes philosophers are too fond of playing games. When we ask ourselves a practical, important question such as how to conduct our lives or how to make our lives meaningful, let us not play games.

also applies to the other types of relativism. According to cultural relativism, our judgments do not have a transcendent, objective, absolute status that is independent of specific cultural standards. Our judgments are true only according to, or relative to, certain criteria or standards, and these criteria are never neutral; they are always culture-specific. In one culture, for example, the assertions "It is immoral to murder unfaithful wives" and "The earth rotates around the sun" are correct (that is to say, for relativists, correct according to the moral and scientific standards of that culture), while in another culture these assertions are incorrect (that is, incorrect according to the moral and scientific standards of that other culture).

One may, of course, point out that one is not interested in what is correct according to this or that culture but in what is correct, period. But that is precisely what cultural relativists say is impossible: according to cultural relativism, we never have *The View from Nowhere* (to use Thomas Nagel's famous term and title), that is, a neutral view that is not from any one particular perspective but is from God's point of view, so to speak. We can never know how things are not from any specific point of view, but from *all* points of view or from no point of view at all. Our view is always from somewhere, always perspectival and situated, and we can only say how things are relative to the standards accepted in a certain culture. According to the relativist, when we claim to have an objective view, "a view from nowhere," we are simply elevating the judgments or standards of our specific culture and granting them, with no justification, an objective, neutral status that they do not in fact have.

Of course, we could try to judge which culture-specific criteria or standards are correct or better. But to do that we would again have to use standards and criteria, and according to cultural relativism those standards and criteria would *also* inevitably be culture-specific (even if, again, they would not be presented as such but disguised as part of "the view from nowhere"). For cultural relativists, then, our judgments are never "just true," "true, period," or what might be called "true with a capital *T*." They are always true for me or true for you, true according to my standards or true according to yours. Put differently, since there is no neutral point of view, no claim can be preferable to another from the neutral point of view. Claims can be preferable to others only according to the nonneutral criteria accepted in my culture or in yours. In my culture and according to my standards, of course, my view is preferable. But in your culture and according to your standards *your* view is preferable. Since there is no way of adjudicating between my view and yours that is not culture-specific, I cannot determine that a view is better, period, but only that a view is better from this or that point of view.

Another, closely related, theory is individual relativism. While cultural relativism rejects "the view from nowhere," individual relativism rejects both "the view from nowhere" and "the view from a culture." An individual relativist is one who judges the truth of statements not relative to the standards of the cultural community to which she belongs but relative to the individual standards that she espouses, even if these differ from the standards commonly accepted in her cultural community. Thus, a certain judgment is true for me if, according to my individual standards, it is true. Of course, you may think that I am wrong. And that is perfectly fine, since a judgment can be true for me and wrong for you. There is no sense in asking whether the judgment is neutrally true, or true, period, or true according to the view from nowhere, since there is no such thing; for an individual relativist, judgments are always true relative to local (individual) standards.

One can apply cultural or an individual relativism to art, science, morality, the meaning of life, or everything. In this discussion I will focus on how relativism can influence views on the meaning of life. Not surprisingly, a cultural relativist would deny that life is "meaningful, period" or objectively meaningful. Instead, she would believe that life can be meaningful only according to the accepted standards of the cultural community to which a certain person belongs. Similarly, for an individual relativist, life can be meaningful only according to the standards that the individual in question espouses. An individual relativist holds that if a person's life fulfills her criteria of meaningfulness, it is indeed a meaningful life (to her), and if that person's life does not fulfill her criteria of meaningfulness, it is indeed a meaningless life (again, to her). I, of course, am free to think that her life is, say, meaningless (to me, by my standards), and thus her life would indeed be meaningless (to me, by my standards), even if, to her, her life is meaningful. This does not involve a contradiction, because for an individual relativist a certain life can at the same time be meaningful to one person and meaningless to another. Of course, if I am an objectivist I would point out that I understand that her life is meaningful to her, according to her standards, and meaningless to me, according to my standards; but as an objectivist I do not want to know whether her life is meaningful to her, or meaningful to me, but whether it is meaningful, period, or meaningful from the neutral point of view. For individual relativists, however, this is a wrong and senseless question, since according to them there is no such thing as meaningful, period, or meaningful from a neutral point of view. There are only local, situated, perspectival points of view, and hence life is always meaningful only from somewhere, according to someone's standards.

But if we accept cultural or individual relativism, it might be argued, we cannot see life as meaningful. First, because relativists believe that every person judges by her own cultural or individual standards, they have to see any view on the meaning of life as acceptable; anything can be valuable if one's standards render it valuable.

But this means that relativists have to endorse highly counterintuitive claims, such as that life can be made meaningful by lining up balls of torn newspaper in neat rows.[2]

Second, because relativists believe that no claim is advantageous to another from the neutral point of view, and that anything can be valuable if one's standards render it valuable, they cannot consider anything to be of less value than what they value. Thus, for them, "anything goes." But this "anything goes" attitude undermines the notion of valuing, for implied in valuing is the possibility of hierarchizing. Valuing presupposes that it is possible to consider some things to be of higher value, others of lower value, and yet others of no value. If nothing can be considered preferable to or more valuable than anything else, we indeed have no reason to prefer or value anything. It does not really matter what we choose or endorse; it's all the same. And if valuing becomes an empty notion, and value and meaning in life are as linked as we have seen them to be, then the meaning of life becomes an empty notion as well.

Third, it might be argued that those who accept cultural or individual relativism cannot take life to be meaningful because relativism excludes rationality, while most people see at least some of their judgments about the meaning of life as having to do with rational considerations. Thus, relativism undermines the ability to see life, or aspects of it, as meaningful.

Fourth, it might be claimed, relativists cannot regard their lives as meaningful because, under relativism, there is no real value, that is, no objective value that is independent of specific cultural or individual standards. For relativists there is only relative value, that is, value dependent on specific cultural or individual standards, which

---

2. The example is taken from John Cottingham, *On the Meaning of Life* (London: Routledge, 2003), 21.

is not real value. But without real value, there is no real meaning and, thus, life is meaningless.

3

Those who believe that life is, or can be, meaningful have two main avenues of response to relativism. The first and obvious one is to join most philosophers in the Western tradition and reject relativism. Some common antirelativist arguments start out by claiming that relativism contradicts itself (since, according to relativism, nothing, including relativism, is objectively true); that disagreement among individuals or among cultures does not prove the truth of relativism (since disagreement may just as well arise when one side is objectively right and the others are objectively wrong); and that many disagreements are only apparent or resolvable. Limits of space prevent me from following these and other arguments and describing some of the many moves and countermoves made in this complex debate. I will only mention that it is not at all clear that relativism holds.[3] The second route is to deny that relativism, even if accepted, renders life meaningless. According to this view, relativism may or may not hold; but even those who believe that it does hold and take themselves to be relativists can still find life to be meaningful. In the rest of this chapter, I follow this second route, and argue that relativism does not render life meaningless.

3. For some discussions critical of relativism see, e.g., Harvey Siegel, *Relativism Refuted: A Critique of Contemporary Epistemological Relativism* (Dordrecht: Reidel, 1987); Christopher Norris, *Reclaiming Truth: Contribution to a Critique of Cultural Relativism* (Durham, NC: Duke University Press, 1996); Thomas Nagel, *The Last Word* (New York: Oxford University Press, 1997); Paul Boghossian, *Fear of Knowledge: Against Relativism and Constructivism* (Oxford: Clarendon, 2006).

The first and second arguments for the claim that relativism undermines meaningfulness were that because relativists allow every person to judge by her own cultural or individual standards, they have to see any view of the meaning of life—including highly counterintuitive ones—as acceptable, and thus also empty the notion of "valuing" of its content. However, relativists can respond that there are sufficient resources within the relativist paradigm to reject other people's views. Relativists may well deny that anything goes: only certain things go from certain perspectives, and that is how relativist value can be retained. Suppose that I am a relativist. As such, I will take some things to be meaningful. I will, of course, take them to be meaningful from my point of view and according to my norms. I may also note that you are a different individual, with a different point of view, and that you take other things to be meaningful. As a relativist, I will hold that no view is superior to any other from a neutral, objective point of view since I believe that no such neutral, objective point of view exists. But that does not mean that I will hold that no view is superior to another from my own, perspectival, point of view. As a relativist, I may well take some activities, such as feeding the hungry, to be—for me—more meaningful than other activities, such as lining up balls of torn newspaper. I may well take lining up balls of torn newspaper to be completely meaningless. Of course, I will not take this activity to be objectively meaningless since, as a relativist, I will not think that there is such a thing as objective meaninglessness. But I will take lining up torn newspapers to be, under the relativist paradigm, meaningless according to my own cultural or individual norms. The rejection of some views and of the "anything goes" mentality under relativism is somewhat different than it is under objectivism, but it is still possible.

It is untrue, then, that by allowing every person to judge according to her cultural or individual norms, relativists have to regard any view on the meaning of life as acceptable. Not everything is valuable from one's cultural or individual point of view, even if others do take it to be valuable from their point of view. Of course, relativists will hold that if some people really take a certain activity, such as lining up rows of torn newspaper, to be meaningful to them, from their point of view, it is indeed meaningful to them (from their point of view). But this is different from accepting this activity as meaningful, period, or as objectively meaningful. It would indeed be odd and very counterintuitive to consider lining up torn newspapers as objectively meaningful. But the relativist would not do that, as the relativist thinks that nothing can be objectively meaningful. The relativist would instead hold the more intuitive and plausible view that lining up torn newspapers may turn out to be meaningful in a certain culture or for a certain individual. And again, this relativist will not accept that lining up torn newspapers is also meaningful for *her*.[4]

4

The third argument for the claim that relativism undermines meaningfulness was that relativism excludes rationality, while most people see at least some of their judgments about the meaning of life as having to do with rational considerations. Thus, relativism undermines the ability to see life, or aspects of it, as meaningful. At least for the sake of argument, we can grant that meaningfulness does presuppose some degree of rationality. However, it is untrue that

4. This is in disagreement with, among others, Cottingham, *Meaning of Life*, 21; Erik J. Wielenberg, *Value and Virtue in a Godless Universe* (Cambridge: Cambridge University Press, 2005), 21–23; Susan Wolf, *Meaning in Life and Why It Matters*, with commentary by John Koethe, Robert M. Adams, Nomy Arpaly, and Jonathan Haidt (Princeton, NJ: Princeton University Press, 2010), 15–18, 36; and Thaddeus Metz, *Meaning in Life* (Oxford: Oxford University Press, 2013), 175.

relativism excludes rationality; one can endorse cultural or individual relativism while subscribing to rationality. As we saw earlier, relativism is the view that all judgments are perspectival, local, situated, "from somewhere," so that no judgments are neutral, transcendent, objective, or "from nowhere." But being perspectival, local, and so on, does not in itself exclude the use of rational procedures (that is, procedures that aim for consistency, are open to criticism, are based on valid rules of inference and on careful consideration of evidence, etc.). A judgment may be "from somewhere" but, at the same time, rational. The rational procedure applied in this "somewhere" will indeed apply only in the context of this "somewhere." It will not have an objective status. But a rational procedure it will still be. Being situated rather than neutral is consistent both with being rational and with being irrational.

Those who hold that life cannot be seen as meaningful under relativism may concede that relativism does not exclude rationality, but argue that it also does not exclude *irrationality*, and that this may pose just as much of a problem. They may point out that although, under relativism, we may disagree (from our cultural or individual point of view) with irrational procedures that other cultures or people engage in, the relativist framework does not in itself exclude the use of irrational procedures. However, that is also true for the objectivist framework in itself. Holding that certain views, standards, or procedures are nonperspectival, or are objectively and neutrally true, does not in itself necessitate that those views, standards, or procedures will be rational. Objectivists may, but need not, rely on reason. Many of them rely, for example, on emotion ("I know it is objectively true because I strongly feel this to be so, and those who say differently are just objectively wrong"), on revelation or what they take to be revelation ("God spoke to me, therefore it is objectively true, and there is no place for a difference of opinion on this matter"), on authority, on tradition, or on any other good or bad method people use to form their views. Many who rely on feeling, whim, fad, insight, intuition, putative self-evidence, pseudoscience, or pseudoarguments are objectivists who take all these to show what is objectively true, and think that those who think differently are objectively wrong. The objectivist paradigm in itself does not shield people from accepting utter nonsense on the basis of irrational procedures, and most people who accept nonsense on the basis of irrational procedures are objectivists. This, of course, does not say much, since most people are objectivists,[5] and hence it is also likely that most people who accept nonsense on the basis of irrational procedures will be objectivists. I have no reliable statistical data, but my experience with objectivists and relativists so far has given me no reason to believe that the percentage of objectivists who hold outlandish views for foolish reasons is lower than the percentage of relativists who do the same.

Some of those who hold that life can be seen as meaningful only under objectivism, and never under relativism, are not thinking of objectivism *in itself* but rather of some specific type of objectivism that is close to their heart, such as a rationalistic objectivism that leads to conclusions with which they agree. And when they consider relativism, they are not thinking of relativism *in itself* but rather of some specific type of relativism with which they disagree, such as a nonrationalistic relativism that leads to conclusions that they find grotesque. But this undermines the comparison between objectivism and relativism *in themselves* because it introduces other, idiosyncratic elements into the comparison. Of course we should

---

5. It is difficult to find cultural or individual relativists outside academia, and even within academia most reject it. Relativism tends to be popular only in departments of anthropology and sociology, as well as literature and cultural studies departments with poststructuralist orientations.

not, when comparing relativism and objectivism, consider specific types of relativism and objectivism and generalize from these specific types to relativism in itself or to objectivism in itself. Rather, we should consider relativism and objectivism *as such*.

Thus, relativists, like objectivists, can consider issues related to the meaning of life in a rational manner. In this respect, too, relativism does not, in itself, undermine the meaningfulness of life.

5

The fourth argument for the claim that relativism undermines meaningfulness was that relativists cannot hold things to be of real value, that is, objective, transcendent value, independent of specific cultural or individual standards. According to this argument, for relativists there is only unreal value, that is, relative value, dependent on specific cultural or individual standards. But without real value, there is no real meaning and, thus, life is meaningless. However, relativists may well reject the supposition that only value that is independent of cultural or individual standards (a value that, according to them, does not exist) is real; they may well take value that is dependent on cultural or individual standards to be quite real and sufficient. They will hold that, as relativists, they take some things to be valuable and important according to *their* individual or cultural norms. But this does not mean that these things are not really valuable and important (although they will be really valuable to agents according to the norms that these agents uphold).

Relativists may also point out that what they are suggesting is not counterintuitive. We frequently do accept that things can be important, valuable, and meaningful to one, even if they are so only from a specific, local point of view. These might include objects that belonged to loved ones who have passed away; pictures, books, and toys from one's childhood; old gifts; and anything else of sentimental value. Likewise, we can see how a person's spouse, parents, and children would be more valuable to her than other spouses, parents, or children are, just because they are hers. What is valuable or meaningful does not have to be objectively valuable or meaningful. Similarly, it may be that *only* within the specific fabric of my culture (that I do not see as having a neutral or universal status) will certain works of literature and visual art be seen as sophisticated, rich, and very rewarding. But that is no reason to see them as nonvaluable or nonmeaningful. I may also find much meaning in other aspects of my cultural heritage, and no meaning in aspects of other cultural heritages, without holding that what I find meaningful is superior to what others find meaningful from any neutral point of view, or that such a point of view exists. We commonly not only accept, but also encourage people to indulge in such nonneutral, local attitudes and experiences, take them to enhance life's meaning, and frequently believe that those who have no such attitudes or experiences lead impoverished lives. Thus, we frequently do see perspectival value and meaning as real in a sufficiently robust and satisfying way. It is local meaningfulness, dependent on one's specific perspective and on individual or cultural norms, and is thus somewhat different from the universal or neutral meaningfulness that we usually think of (and which, relativists claim, does not exist). But as localized meaningfulness, it is real.

Those who hold that meaning is not real under relativism may still claim that, as Charles Taylor has argued, taking something to be meaningful presupposes that its value is at least partly independent of one's free choice; otherwise, it would not matter what one chooses and one could just as well choose something else. However, they may argue, relativists are committed to the view that what is valuable to them is completely dependent on their free choice. Hence, the argument will go, what relativists take to be valuable is not really valuable.[6] But it should be noted that Taylor does not raise his argument in order to criticize cultural or individual relativism: he uses it only to criticize the ideal of radical authenticity that advocates pure self-determining freedom, self-creation, or self-expression.[7] Relativists may, but do not have to, subscribe to what Taylor calls radical authenticity. Relativists need not hold that what is valuable to them is completely dependent on their free choice. A cultural relativist, for example, may accept that what he considers to be honorable, admirable, valuable, and so on, is not freely chosen but, rather, largely dependent on, moreover determined by, the culture in which he grew up. He may accept that rather than choosing many aspects of his culture, he grew up into them. Nor do individual relativists need to subscribe to the radical authenticity that Taylor criticizes. They, too, may hold that they *find* themselves valuing different things rather than engaging in pure free self-determination or self-creation. They may well accept, for example, that they love their mother and not another one not because they chose her from among many, but because they were born to and raised by her. Had they been born to and raised by another mother, they would have loved that other one, not the mother they now love. Likewise, had they grown up with different childhood toys, books, and songs, or had they themselves had different children, they would have cherished

---

6. Charles Taylor, *The Ethics of Authenticity* (Cambridge, MA: Harvard University Press, 1992), 38–41. For a discussion see Metz, *Meaning in Life*, 173.

7. A reply to Taylor may suggest that choosing without relying on anything independent of one's choice, thus expressing only one's pure self-determining freedom, may still be taken to be of real value (even if the choices are arbitrary) if pure self-determining freedom is deemed as valuable. But my discussion here does not follow this direction. It grants that taking something to be meaningful presupposes that its value is at least partly independent of one's will, and only claims that this does not conflict with individual or cultural relativism.

those, and not the ones they now cherish. Relativists can accept, then, that what they value is not dependent only on them, and they need not rely on notions of radically free self-determination or pure self-creation. But since neither cultural nor individual relativism is committed to the ideal of radical authenticity, Taylor's criticism of this ideal does not show (nor, I believe, did Taylor intend it to show) that relativism excludes real value.

6

Relativism, then, does not jeopardize the meaning of life. Moreover, I believe that choosing between relativism and objectivism is irrelevant for most issues related to the meaning of life. Consider the example of Amy and Jane. Suppose that Amy believes that life is meaningful if and only if one makes one's first million by the age of twenty-five, while Jane believes that life is meaningful if and only if one feeds the hungry in Africa. Amy and Jane have, then, very different standards of meaningfulness, and hence they also have very different views on which specific behaviors make life meaningful.

Amy and Jane can be either objectivists or relativists when it comes to the meaning of life. First suppose that, like almost all people and philosophers, they are objectivists. Thus, Amy thinks that her views and standards of meaningfulness are objectively correct, while Jane's views and standards are objectively incorrect; and Jane thinks that *her* views and standards are objectively correct, while Amy's views and standards are objectively incorrect. Objectivist Amy and Jane, then, do value some things more than others, and do not accept that "anything goes."

Now let us suppose that Amy and Jane are relativists rather than objectivists when it comes to the meaning of life. While this might seem to be the complete opposite of the previous situation, in fact not much changes; the same statements about Jane and Amy still hold, with only small modifications. Relativist Jane and Amy each still thinks that she is right and that her interlocutor is wrong, but each of them holds that this is so according to her own cultural or individual standards. In other words, Jane thinks that she is right by her own standards, and rejects Amy's views also in the light of her own (Jane's) standards, while being aware of the fact that what she, Jane, considers to be wrong is right by Amy's standards. The same is true, of course, of relativist Amy's views vis-à-vis herself and Jane. Thus, like objectivist Amy and Jane, so also relativist Amy and Jane do value some things more than others, and do not accept that "anything goes."

Objectivist Amy and Jane may relate to each other's positions in an irrational or a rational manner. They may just roll their eyes, sigh with frustration, mock, and thoughtlessly reject each other's positions. Or they may try critically and cautiously to identify inconsistencies, false descriptive claims, implicit suppositions, unheeded implications, and unwarranted conclusions in each other's as well as in their own positions. Again, however, let us now suppose that Amy and Jane are relativists rather than objectivists. Once more, hardly anything changes; what has been written above about objectivist Jane and Amy still holds, with only very small modifications. Relativist Amy and Jane may consider their own and each other's positions, and communicate about them, as irrationally or rationally as objectivist Amy and Jane do. They may roll eyes, mock, and so on, or they may try critically and cautiously to identify inconsistencies, unwarranted conclusions, and so on, in each other's as well as in their own positions. Again, being a relativist rather than an objectivist does not make much of a difference.

Likewise, objectivist Amy and Jane each believes that the path she chose makes her life really valuable or meaningful. But this is true also of relativist Amy and Jane. Of course, objectivist Amy and Jane each holds that the path she chose makes her life objectively valuable and meaningful, while relativist Amy and Jane do not think that there is objective value or meaning; relativist Amy and Jane each believes that the path she chose makes her life valuable or meaningful according to the norms she endorses. But like objectivist Amy and Jane, relativist Amy and Jane can each believe that the path she chose makes her life really valuable or meaningful.

Thus, relativists and objectivists are more similar to each other than may at first appear. This is why relativists as regards the meaning of life, such as Aldous Huxley, A. J. Ayer, E. D. Klemke, and Brooke Alan Trisel, present their paradigm not as destructive or subversive but, rather, simply as another paradigm for understanding how life can be meaningful.[8] Some people worry that if what is meaningful to them is so only from somewhere, and not from nowhere and to everyone, life cannot be taken to be meaningful. They treat the relativism-objectivism debate as having enormously significant implications for many issues regarding the meaning of life. I suggest, however, that although the debate is interesting in itself, it has hardly any consequences for most issues regarding the meaning of life. One can be an objectivist, or a relativist, and still

---

8. Aldous Huxley, "Swift," in *Do What You Will* (London: Watts, 1936), 80–81; A. J. Ayer, "The Meaning of Life," in *The Meaning of Life and Other Essays* (London: Weidenfeld and Nicolson, 1990), 196; E. D. Klemke, "Living without Appeal: An Affirmative Philosophy of Life," in *The Meaning of Life*, ed. E. D. Klemke, 2nd ed. (New York: Oxford University Press, 2000), 195–197; Brooke Alan Trisel, "Futility and the Meaning of Life Debate," *Sorites* 14 (2002): 79; Trisel, "Human Extinction and the Value of Our Efforts," *Philosophical Forum* 35, no. 3 (2004): 379. Note that some people are relativists not because they like the position but because they do not think that objectivism can be defended in good faith. They would like for some views to be true in a nonperspectival way, but cannot see how that could be possible.

accept (or reject) all that has been said in the other chapters of this book, and for more or less the same reasons. If, after having formed a view about the issues discussed in this book, one changes from being an objectivist to being a relativist, or vice versa, one need not change any of one's former views. Little hangs on whether one is a relativist or an objectivist. The relativism-objectivism debate, then, is not very consequential for issues relating to the meaning of life. And relativism does not entail that life is meaningless.

I should point out that I have not been arguing in this chapter for relativism. I have only suggested that even if relativism is true, life need not be seen as meaningless. Just as one does not have to accept determinism, so, I believe, one does not have to accept relativism. But just as one can accept determinism and still see life as meaningful, even if in somewhat different ways than before, so can one accept relativism and still see life as meaningful, even if somewhat differently than before.

Chapter 10

The Goal of Life

1

Many associate the meaning of life with the goal, purpose, aim, or end of life. People frequently wonder what the end of their life is, sometimes asking questions such as "What am I living for?" or "What is the purpose of my life?" It is not surprising that they relate meaningfulness to ends, since we commonly attribute value to things by using teleological (from the Greek *telos*—end), instrumental explanations that relate means to ends. For example, the value of a certain cog in the car's motor has to do with its purpose or end: it helps the car stop when we press the brakes. If the cog did not serve any end, and just sat there, we would consider it worthless or pointless. Similarly, I am not "just hurrying." If I did, it would be pointless for me to hurry. I could just as well not hurry. But my hurrying has a point, or value, which has to do with my goal in hurrying: I am hurrying in order to catch the bus. If that bus line were to be canceled, one might tell me that there was no reason for me to hurry. But catching the bus is also not something that I just do for no end. Why catch the bus? To arrive in class on time. Why arrive in class on time? To learn. Why learn? To know. And so on. As with other instrumental, goal-oriented explanations, so it is for the ones just given: the goal (which, in the final example, was knowledge) both explains the activities engaged in for the sake of achieving it and transmits some of its value to those activities (such as hurrying or catching the bus). Once we accept that the end—knowing things—is valuable, we often accept that the means for achieving it are of value as well.[1]

The teleological paradigm, then, is one that we commonly use to ascribe value to things; to understand why things are of value, we often search for their goal. It is not surprising, then, that many apply this paradigm not only to specific items or behaviors in life but also to the value of their lives as a whole.[2] They wonder, as part of their queries about the meaning of life, what the end or purpose of their life is. And if they cannot find a reply to questions such as "What is the purpose of my life?" or "What do I live for?" they feel uncomfortable and suspect that their life is meaningless. Without an end to which their life is a means, some feel, they do not have a meaningful life.

2

One good option, for those who feel that their lives are meaningless because there are no ends to which their lives are means, is to find such ends, whose value will then be transmitted to these lives and

---

1. Of course, it is not always the case that once we accept that the end is valuable we also accept that the means for achieving it are valuable, since some means are otherwise harmful or problematic (valuable ends do not justify all means). For simplicity's sake I will be discussing in this chapter only means that are not otherwise harmful or problematic.

2. Some scholars, too, state that meaningful activities often have goals or that having a purpose in life is necessary for meaning in life, or use the terms "meaning of life" and "purpose of life" as equivalent. See, e.g., John Cottingham, *On the Meaning of Life* (London: Routledge, 2003), 21; Viktor Frankl, *Man's Search for Meaning* (New York: Washington Square Press, 1985), 87–88, 98, 122, 166; Lois Hope Walker, "Religion Gives Meaning to Life," in *Philosophy: The Quest for Truth*, ed. Louis P. Pojman, 6th ed. (New York: Oxford University Press, 2006), 552; and L. J. Russell, "The Meaning of Life," *Philosophy* 28, no. 104 (1953): 32, 38–40.

make them valuable. People endorse many different ends, including the advancement of science, liberating their country, serving God, ending world poverty, maintaining a clean environment, and building a just society.

But suppose that my life is not dedicated to a goal beyond itself, to which it is a means. Should I feel, because of this, that my life is meaningless? As Kurt Baier has pointed out, it is incorrect that a meaningful life must have any end or purpose to which it is a means.[3] A life, like anything else, may be of much worth even if it is not geared toward and does not serve any ulterior purpose. Value theory distinguishes between instrumental or extrinsic value, on the one hand, and terminal or intrinsic value, on the other hand. We can take something to be of value because it is a good instrument for enhancing or maintaining something else that we take to be of value. But we do not take only instruments to be of value; we take also what the instruments are instruments of to be of value. The latter have noninstrumental or intrinsic, terminal value. Instrumental explanations do not presuppose that instrumental chains must continue forever, and hence do not presuppose that everything must have an end external to itself; they accept that some ends have no further, ulterior ends to them.[4] Things can be worthy when they are not means to something else. They are worthy because they are the ends. Their worth is intrinsic to them.

Consider the following example: I am going to the store. To what end? To buy candy. To what end? To eat it. To what end? To enjoy myself. To what end? Most of us would not think that that last question need be asked or answered. We would close the explanation

---

3. Kurt Baier, "The Meaning of Life," in *The Meaning of Life*, ed. E. D. Klemke, 2nd ed. (New York: Oxford University Press, 2000), 119–120. The following discussion owes much to Baier's claims.
4. Cf. Aristotle, *Nicomachean Ethics*, 1094a20ff.

at that stage and reply with something like "I do not enjoy myself for a certain end or purpose. I just enjoy; it is worthy in itself" or "Enjoyment is the purpose of the whole endeavor, it does not have any further purpose beyond itself." Some might wish to continue one or two steps more beyond this explanation, but they too would then close it at that point. The same is true of the chain whose end is knowing, mentioned earlier in this chapter. It too may perhaps continue a step or two further, but will then end.

Even for instrumental chains that *do* take life to be the means to a further end—such as creating a just society; service to God; or freeing one's nation—the chain of ends stops somewhere. Suppose that I take my life to be a means to forming a just society. What for? So that envy, suffering, injustice, and pain will end. What for? So that people will thrive to their fullest degree. What for? Most will close the instrumental chain here or very soon after this. Or suppose that I take my life to be a means to serving God. What for? So that God will be pleased. What for? Again, most explanations will close at this stage or soon after it. Instrumental chains end somewhere, and there is nothing wrong with that.

Some may think that enjoyment, a just society, a liberated nation, and God are not ends that have no end, or goals that have no goal, but that they are *their own* ends or goals. Those who accept this can hold, if they so wish, that all things have ends or goals, even if sometimes the goals are the means themselves. I have no quarrel with this suggestion. It suffices for me that it be realized that not everything needs to have an external end or a goal beyond itself; whether some things have no ends at all or are their own ends is irrelevant to me for the purpose of the present discussion.

Thus, there are means that are not ends for anything else; they are only means. They start the instrumental chains. There are also ends to means that are themselves means to further ends. They are the middle links in instrumental chains. And then there are the ends that are not means to anything else beyond themselves. They are just ends, or they are their own ends, and they close the instrumental chains. This does not make the final links in the chains valueless. They may well have much value, and moreover impart some of it to the means used to achieve them. Nor does the whole instrumental chain become incomprehensible because its end is not a means to a further end but is simply the end (in both senses of the term) of that chain, an end that has worth in itself. Not everything worthy has to have a goal or an end beyond itself.

Even according to the instrumental paradigm, then, life may be meaningful if it is not an instrument for anything beyond itself and serves no external purpose.[5] Alternatively, the purpose or end of a meaningful life could be seen as itself, that is, as having a meaningful life. We need not feel that our life is meaningless just because we cannot name an ulterior goal or end for it, since the supposition that in order to be meaningful a life must have an external goal or purpose is incorrect. The assertion, "I have no general goal or purpose to my life, I just live a life that includes a sufficient number of aspects of sufficient value" can be a good reply to questions such as "What do you live for?" or "What is the goal of your life?" A person may not have an end to which his life is a means, but that does not entail that that person has a meaningless life. His life could be meaningful because it includes great worth deriving, for instance, from the love he feels toward people close to him, his reading, and his enjoyment of beauty. Life can be valuable enough to be of sufficient worth as an end, rather than as an instrument for something else; or it can be its

---

5. Moreover, as Baier ("The Meaning of Life," 120) suggests, seeing people merely as means to something else rather than also as ends is, within a Kantian paradigm, morally problematic and detracts from their value.

own end. Hence, a life with no end beyond itself may well be a very meaningful one.

Taking one's life not to be lived for something beyond it—that is, not having an end to which that life is a means but rather being its own end or not having any end at all—does not of course entail that one's life may not include efforts to achieve many local, specific ends, the achievement of which increases value in one's life. We may distinguish between the ends or goals *of* a life, to which that life is a means, and the ends or goals *in* a life, which are aspects of value in one's life and to which one's life is not a means.[6] One may have as one's ends *in* life, for example, to develop a deep friendship, finish one's studies, increase one's musical sensibility, or even participate in or complete rehab. Increasing the value, and thus the meaningfulness, of one's life through the achievement of such ends or goals is different from seeing life as a means to or an instrument of a certain end beyond itself that we frequently cannot identify.

The discussion above is also relevant to some people's feeling that all their actions are meaningless since the chain of goals goes on indefinitely and no final goal can be identified. Their actions, they believe, must be directed at goals in order to be meaningful. But those goals, too, must have goals in order to be meaningful, and those, too, in turn, must have further goals, ad infinitum. And if there is no final goal to give meaning to the entire chain, no actions can be meaningful, and hence life is meaningless as well.[7] However, here too the reply is that not all goals must have further goals in order to be meaningful, for goals can be intrinsically

6. This distinction is highly influenced by Baier's distinction between purposes attributed to things and purposes attributed to people ("The Meaning of Life," 119–120).

7. Cf. Moritz Schlick, "On the Meaning of Life," in *Philosophical Papers*, ed. Henk L. Mulder and Barbara F. B. van de Velde-Schlick (Dordrecht: Reidel, 1979), 2:113–114.

valuable or meaningful, thereby making the actions geared toward them meaningful as well. Such intrinsically valuable ends of our actions could include serving God, enjoying personal warmth, having aesthetic experiences, understanding something, or leading a valuable, meaningful life.

3

What has been said in the previous section about the goal of life is relevant also for a host of other, somewhat similar questions. People sometimes ask why they are here, what they were created for, why they are alive, or what the reason is for their existence. "We are in the world for some reason, aren't we?" The questions are not always completely clear, but one way of replying to them is to find such a reason. The reason we are here could be to praise the Lord, to help other people, or to liberate our country. This is also why we are alive or what we were created for.

But another option is to deny that we were created, or are here, for any particular reason. Just as statements can be wrong, so can questions. Questions rely on presuppositions, and if the presuppositions are wrong, so will be the questions that rely on them. ("When did he steal the book?" for example, presupposes that he stole the book, and thus may be a wrong question if, in fact, he did not steal it.) Thus, questions such as "What is the reason for our being in the world?" or "What were we created for?" may be wrong questions. It is not clear at all that we are here, or are alive, for any particular reason. But if these are wrong questions, there is no need to find their answers, and those who cannot find a reason for their being in the world should not believe that their life is meaningless because of that. We do not have to be here for a reason in order to have a meaningful life. We can have a meaningful life, in the sense that it includes enough aspects of sufficient value, without there being a reason why we are alive; we are here, and our life is of high value, even if there is no special reason for our coming into the world.[8] The same is true for the question "What have we been created for?" It may well be that we were not created *for* anything, yet our life is nevertheless very meaningful. Another possibility is to see life itself, or having a meaningful life, as the reason for living, or as the reason for which we were created. We are alive in order to have a good, meaningful life.

Likewise, people sometimes think of their lives as a journey, but feel at a loss because they cannot find a destination for that journey. This sometimes leads them to see their lives as meaningless. Although I agree that a meaningful life may be seen as a journey, I do not think it must be seen that way. A life may be meaningful, that is to say, of sufficient value, even if one does not metaphorically go from one point to another but instead inhabits one or a few worthy "places" in a valuable way.

4

Yet others consider life as meaningless because they suppose— perhaps influenced by evolutionary biology—that the end of life is merely producing the next generation, and thus contributing to the persistence of the species. But then what is the end of the next generation's lives? Again, it is to produce another generation of descendants, whose sole purpose is to produce yet another generation of descendants, whose sole worth is in producing even more descendants. In this view, our lives have no inherent worth, since we are

8. But note that, as above, even if there is no special reason for one's coming into the world, there can be very good reasons for various decisions and actions one takes *within* one's life.

merely the means for the lives of the next generation. But those lives, too, would seem to lack any worth in themselves, since they too are just means for something else, which is in itself, again, worthless. No one's life, in this chain, seems to have any worth in itself, which suggests that our lives—and even human life in general—are worthless.[9]

But as Oswald Hanfling points out, it is doubtful that many see the biological persistence of the species as the *sole* element of value in their lives and in the lives of their descendants.[10] For many, lives are meaningful because they include many activities and experiences such as those having to do with intellectual understanding, aesthetic enjoyment, humanitarian activity, courage and persistence in the face of difficulty and unavoidable pain, or emotional contact. Others also find meaning in goals such as those mentioned in the previous section (for example, the advancement of science, service to God, or the liberation of one's country). People rarely take the continuation of our biological species to be the sole, or as even a necessary, issue of worth in their own lives or in the lives of the next generations. They want the species to continue because they see its continuation as a necessary condition for the good, worthy moments and experiences that can be had by future human beings. Suppose we were to learn that, because of a radioactive catastrophe, all human offspring from now on would live without any emotional and intellectual capabilities, more or less like mosquitoes, bereft of love, aesthetic enjoyment, intellectual appreciation, or moral fulfillment. Suppose we also learned that, notwithstanding this catastrophe, the biological, genetic continuation of the human race (in the physical sense) was going to be very safe for eons and eons. Most people would see this as a terrible calamity, and it would then not be that important

9. Richard Taylor, "The Meaning of Life," in Klemke, *The Meaning of Life*, 171.
10. Oswald Hanfling, *The Quest for Meaning* (New York: Blackwell, 1988), 24–26.

to them that the human race (if it could still be called by that name) continue to exist. We want the human race to continue because we value particular aspects in the lives of future generations.

Likewise, people can have meaningful lives even if they do not have children, or after their children have grown up and are no longer dependent on their parents, since there are many worthy aspects of life besides those that have to do with the continuation of the species. And many people want to have children not only, or not at all, because they want to ensure the continuation of the species. Even if I knew for certain that the world was going to be destroyed three hundred years from now, I would still raise children and educate them to live meaningful lives, since I take their existence and their own children's existence to be valuable, and the experience of being with children itself to be valuable. If my sole interest in raising children were merely that the species would persist, however, I would have no reason to do so once I learned of this inevitable catastrophe. If the only thing that moved us in life were indeed the urge to satisfy an instinctual drive that exists in mosquitoes and humans alike to proliferate more samples of their biological type, our lives would have indeed been meaningless. But this is not the case for most people.

I have criticized in this chapter arguments that focused on the goal of life. Some arguments claimed that life is meaningless because there is no external goal for which life is a means. Other arguments claimed that life is meaningless because there is a goal for which life is a means—the mere continuation of the species—and this goal is unworthy. In the next chapter I criticize another type of argument that focuses on goals. It suggests, paradoxically, that life is meaningless because we sometimes *succeed* in attaining our goals.

Chapter 11

The Paradox of the End

1

People set ends for themselves and try to achieve them in the hope that the attainment of those ends will improve their condition. The closer they get to achieving their goals, the more meaningful they feel their life to be. Paradoxically, however, when they finally achieve them, their sense of meaning in life is sometimes diminished. They have a sense of insignificance and emptiness and feel that in attaining their goal they have *lost* the meaning they experienced while they were striving toward it. Paradoxically, it seems as if the struggle to achieve the end was more meaningful than the achievement of the end.

This view has found expression in both philosophy and literature. Rousseau writes that "one enjoys less what one obtains than what one hopes for."[1] Schopenhauer argues that "attainment quickly begets satiety. The goal was only apparent; possession takes away its charm."[2] Shakespeare's Cressida remarks, "Things won are done, Joy's soul lies in doing," and Robert Louis Stevenson writes, "To

---

1. Jean-Jacques Rousseau, *Julie ou la Nouvelle Héloïse* VI, viii (Paris: Garnier, 1960), 68.
2. Arthur Schopenhauer, *The World as Will and Representation*, trans. E. F. J. Payne (New York: Dover, 1969), 1:313–314.

travel hopefully is a better thing than to arrive."[3] George Bernard Shaw acknowledges the same problem, writing, "There are two tragedies in life. One is not to get your heart's desire. The other is to get it." And Oscar Wilde puts the sentiment even more sharply: "In this world there are only two tragedies. One is not getting what one wants, and the other is getting it. . . . The last is a real tragedy!"[4]

Let us call this phenomenon the *paradox of the end*. If the goal is uncovered as having, in fact, little or no worth, then all our efforts to achieve it are rendered of little or no worth as well. Much of what we do, then, is worthless. This is one way of experiencing the paradox of the end. But if achieving our ends makes us lose meaning, then it seems that we should *not* try to achieve them, or even try *not* to achieve them. But if we do not try to achieve the ends (or if we try not to achieve them), we again lose the feeling of purposefulness and significance we wanted to retain. This is another way of experiencing the paradox of the end. To guard ourselves against the loss that awaits at either end of this paradox, then, we ought both to try and not to try to achieve our ends, at one and the same time. And this is yet another way of experiencing the paradox.

But this also means that the end of the activity is, in fact, its means, and what has been previously seen as its means is the end. The end is not valuable in itself; its value lies in giving significance to our efforts to achieve it (as long as the end is believed to be important). It is our efforts, which until now we had seen as means, that

3. William Shakespeare, *Troilus and Cressida*, I, 4; Robert Louis Stevenson, *Virginibus Puerisque* (London: Thomas Nelson, 1932), 184.
4. George Bernard Shaw, *Man and Superman* IV (New York: Brentano, 1922), 174; Oscar Wilde, *Lady Windermere's Fan* III, in *Complete Works of Oscar Wilde* (London: Collins, 1966), 417. See also Constantine Cavafy's *Ithaca*, in *The Complete Poems of Cavafy*, trans. Rae Dalven (New York: Harcourt Brace Jovanovich, 1976), 36–37.

are really the end. Here we find yet another expression of the paradox of the end.

But once the means and ends of an activity are understood in this way, we sense that the meaning that we used to feel in our activities vanishes. The moment we know that we do not really want the end itself, but have a need of it only so that our lives should have some meaning, the end stops being important and significant. And when that happens, the end ceases to bestow importance and significance on the efforts to achieve it. We feel, to change Voltaire's dictum, that if there were no ends we would have had to invent them. But once we understand ourselves as inventing ends, there is no point in our doing so. All these are further expressions of the paradox.

This paradox brings to mind again the story of Sisyphus, which we explored in the context of another possible interpretation in chapters 5 and 6. Sisyphus was condemned by the gods to push a huge rock uphill, but whenever he managed to reach the top of the mountain, the rock would roll back down and he would have to start his labors all over again. In the context of the paradox of the end, Sisyphus's task is analogous to our lives. Like Sisyphus, we spend our lives in continual, unending exertions only to lose meaning and fulfillment just when we think we have attained them. We perpetually have to go back and start pushing the stone uphill again. But the myth would portray the paradox even better had it continued thus: one day, Sisyphus succeeded in stabilizing the rock at the top of the mountain. He realized, to his surprise, that this time the rock was not rolling back down. He was surprised at first, then jubilant. He had finally made it. Very tired but excited, he lay down next to the rock whose weight he had overcome, happy that his unceasing toil had at last ended. He slept for many hours and then, waking up, he again looked triumphantly at the rock and the slope of the mountainside. After having rested some more, he looked around unhurriedly for the first time in a very long while at the beautiful view from the top of the mountain. He continued to rest, savoring this new experience, enjoying the thought that he had conquered not only the stone, but also the gods. He had finally managed to lift the curse. He relaxed some more, but oddly, he found that he was starting to feel less and less comfortable. As time passed, he became, to his astonishment, increasingly restless. Slowly, he began to understand that the curse the gods had placed on him was in fact much subtler and more terrible than he had ever imagined, and that he had not managed to break the curse at all but only to worsen his position. He stood up, sighed, went over to the stone and pushed it off the top of the mountain himself. He watched it roll down, walked down slowly after it, and then started pushing it uphill again.

In his *Autobiography*, John Stuart Mill recounts how the paradox of the end led him to suffer a mental breakdown at the age of twenty:

> From the winter of 1821, when I first read Bentham, ... I had what might truly be called an object in life; to be a reformer of the world. My conception of my own happiness was entirely identified with this object. ... [A]s a serious and permanent personal satisfaction to rest upon, my whole reliance was placed on this; and I was accustomed to felicitate myself on the certainty of a happy life which I enjoyed, through placing my happiness in something durable and distant, in which some progress might be always making, while it could never be exhausted by complete attainment. This did very well for several years, during which the general improvement going on in the world and the idea of myself as engaged with others in struggling to promote it, seemed enough to fill up an interesting and animated existence. But the time came when I awakened from this as from a dream. It was in the autumn of 1826. I was in a dull state of nerves, such

as everybody is occasionally liable to. . . . In this frame of mind it occurred to me to put the question directly to myself: "Suppose that all your objects in life were realized; that all the changes in institutions and opinions which you are looking forward to, could be completely effected at this very instant: would this be a great joy and happiness to you?" And an irrepressible self-consciousness distinctly answered, "No!" At this my heart sank within me: the whole foundation on which my life was constructed fell down. All my happiness was to have been found in the continual pursuit of this end. The end has ceased to charm, and how could there ever again be any interest in the means? I seemed to have nothing left to live for.[5]

When we experience our lives as meaningful, then, we may well be cheating ourselves, pretending to ourselves and others that the paradox does not really exist and disregarding our forthcoming experience that the ends we are striving for will not be of much worth. But if we look at the issue sincerely, we realize that the worthlessness of our ends, and therefore of the means to attain them, makes our lives meaningless.

2

We should not settle for this argument, however. There are indeed cases in which people feel, once they have achieved a goal, that it is less worthy than they had taken it to be. But like many other arguments for the meaninglessness of life, this one, too, wrongly

---

5. John Stuart Mill, *Autobiography* (New York: New American Library, 1964), 106–107. Note, however, that, strictly speaking, Mill is discussing happiness here rather than meaningfulness.

generalizes from some cases to all: it presents people as sensing the paradox all the time, while most sense it only part of the time and only after attaining some ends. It is simply not the case that the worth or meaning of all goals disappears after they have been achieved.[6] Many achievements continue to seem valuable to us for a long time after they have been achieved. Thus, even if there were no other problems with the argument, it would show not that our life is meaningless but only that some parts of it are. But the fact that some parts of life are meaningless does not show that life as a whole is meaningless, since—unless one is a perfectionist—a meaningful life need not be completely and wholly meaningful; it may include some parts that are meaningless.[7]

For example, many people experience the worth of having raised children successfully, of having had satisfying personal encounters with other people, or of moments, hours, or weeks of grace they have had, for a long time after those events or processes are over.[8] These aspects of worth in our lives can shine and emanate some of their worth for a long time and even onto the rest of our lives. Many people, similarly, remember and appreciate, for a long time afterward, the beautiful aesthetic experiences they have had and the good deeds they have done that made a difference to other people. Many are justly proud of having been decent, honest people or having been part of helpful social or political movements. Likewise, many who have recovered from a difficult sickness, or overcome a great obstacle, are pleased with that achievement for a long time afterward, even for the rest of their lives. Every time they remember

6. See Oswald Hanfling, *The Quest for Meaning* (New York: Blackwell, 1988), 7.

7. Moreover, even when the paradox is experienced, the attained ends are often not experienced as completely worthless but merely as having a value that is somewhat lower than what was initially expected. That value, too, may be sufficient for meaning.

8. See Hanfling, *The Quest for Meaning*, 7.

it, they are pleased, or see the worth of it, to some extent. Note that in many cases the happiness and recognition of worth at achieving something are indeed greater in the first seconds after it has been achieved than after several days, but then the happiness and recognition or worth remain constant.[9]

Not only does the paradox not affect the many cases in which the ends we have achieved continue to be deemed worthy, it also fails to affect those cases in which ends are achieved but have no terminus, such as being and remaining a good and loving husband or being and remaining a good teacher. These are goals we may achieve every day and never cease achieving, so that they are never "over and done with." Nor does the paradox affect the many cases in which our actions do not lead to the achievement of ends at all. Some of our efforts are geared toward regulative ends, that is, ends that we know we can never achieve and toward which we can only, at best,

9. The claim that in many cases we do not experience the paradox seems to conflict with what has come to be called in experimental psychology "hedonic adaptation" or "the hedonic treadmill," that is, people's tendency to return to their previous degree of happiness regardless of the happy or sad events that they may have experienced. For example, several findings suggest that people who win the lottery or become paraplegic quickly return to the level of happiness that they experienced before winning the prize or becoming disabled. See, e.g., Philip Brickman, Dan Coates, and Ronnie Janoff-Bulman, "Lottery Winners and Accident Victims: Is Happiness Relative?" *Journal of Personality and Social Psychology* 36, no. 8 (1978): 917–927. However, more recent studies show that although there are some cases in which hedonic adaptation does occur, there are also many in which it does not. See, e.g., Shane Frederick and George Loewenstein, "Hedonic Adaptation," in *Well-Being: The Foundations of Hedonic Psychology*, ed. Daniel Kahneman, Edward Diener, and Norbert Schwarz (New York: Russell Sage, 1999), 319; Ed Diener, Richard E. Lucas, and Christie Napa Scollon, "Beyond the Hedonic Treadmill: Revising the Adaptation Theory of Well-Being," *American Psychologist* 61, no. 4 (2006): 309–311; Bruce Headey, "Life Goals Matter to Happiness: A Revision of Set-Point Theory," *Social Indicators Research* 86, no. 2 (2008): 221–227; Anthony D. Mancini, George A. Bonanno, and Andrew E. Clark, "Stepping Off the Hedonic Treadmill: Individual Differences in Response to Major Life Events," *Journal of Individual Differences* 32, no. 3 (2011): 146–151; and Frank Fujita and Ed Diener, "Life Satisfaction Set Point: Stability and Change," *Journal of Personality and Social Psychology* 88, no. 1 (2005): 162–164.

make consistent progress. This is true of such efforts as attempts to become a more moral person, to understand music ever more deeply, to learn more, to increase a certain ability or sensitivity, or to come nearer to God. Having such aims in life can give people meaning, but the slow progress toward an end that practitioners accept they will never reach is not vulnerable to the mechanisms of the paradox of the end. This is also true for people who are not progressing toward such a regulative end but are in a stable relation of engagement with the end or even, because of sickness or old age, are slowly regressing from it. The engagement with the worthy goal endows their lives with worth, but the end will not be reached and thus the mechanism of the paradox cannot operate.

Furthermore, some acts and experiences do not follow the instrumental, means/ends structure at all and, for that reason, do not give rise to the paradox. Some acts are taken to have their worth in themselves and not in an end that is outside them. This is, for example, how Kant understands moral activity. Some people also see other activities, such as studying, having aesthetic experiences, being good parents, or showing courage in the face of difficulty, pain, or disappointment as falling into this category, that is, as activities worthy in themselves, quite apart from what they may or may not produce.

Other noninstrumental experiences or activities are not intended at all, but just happen to us.[10] We are sitting in a bus and happen to see a sunset or a beautiful garden through the window. Or we muse, and an interesting thought or pleasant recollection comes to mind. Perhaps we just happen to have a very nice and enjoyable conversation with someone, or overhear a deep remark. These are all meaningful experiences and do not involve great expectations,

10. See Hanfling, *The Quest for Meaning,* 6.

significant efforts, or subsequent disappointments. The paradox of the end is untrue for such events as well.

3

But this argument for the meaninglessness of life is problematic not only because it wrongly universalizes from some cases to all but also because it presents the paradox as if it were an inherent and unchangeable part of our life. However, the paradox is not a constant in human life. It is, rather, a variable that can be changed—the result of several factors that can be largely controlled. Many of these factors are related to education: there are several problematic elements in education that exacerbate the tendency to undervalue achieved ends, and changing these elements will decrease the extent to which the paradox is experienced.

Workaholism, that is, the tendency to work too much, increases people's tendency to become uninterested in and unappreciative of what they have achieved. Just as some people are lazy, others are overdiligent. They feel uneasy when they are not working. Since it conforms to many social and, at times, religious mores, and is materially productive, many do not identify overwork as a problem or even praise it. Yet one indication that some people are too committed to working hard is their experience of the paradox of the end. People who are habituated to working most of the time and who thus feel anxious or guilty when not working will not be able to derive much enjoyment from their attained goals. Although the restlessness that they sense soon after they have achieved an end results from their overdiligence rather than from a correct assessment of the worth of their achievement, they can easily mistake the former for the latter.

Experiencing the paradox of the end can also have to do with the tendency of some educators to be too stingy with compliments. This differs from pushing children into an overcommitment to work, but the two practices often share the same motivation: namely, the wish to create industrious, productive people who are resolved to work hard. Some instructors and parents fear that children or students will rest on their laurels, becoming complacent, overconfident, and so pleased with what they have already achieved that they stop trying to improve further. Another reason why educators may be sparing in their praise for children's achievements has to do with religious emphases on modesty and objections to pride. In the latter cases, too, educators may communicate messages in the vein of "Don't be so pleased with yourself," which children may internalize all too well. Those who are excessively careful not to take pride— even deserved and appropriate pride—in their achievements may develop the mental habit of "spoiling" their achievements for themselves by denying their worth, thus causing themselves, again, to feel that what they have worked for so long and hard is not really all that valuable.[11]

Some people are also educated "too successfully" to delay gratification. As many parents and teachers can confirm, the more common problem is the opposite one, the inability to delay gratification; many people have such a strong tendency toward instant pleasure that they cannot defer it. The lure of immediate gratification is so strong that they fail to find the power to engage in anything else, not even activities that would result in far greater gratification at a later point. This tendency is more common in childhood, but some carry it into adulthood: as adults, they constantly put off work, duties, and anything that is even a little unpleasant or difficult. Yet

11. For a discussion of the legitimacy of deserved, appropriate pride see chapter 14 section 5.

sometimes children are too successfully educated to combat this tendency. They learn too well to delay immediate gratification for the sake of greater future gratification, and become adults who have difficulty accepting and enjoying their achievements. People who suffer from this curse keep telling themselves, perhaps in an echo of the adult voices they heard in childhood, that they will not reward or congratulate themselves just *yet*; they will only celebrate sometime in the future, when another, even more difficult task has been achieved. Like those who put off work, they put off reward. Whereas some cannot delay gratification, they cannot accept it. Such people are also likely to experience the paradox of the end.

Educators may also inadvertently make their students more predisposed to suffer from the paradox of the end by habitually overstating the satisfaction that their students are going to feel once they achieve their goals. The educators who do this are of course aiming to boost their students' motivation to work. But by repeatedly predicting that future gratification will be extreme, they may foster in students the mental habit of forming unrealistic expectations that are bound to be disappointed. If one imagines the fulfillment one is likely to feel from a new romantic relationship, a higher-level job, or having completed a doctoral dissertation in idealized rather than realistic terms, one is likely to be disappointed, and might interpret that disappointment as the paradox of the end. Those who keep their expectations realistic, on the other hand, are more likely to enjoy the ends that they attain.

Some people are so competitive that it is difficult for them to feel satisfaction even when they attain a goal long sought after. They constantly interpret their own and others' behavior in competitive terms, sometimes even engaging in secret competitions with others who are unaware that anyone is competing with them. At other times, they compete with themselves, against their own earlier performances. It is hard for such people to enjoy for a long period of time a situation in which they are not competing. Soon after they have attained any given goal, they feel unsettled and in need of yet more competition. This, however, can prevent the prolonged enjoyment of what has been achieved. Competitiveness can make it harder for them to appreciate what they have achieved also by leading them to compare themselves with those who have achieved even more than they have. If they earn a lot of money, for example, they quickly feel that they have lost the competition with those who have done even better. This habit is not unique to overly competitive people interested in material goods; it is also common among those who focus on intellectual accomplishments. I know university professors who are miserable because others have published a few more papers than they have or in slightly more prestigious journals. Those others, if they are also highly competitive, may be very dissatisfied with their own achievements, too, contemplating in dismay those who are doing slightly better than they are academically and to whom they have lost in their own hidden competitions. It should come as no surprise that this attitude leads people to experience the paradox of the end: it will be difficult for such people to sustain their appreciation of what they have achieved for long, and they will quickly experience the achieved end as uninteresting or of insufficient worth.

Some people cannot enjoy the fruits of their labor because of simple nervousness that sends them off into further activity immediately after they have reached a goal. (In some cases, "being energetic," "being productive," and "being driven" are euphemisms for such nervousness.) This nervousness has no relation to the worth of the end itself; it is a manifestation of the condition of the person experiencing it rather than an indication of the value of what that person has achieved. And yet others cannot enjoy sufficiently what they achieve because of the power of routine, discussed in chapter 2 section 7: we are built psychologically so that after we have been exposed to something ceaselessly and for a long time, our pleasure or interest in it often wanes; in some cases, we stop noticing it (as with the painting that we "don't even see anymore" after it has been on the wall for a while).[12] This does not mean that what we have been exposed to is not pleasurable or valuable, however; it only means that we have a psychological need to alternate from time to time among worthy achievements in order to continue to enjoy each of them. Achievements, then, *can* be experienced as pleasurable and worthy over a long period of time, but not usually without breaks. A failure to realize this, too, could lead people to become disappointed in their achievements, wrongly interpreting what they have gained as being of no value.

While we are devoting strenuous effort to achieving goals, we often have a tendency to disregard or suppress feelings that are not conducive to this effort: our resolution and concentration often numb us to our accumulated fatigue, to minor discomfort, and even to the normal ambivalence that we might feel toward our goal and our efforts to achieve it. For example, a person focusing on coping with a difficulty at work or on completing a PhD may ignore, while focusing on that goal, his weariness, small irritations, and uncertainty whether that line of work or study is the right one for him. But once he has achieved his goal and relaxed his determined concentration, his exhaustion and previously blocked feelings are allowed to surface, creating a sense of anticlimax. This too could, to some extent, spoil the contentment we feel after we have attained a

---

12. Of course, there are exceptions. It also happens that the impact of shrill noises, inconsiderate roommates, inefficient bureaucrats, or overheated rooms, on the one hand, or of profound ideas or good friendships, on the other, intensifies over time, so that rather than becoming numb to these things, we experience them more sharply.

goal. Again, however, such feelings should not be understood as an indication of the worthlessness of the end itself; after some rest, we will be able to appreciate it.

And some ends are in fact disappointing. We cannot always accurately estimate how worthwhile a certain achievement is going to be. Some of the goals we realize are bound not to turn out as we had hoped. It is only sensible to expect that over the course of a lifetime we will sometimes experience that.

Recognizing these processes helps understand better why John Stuart Mill paradoxically felt so uneasy at the prospect of succeeding in his efforts to improve the world. In his *Autobiography* he recounts how his overbearing father educated him to be a workaholic and to delay gratification, demanding extremely high achievements from him. That education then made it difficult for Mill to imagine himself enjoying a state of affairs in which the world was economically, socially, and morally thriving and just. For him, a state of affairs in which he was not working hard or striving for something must have felt awkward, tense, or even sinful.

4

I am sure that I have not presented an exhaustive list of the phenomena that lead some people to feel, in some instances, that the goals they have achieved are of little or no worth, but I believe I have covered most of the patterns that lead to this feeling. Being aware of these patterns should allow us to counter them both in our own lives and, through the education of children and students, in the lives of the next generation. Educators should pay attention to whether their educational approaches might be inadvertently encouraging these patterns. Admittedly, it is difficult to find the right measure. Some degree of ambition is good, and the same is true for competitiveness, diligence, and the ability to delay satisfaction. In many cases, the paradox of the end results from an overcultivation of habits and personality traits that are productive and positive when present to a moderate degree; just as we would not want to have too much of these habits and traits, so would we also not want to have too little of them.

But whatever strategies we adopt for coping with the paradox of the end, I take the discussion to have shown that the paradox is not a necessary element of human existence. This is also shown by its non-universality. As Hanfling points out, different people experience the paradox to different degrees.[13] Moreover, people who have not had a strong work ethic inculcated in them from a young age and who are not achievement-oriented often appear not to suffer from the paradox of the end at all. They are quite content with an unchallenging life; they are not programmed to look incessantly for new challenges.

Note the general faults in the argument for the meaninglessness of life criticized here. First, the argument represents difficulties as completely destructive of the meaningful life when in fact they merely diminish meaning in life. Second, the argument represents difficulties as universal, that is, as affecting all people, whereas in fact those difficulties only affect some people. Third, the argument represents the difficulties as necessary and unchangeable, whereas the difficulties can in fact frequently be overcome: they do not have to do with some deep-seated metaphysical element of reality but, rather, with contingent and frequently alterable empirical facts. These characteristics of the argument discussed here are also true of some other arguments for the meaninglessness of life considered in other chapters.

13. Hanfling, *The Quest for Meaning*, 20, 27.

5

I have argued that it is not an essential part of being human to sense boredom or disappointment once we have achieved an end. But suppose that some of us are, in fact, "wired" to suffer the paradox of the end. Let us call these people, who have an urge to keep overcoming challenges even when it is not necessary to do so, *challengers*. Like Mill, they have to improve or achieve something every once in a while in order not to feel restless; they find it hard to just sit down and enjoy the world. After they achieve something, they rest a little and then have to go on and achieve something else.

But this does not mean that their achievements are not valuable or that their lives are not meaningful. It may well be that they have a constant need to overcome challenges *and* that some of the challenges they successfully cope with (and the achievements they attain) are highly meaningful. Let us take the specific example of a person who has, say, an obsessive need to read. Shortly after finishing a book he has to start reading another, so as not to feel restless. If he has no good books to read, he will read bad ones. That does not mean that his reading is worthless. He may well read a large number of good books that develop his mind and make his life more meaningful. Challengers, like this book reader, should of course try to engage with positive challenges. But knowing that if they do not engage with good challenges they will engage with bad ones or be restless does not diminish the worth of their good achievements. Likewise, it is true that challengers, being obsessive about challenges, would find it somewhat stressful to live in the kind of morally perfect world that Mill contemplated (although they might, with some time and treatment, eventually feel less stressed and thus enjoy this world more). But that does not show that it would be a meaningless world.

Thus, some people who are used to finding meaning in achieving should continue to do so while noting the sources and the unreliability of their feelings of disappointment after achieving goals. For them, a good way to stop feeling that life is meaningless is to set themselves worthy goals and try to achieve them while remembering that the restlessness and the urge to set themselves more goals does not mean that the goals they are pursuing are not valuable. Nor do the restlessness and urge to set new goals after achieving old ones mean that they are not improving the world and themselves by pursuing worthy goals. In our world there are too many valuable goals toward which not enough people are working; pursuing those goals is highly worthwhile.

Chapter 12

Suffering

1

Some people feel that life is meaningless because there is so much pain and evil all around. The world is too nasty and horrible. Some are more troubled by the pain and suffering in human life, and for others this feeling has more to do with the vileness of human beings. I will address the issue of suffering first and discuss the dark side of human nature in the next chapter.

Probably the most famous modern philosopher to have argued that suffering predominates in life is Schopenhauer.[1] One of his arguments starts with an analysis of pleasure. Pleasure, Schopenhauer argues, does not appear independently; it is always the satisfaction of a desire or a need.[2] But the state of desiring is frustrating because it involves not having what we want or need. For example, in order to feel pleasure when I quench my thirst I have to be thirsty, that is, to want water but not have it, which is unpleasant. Likewise, in order to feel pleasure when I sit down to rest after a long day I have

---

1. My discussion of Schopenhauer is influenced by (and adds to) Oswald Hanfling's discussion in his *The Quest for Meaning* (New York: Blackwell, 1988), chap. 1.
2. Arthur Schopenhauer, *The World as Will and Representation*, trans. E. F. J. Payne (New York: Dover, 1969), 1:196, 312, 363.

to be tired, that is, to feel the as-yet-unsatisfied need to rest, which is unpleasant. Relying on a version of the paradox of the end, discussed in the previous chapter, Schopenhauer adds that when we achieve what we desire, after having suffered for it, we do not enjoy the pleasure for long: it dissipates very quickly. Thus, there is more suffering than pleasure in life.

There are problems with this argument, however. First, as we have seen, not everyone experiences the paradox of the end, and those who do experience it feel it, or can often educate themselves to feel it, to different degrees. Thus, in some cases the dissatisfaction experienced before attaining a goal will *not* exceed the satisfaction experienced in attaining it and afterward. This means that in some cases, the pleasure will outweigh the suffering; the gain will exceed the pain.

Second, as Oswald Hanfling has already argued, it is not true that all pleasures presuppose prior suffering.[3] Although some do, many do not. Some pleasures are not a response to striving at all; they just appear. For example, we may enjoy a pleasant conversation with an acquaintance we happen to meet on the street. We may just overhear an interesting analysis on the radio. We may be offered and enjoy tasty food without being hungry. We can enjoy unanticipated pleasures. In some other cases, pleasures indeed involve desiring, but the desiring is not painful. For example, when I plan a trip abroad, the anticipation does not usually involve suffering. On the contrary, the anticipation is itself pleasurable, and thus I enjoy myself both during the trip and ahead of time, when I am planning and looking forward to it. People frequently also enjoy anticipated games, church gatherings, concerts, a good class, or sex. Much depends on the specifics of the expectation and of the attained

---

3. Hanfling, *The Quest for Meaning*, 5–6.

pleasure. When one waits for food for a very long time the suffering may be greater than the pleasure gained in eating, but when the wait is short pleasure may exceed suffering. If we have to wait for a long time to be hugged, we will suffer more than if we only have to wait for a short time. Likewise, temperament, the specific activity at hand, the types of effort required, and the urgency of our need all affect the degree of our overall pleasure. Schopenhauer's argument is only true, then, for some pleasures.

But not only is Schopenhauer wrong in presenting all pleasures as involving prior pain, and in supposing prior pain that always exceeds later gain, he is also wrong in presenting his claim as if it were a necessary truth about human experience. He ignores the significant degree to which we can affect the pleasure and suffering that we experience. As with the paradox of the end, so too with our efforts to achieve ends: we have some control over what happens to us and can use this control to increase our pleasure. We could, of course, choose objects of desire and yearning whose attainment requires torturous means, and we could lengthen the duration of our wanting until it becomes painful. (We could also choose to follow goals we will never achieve.) Then, of course, pain would exceed gain. But we could also choose not to do so and have our gain exceed our pain. Since we have control, to a large extent, over what we choose and aim for, we can find ends, and roads to ends, that are more enjoyable than others.

Note that Schopenhauer's argument fails here not because of sophisticated or subtle problems with a logical inference or a metaphysical claim, but because his description of the facts clashes with empirical reality.[4] His argument, like many other arguments for the

---

4. Schopenhauer's views about our extensive and intense suffering are also based on his metaphysical theory. I do not have here the space to discuss this metaphysical theory, but will just note that the falseness of the empirical claims he makes weakens it.

meaninglessness of life, fails for this simple reason: he describes facts incorrectly and ignores relevant issues.

2

Another of Schopenhauer's arguments focuses on the subjective passage of time.[5] Even if objectively the number of hours in which we suffer is equal to the number of hours in which we enjoy ourselves, since time passes more slowly when we are suffering than when we are enjoying ourselves, subjectively we suffer more, as we experience suffering for a longer (subjective) time than we experience joy. However, this is also insufficient to prove that there is more suffering than joy in our life overall, since it may be that our life includes significantly more hours of joy than of suffering. Assume, for example, that in a certain batch of a hundred hours there are forty that are neither painful nor joyous, forty that are joyous, and twenty that are painful. There are, then, twice as many joyous as painful hours. Assume also that the subjective duration of a painful hour is one and a half times as long as that of a joyous hour. There is still more enjoyable subjective time in those hundred hours than there is painful subjective time. Thus, although Schopenhauer is right that, as a rule, unpleasant hours are subjectively experienced as longer than pleasant hours, he does not show that, for all people, life is indeed more painful than pleasant.

Note that the rate at which subjective time passes also depends on the types of pleasant and unpleasant activities in which we are engaged: physical pleasure seems to pass subjectively more quickly than does intellectual, emotional, or spiritual pleasure. The rate of

5. Schopenhauer, *Will and Representation*, 2:575.

the subjective passage of time also has a great deal to do with our level of boredom versus interest rather than simply with suffering versus pleasure: a painful but challenging activity on which we have to concentrate can pass very quickly. Furthermore, people differ from each other in the pace at which subjective suffering and pleasure pass for them; many people are even able to influence that pace by, for example, focusing on and holding on to the "taste" and "aftertaste" of a pleasure. Schopenhauer's argument, however, ignores all these differences, as well as people's ability to affect the duration of various pleasures and pains in their lives.

3

Schopenhauer argues that pleasure and suffering are also asymmetrical in another way: we are much more sensitive to what is unpleasant than to what is pleasant. We feel pain, but do not feel nonpain. We are conscious of our worries but not of our nonworries. We sense fear, but do not sense a feeling of security, or at least we do not sense it as strongly. We remember bad things that happened to us very vividly and sharply and continue to be distressed by them for a long time, but the memory of good things that happened to us is vague and weak and does not please us for long after they have happened. When an unpleasant event that caused us suffering ends, we have a positive feeling. However, this positive feeling does not persist for long and is not intense; after a short time it dissipates. On the other hand, when a pleasant event that caused us happiness ends, we have intense negative feelings that remain with us for a longer time.[6]

6. Schopenhauer, *Will and Representation*, 2:575.

However, there are problems with Schopenhauer's claims. He points out that although we feel pain, we do not feel absence of pain. But the opposite of pain is pleasure rather than a state of neither-pleasure-nor-pain. Schopenhauer may be right that we remember and are displeased with pain more than we remember and are pleased with a situation of neither-pain-nor-pleasure; but it is not clear that we remember and are displeased with pain more than we remember and are pleased with pleasure. Furthermore, contrary to Schopenhauer's claim, many people do not in fact remember past negative experiences in the way that he describes. My detailed diaries from my early twenties show that this era was very confused and tortured for me. But today I remember those years quite differently, as somewhat hard but still as exciting, fun, and interesting years filled with new experiences, during which I encountered many stimulating if challenging events and was enthusiastic about almost everything that happened to me. Many of us tend to beautify, sentimentalize, and romanticize the past. We frequently redescribe the suffering we have gone through in a way that helps us to desensitize ourselves to it, while exaggerating to ourselves the pleasures we have had.

Furthermore, just as we can become accustomed to many types of pleasures, successes, and gains and stop feeling them quite so strongly after a while, so too do many of us become accustomed to many types of pains, failures, and losses and stop sensing them quite so strongly after a while. Frequently, as days and months pass, we become used to hardships and come to accept them, thus becoming less troubled by them. Losses and failures are usually most painful when fresh. In some cases, after a while, we hardly even feel the distress. It is not clear that time numbs happiness more than it does sadness. Of course, much depends on the types of gain and of loss. Some losses are very strongly felt even after significant time has elapsed. But that is also true of some pleasures and gains. All of this conflicts with Schopenhauer's claims. And as in many of his other claims, here too Schopenhauer ignores the variety among people and generalizes from some cases to all, presenting universal, totalistic claims about the way all human beings are. But people are highly varied. Some people are more inclined to be bitter about whatever has gone wrong and refuse to forgive the world or themselves for a very long time, while others are more forgiving and better at overcoming disappointments. Likewise, some are more thankful and happier than others about everything that goes well in their lives. Part of our reaction to gains or losses has to do with our expectations. If we have perfectionist and unrealistic expectations, according to which we will fail at nothing, excel at everything, never become unhealthy, and so on, we are likely to be distressed at everything that is not going according to plan and are likely not to be satisfied about the good things that do happen to us.

And as in many of his other arguments, here too Schopenhauer describes the variables of human life as stable or even inherent to human experiential reality, thus ignoring people's ability to change their emotional habits. People can often educate themselves or be educated to appreciate that they have not been harmed (or have not been as harmed as they could have been) by many types of misfortune and to become more sensitive to the good aspects of life. What Schopenhauer describes is not the necessary structure of human nature but largely mutable psychological characteristics of some people. He does not show that all people's lives are full of suffering, but only that some people's lives are so, in a way that is frequently alterable.[7]

---

7. According to Schopenhauer, there are two ways to transcend experiential reality and the suffering inherent in it. First, artistic geniuses can (temporarily) do so by adopting an aesthetic attitude whose objects are "the eternal Ideas, the persistent, essential forms of the world and of all its phenomena" (*Will and Representation*, 1:186). Second, some people can, through harsh asceticism and self-abnegation, adopt an attitude of "voluntary renunciation,

4

Even without these analyses of what precisely is wrong with Schopenhauer's arguments, we can tell that they are wrong simply by the fact that many people experience their lives as more enjoyable than painful. It may be plausible to argue that people *should* not feel as they do; but this is not Schopenhauer's argument. He is telling such people that they do not in fact feel as they do.

Like many others who argue for the meaninglessness of life, Schopenhauer puts himself in a difficult position by presenting very ambitious claims: he argues that *all* people are in a certain state and that they are *necessarily* so. The claims presented in this book, however, are much more moderate, and thus easier to defend. They are not diametrically opposed to his, since I do not claim that *all* people have happy lives or that they necessarily have them. I claim only that some people have happy lives, and that some others who do not can make their lives happy; I make no claims for any deep necessities about the human condition.

I have suggested in this chapter that not all people's lives have to be, or are, more painful than pleasurable. But it is important also to note that painful lives are not always meaningless. Admittedly, in many cases, suffering diminishes or even completely undermines people's ability to sustain valuable activities and attitudes and, therefore, meaning in their lives. Sometimes pain can be incapacitating; people sense only the pain (or, occasionally, numbness), as if it has destroyed everything else in them, and they do not have

resignation, true composure, and complete will-lessness" (*Will and Representation*, 1:379; see also 1:383), thus reaching a state in which there is "no will: no representation, no world" (*Will and Representation*, 1:411). But if what has been argued in this chapter is correct, then, at least in many cases, it is not in fact necessary to transcend experiential reality.

the ability to do or to feel anything of value. Moreover, pain often breeds aggression, hard-heartedness, or even cruelty, all of which decrease or undermine meaning in life. But this is not always the case. Suffering and meaninglessness are distinct from each other, and although the former frequently breeds the latter, it does not have to do so; there are many cases in which suffering coexists with meaning.[8] This, indeed, is one of the themes of Viktor Frankl's work on the meaning of life in the concentration camps. Despite the immense suffering people endured in the camps, some managed to retain meaning in their lives.

We can also think of other examples in which people may have painful but meaningful lives. Consider a woman who, after being sexually assaulted, is herself blamed for that attack by the conservative community in which she lives. But she rises to the painful challenge of defying that attitude and dedicates her life to changing the mores of that society, educating young people about sexual assault, helping to prevent similar attacks from happening in the future, and supporting other victims. She may, because of the attack she has suffered and because of her constant conflicts with conservative members of her community, experience great anxiety and pain; she may not have a pleasurable life. But it still would be plausible to describe her life as meaningful. Similarly, there is evidence that, at different points, Mother Teresa experienced her life as painful rather than pleasurable because she felt deep spiritual emptiness and desolation, perhaps even thinking that she was not living under the grace of God.[9] Yet it is plausible to suggest that, because of her important work and commitment, her life was meaningful even at

8. See Thaddeus Metz, *Meaning in Life: An Analytic Study* (Oxford: Oxford University Press, 2013), 60–74.

9. Mother Teresa, *Come Be My Light*, ed. Brian Kolodiejchuk (New York: Doubleday, 2007), 149, 164, 182, 186–188, 192–194.

those points. A former Soviet dissident who suffered greatly in his struggle for human rights could also be said to have led a painful but meaningful life. I have described here mostly moral or political endeavors as creating meaning despite life's suffering. But a painful life can also be made meaningful by writing or reading poetry, by learning and knowledge, by religious belief, or by showing persistence and courage in the face of suffering. There are many aspects of value in life, of which pleasure is only one. It is usually an important and good aspect of life. It is frequently easier to maintain meaning when pleasure persists, and it is usually important to try to guard and enhance pleasure. But for many people, pleasure is not a necessary condition for meaning. Despite their suffering, many can maintain and even considerably increase the meaning in their lives.

I was born in the late 1950s and spent most of my childhood and youth in Jerusalem. Many of our neighbors, and some relatives, were Holocaust survivors. I remember being impressed as a teenager by the ability some of them had, even some of those who had lost their families and gone through very traumatic experiences, to lead meaningful (and sometimes even happy) lives. Many of them had gone on to create new families and new lives. I am certain that they never stopped feeling intense sorrow and having painful memories, but some of them found or created happiness as well and, according to what they told me, led lives that were happy overall. Others could not be said to have had happy lives, but did have meaningful ones. Meeting some of these people in my youth left on me a strong impression that has lasted to this day.

Chapter 13

Human Evil

1

While the previous chapter focused mainly on suffering, the present one discusses mostly the feeling that life is horrible because there is so much evil in the world (and perhaps also within us). Humanity is too vile to bear.[1] One need only open almost any newspaper and see for oneself the overwhelming number of terrible events happening every day. The news media are filled with stories about natural and human mishaps and disasters, reporting mostly on earthquakes and floods, rapes and murders, felonies and embezzlements, delinquent negligence, manipulation, corruption, hypocrisy, and betrayal of trust. It is realistic to assume that, because people usually try to hide the nasty things they do, much wrongdoing is not reported at all, so that the extent of suffering and evil is, in fact, even more widespread than reported. Newspapers report on the present or the very recent past; but history books are also filled with stories of natural

---

1. A literary depiction of this sentiment can be found in Dostoevsky's *Brothers Karamazov*, where after describing to Alyosha the atrocities committed during the wars in the Balkans, cruelty to children, and other dire realities, Ivan asserts, "I hasten to return my ticket. And it is my duty, if only as an honest man, to return it as far ahead of time as possible." Fyodor Dostoevsky, *The Brothers Karamazov*, trans. Richard Pevear and Larissa Volokhonsky (San Francisco: North Point Press, 1990), 208.

and human-caused calamities such as floods, earthquakes, epidemics, famines, wars, genocides, usurpations, murders, and oppression. This does not paint a pretty picture of the human condition.

I suggest, however, that newspapers and history books give the wrong impression of what the world is like. They represent the world in a biased way that filters out most of the good aspects of reality. Take newspapers first. They write more about negative events than about positive ones, and they emphasize the negative ones with larger headlines that we remember better. Increases in unemployment receive bigger headlines, and are discussed in longer articles, than decreases in unemployment. The paper will not record the many cases in which someone helped an old person, but only the one case in which the "helper" ran away with the senior citizen's money. A good person who has behaved justly all her life but then slipped and committed one felony will have none of her good years reported ("Jane Smith did not embezzle anything this year"), but this one wrongdoing of hers will be discussed at length. The orderly behavior of ten thousand people is not reported; one person's disorderly behavior is. Newspaper reporting, then, is heavily biased toward the representation of the evil aspects of social reality. The picture they present of the world is much bleaker than the world really is.

Why do papers present such a selective and slanted description of reality? One motivation for doing so is moral. Many journalists and editors see the papers as tools for improving society and for guarding it against corruption, callousness, and other types of evil. They do so by pointing out and criticizing what is wrong and dysfunctional and, thus, focus on it rather than on what is working well. In this way, papers fulfill an important social and moral role. The media is called the watchdog of democracy for a good reason. However, this selective overemphasis on the bad aspects of human behavior can also have a negative byproduct: presenting wrong behaviors as prevalent leads some people to believe that "that's just the way things are" and "that's what everyone does." Believing that certain wrong behaviors are very common, some people see them also as the social (even if not the legal) norm, and believe that those who do not engage in them are only a minority of dupes.

But another motivation for the almost exclusive presentation of negative facts in the media is financial. Newspapers, magazines, and television stations want to be as profitable as possible; therefore, they cater to people's tastes. And people enjoy reading about the evildoings of others. This is partly because bad behaviors are rare in comparison to good or morally neutral behaviors, and we frequently find the rare more interesting. (As pointed out in the first week of any intro-to-journalism class, "Dog bites man" is not news, but "Man bites dog" is.) But evil is also interesting because of the drama involved in it. Interesting stories are not, usually, about good people who meet good people and agree with them peacefully about most things, but about bad people who enter into conflict with and do bad things to other people (preferably to good people). Conflict, catastrophe, and crime are exciting. Reading about crime and immorality also brings readers a pleasant feeling of self-righteousness: it is pleasant to feel that others are wrong and bad while we, the nice and decent, are superior. People feel proud that they have remained an island of golden virtue in a grimy sea. Another cause for our interest in evil and pain may have to do with a sense of self-preservation; we may be psychologically "wired" to take an interest in those things that may endanger us personally someday.

But whatever the causes of this phenomenon, it is an empirical fact that many are much more curious about that which is painful and evil than about that which is secure and good. News media cater to this curiosity. Thus, if we rely too much on news coverage, we can easily get the impression that the out-of-the-ordinary is quite ordinary, while the ordinary hardly exists at all; the world may then seem to be an almost wholly evil place.

History books, too, especially those of political and military history—often the "dirtier" spheres of human activity—tend to ignore the more positive realities. They are full of stories of usurpations, treasons, murders, and wars. (Books of art history, on the other hand, are selective in the other direction: they focus on achievements and underreport failures or trivialities.) As with news reportage, so it is with many political and military history books: the things that are considered to be historical events usually have to do with conflicts and tragedies. A historical event usually has to do with some kind of a problem, solved or unsolved. Oddly, if a kingdom is passed without conflict from one legitimate heir to another, that is considered to be a lesser historical event. If there are no wars or turmoil, there is not much to report; nothing seems to be happening. Considered as a description of reality, then, many history books tend to employ a problematic principle of selection: the nicer aspects of life are not represented. Again, we receive a skewed picture.

I should point out that I do not aim to ignore here the many terrible aspects of human reality. There are indeed many of them. John McDermott points out that many of what seem to us to be wonderful human achievements are built on terrible suffering, for example the Egyptian pyramids, the Great Wall of China, and the railway from Chicago to Los Angeles.[2] Today there continues to be a great deal of suffering and injustice, much of it unreported or invisible to us, created by both military and economic oppression (some examples are the oppressive regimes in contemporary Africa and sweatshops

2. John J. McDermott, "Why Bother: Is Life Worth Living?" *Journal of Philosophy* 88, no. 11 (1991): 682.

in Southeast Asia). Thus, we should reject rosy descriptions of the world that present it as all hearts and flowers. But it would also be incorrect to present a completely dismal picture of the world. The world is terrible, and the world is wonderful. Both statements are true. It includes evil, injustice, pain, cruelty, and frustration, but also beauty, kindness, friendship, dedication, courage, inspiration, human closeness and warmth, justice, generosity, fairness, knowledge, responsibility, and depth. Many of these we can either choose to find in the world or create ourselves. And although the world is frequently painful, sometimes significantly and sharply so, many aspects of it can also provide a great deal of gratification and meaning (even for people whose lot is bad), if we are only ready to look for or feel them. When we encounter evil and suffering, we often have ways of dealing with them: we can sometimes fight them, distance ourselves from them, draw some good results from them, balance them to a certain degree with good aspects of life, or learn to live with them. It is true that many people completely ignore the evil and painful aspects of reality, pretending to themselves that these do not exist. But many others make a similar mistake by ignoring the many positive aspects of reality or the possibility of enhancing those aspects.

2

Some people despair when they discover that someone whom they admired has faults, many of them significant. Many luminaries were far from perfect. Martin Luther King Jr., although a preacher, was an adulterer.[3] Gandhi beat his wife and was, in general, a bad

3. Ralph David Abernathy, *And the Walls Came Tumbling Down: An Autobiography* (New York: HarperPerennial, 1990), 470–475.

husband.[4] Mother Teresa showed sympathy and support to the Duvalier family during its cruel dictatorship over Haiti; it is also claimed that she initiated the Christian baptism of dying patients without their consent.[5] Krishnamurti had an affair with Rosalind Rajagopal, wife of his associate Desikacharya Rajagopal, for many years.[6] One could go on; when we scrutinize lives more closely, even the lives of those people whom we usually see as having had paradigmatically meaningful lives, they emerge as flawed, and sometimes severely so. One by one they disappoint us, which can give us the feeling that there is no one to revere or look up to. This disheartening disillusionment can make it feel as though we are left with an unworthy world, bereft of meaning.

However, this conclusion, again, seems to be based on a perfectionist attitude that understands only the "greats" to have had meaningful lives and, furthermore, accepts even their lives as having been meaningful only if they were not flawed in any way. A non-perfectionist will find a lot of meaning also in the lives of ordinary people like you and me, and will not hold that lives such as Martin Luther King Jr.'s, Gandhi's, or Mother Teresa's are meaningless just because they are not perfect. By this I do not mean to belittle their flaws; young Gandhi's wife-beating, for example, seems to me to have been a very serious failing (and in Gandhi's later years he, too, saw it as such). It would have been much better if this great person, who opposed violence so strongly in his later years, had not himself used it against his wife in his early years. Thus, I am in no way

4. Stanley A. Wolpert, *Gandhi's Passion: The Life and Legacy of Mahatma Gandhi* (Oxford: Oxford University Press, 2001), 15, 29, 52–53, 104–106.
5. Christopher Hitchens, *The Missionary Position: Mother Teresa in Theory and Practice* (London: Verso, 1995), 3–6, 48.
6. Mary Lutyens, *Krishnamurti and the Rajagopals* (Place of publication unmentioned: Krishnamurti Foundation of America, 1996), 4, 58.

proposing that Gandhi's failing is minor or that we should not be troubled about wife-beating. But I do not think that this very significant flaw overrides all that is valuable in Gandhi's life. Just as we should not ignore Gandhi's failing in this sphere because of his greatness in other spheres, neither should we ignore Gandhi's greatness in other spheres because of his failing in this one. Our sorrow over Gandhi's treatment of his wife does not invalidate our appreciation of his greatness in so many other spheres. We can still appreciate him very much even if we treat him not as a saint but rather as a flawed but in many ways great person. We can appreciate those we do not idolize; we can respect those we criticize. While perfectionists, disgusted with those whom they cannot idolize, hold that no meaning can be found in this world, nonperfectionists hold that the less-than-perfect can have meaningful lives if there is enough that is valuable in them. Moreover, the less-than-perfect can have extremely meaningful lives if there is a high degree of value alongside the flaws. Again, we should recognize and reject the tendency, typical of perfectionism (but not only of perfectionism), to blind ourselves to much of the value that exists.

3

Another argument for the notion that people are evil may be based on psychological egoism. According to this psychological theory, everything we do is based, in the final analysis, only on the egoistic urge to increase the ratio of pleasant to unpleasant feelings we experience. (The pleasant or unpleasant feelings may be physical, emotional, intellectual, or spiritual.) This is true of all activities, including philanthropic or self-sacrificial ones. A person who gives money to a beggar, for example, may thereby secretly be enjoying her superiority over him (she is richer and she has control of the situation) and over the many other people who walk through the streets without giving money (she is a good, charitable person, while they are not). She may also receive some admiration for her charity, both from the beggar and from others who see her giving him money. If she donates anonymously, she may admire herself for being so noble as to give without needing any external recognition, but simply for giving's sake. She may also have guilt feelings about what she perceives as her own insufficient morality, and the charity that she gives may relieve some of those guilt feelings and thus, again, allow her to feel better about herself. But the pleasant feelings felt by those who do good deeds need not derive only from a sense of superiority or the relief of guilt. Philanthropists may well feel real compassion, so that giving satisfies their compassionate desire to give, which again is a pleasant feeling. They may also be empathetic people, and thus genuinely share the joy the beneficiaries of their good deeds feel and experience it themselves. According to this theory, even people who sacrifice their health or even their life, or go through a great deal of suffering, are acting out of an egoistic urge to increase pleasant feelings and decrease unpleasant ones, in the final analysis. Otherwise, they would not do what they do. At the end of the day, people do whatever we do out of egoism.

According to an oft-repeated story, Abraham Lincoln professed the theory of psychological egoism to a fellow passenger on a coach, claiming that all good deeds are prompted by selfishness. Later, while the coach was going over a bridge, the passengers noted a sow squealing loudly because her piglets were caught in the mud and about to drown. Lincoln stepped down from the coach, walked into the mud, and saved the piglets. When he got back into the coach his fellow passenger asked him what egoism there had been in his deed, and he replied that if he had not saved the piglets, the suffering of the sow would have undermined his peace of mind.[7] Thus, although he went through significant discomfort, he acted in the way he expected to maximize the ratio of pleasant to unpleasant feelings he would experience. In the final analysis, then, he did it for himself.

According to psychological egoism, what has been written here about moral endeavors is also true of composing a sonata, writing a poem, or finding an explanation for a natural phenomenon. What motivates composers, poets, and scientists, as well as their audience, is the wish to feel gratification. This good feeling may have to do with one-upmanship (they may think, "I am an artist, while they are not"; "I am a better artist than Tom, Dick, or Harry"), but it does not have to. People may compose sonatas or write poems because they deeply enjoy the process or the product. But their ultimate motive in everything they do, the theory suggests, is only egoistic: they want to feel satisfaction, or to decrease their unpleasant feelings, and this, in the final analysis, is what moves them to do whatever they do.

Thus, it might be argued, all people act only from the same basic impulse: not moral, intellectual, aesthetic, or religious interest but rather self-interest in increasing the ratio of pleasant to unpleasant feelings they experience. And if that is the case, then much of what we take to be worthy, such as moral or artistic work, could be argued to be not worthy, and thus also not meaningful, since it is based on nothing more than a self-serving effort to feel gratification. If our real motivation is not to decrease world hunger, produce good literature, gain knowledge, have warm emotional connections, or please God but rather the egoistic urge to experience more pleasant feelings (and less unpleasant ones), then perhaps our efforts to bring

7. Joel Feinberg, "Psychological Egoism," in *Reason and Responsibility*, ed. Joel Feinberg, 6th ed. (Belmont, CA: Wadsworth, 1985), 483.

about those results should not be appreciated so much. This is true not only of our own endeavors but also of Shakespeare's sonnets, Bach's cantatas, Meister Eckhart's mystical teachings, and Albert Schweitzer's philanthropic work. Moreover, if the egoistic thesis is correct, then it could be argued that there is not that much difference between, say, Mother Teresa and Genghis Khan. In essence, they are both moved by the same urge: egoism. True, what made Mother Teresa feel satisfaction was saving people's lives, while what made Genghis Khan feel satisfaction was killing people. But in the final analysis they both wanted the same thing, which was to feel satisfaction.

However, it is not clear how the supposition that everything people do is ultimately based *only* on their egoistic urge to increase the ratio of their pleasant to unpleasant feelings can be defended.[8] We may accept that an egoistic urge is *also* present in everything we do (otherwise, perhaps, we would have not done it) without accepting that the egoistic urge is the only or ultimate motivating force behind our activities. There may well also be other basic, ultimate urges besides it, some worthy and some unworthy, that motivate us to behave as we do. These urges could direct some people to find egoistic satisfaction in sadistic murders and other people to find egoistic satisfaction in saving lives, painting pictures, or reading poems. It is the worthiness or unworthiness of those other forces that determines whether our life is meaningful. Thus, even if there is always indeed an egoistic motivation present alongside our worthy or unworthy motivations, that does not cancel out the positive or negative value of the other motivations. The desire to feel satisfaction may well be seen as merely one factor among many that

---

8. For a more detailed version of this criticism and for some other criticisms, see Feinberg, "Psychological Egoism."

determine our activities; there is much more than that within us, and some of that "much more" may well merit being seen as meaningful. Perfectionists, of course, may insist that a meaningful life must be driven solely by worthy motivations (such as philanthropy or an aesthetic drive), with no element of egoistic motivation, which they may hold to be insufficiently worthy. But the problems inherent in perfectionism have already been discussed.

Let us, however, for the sake of argument, grant that there is no activity of ours which is not *ultimately* based solely on the egoistic urge to increase the ratio of our pleasant to our unpleasant feelings. This still does not show that life is meaningless or of insufficient worth. The wish to feel good about oneself or achieve a high ratio of pleasant to unpleasant feelings is not in itself a bad or a worthless motive. Thus, it in no way undermines the worth of what we do or achieve. Further, the fact that some people satisfy their egoistic urges by doing *worthy* activities can be seen as making their lives meaningful. Again, compare Mother Teresa with Genghis Khan. True, according to psychological egoism, they shared the desire to feel satisfaction, and both were ultimately motivated to do whatever they did by that desire. In this they were indeed similar. However, there are also some differences: whereas what made Mother Teresa experience satisfaction was saving people, what made Genghis Khan experience satisfaction was killing them. But this is an important difference: we take Mother Teresa's inclination to be worthy and Genghis Khan's inclination to be unworthy. Of course, if we choose to ignore how Mother Teresa and Genghis Khan differ and focus exclusively on what they share, then they indeed emerge as very similar, and we have no reason to see her life as more meaningful than his. But it is unclear why we should focus only on what these two individuals share while ignoring all the ways in which they differ, as if the differences did not exist at all; the differences do seem to be important and relevant. Thus, a person who finds worthy activity satisfying can be seen as having a meaningful life even if that feeling of satisfaction is the driving force of her worthy activity.

4

Some are exasperated by humanity because people, even people who behave well, seem to be morally malleable or corruptible. The goodness in our moral character frequently succumbs to pressure. Some findings in social psychology experiments such as those carried out by Stanley Milgram seem to support this view.[9] Famously, Milgram found that when ordinary people were directed by experimenters in a position of authority to deliver strong electric shocks to people in another room, they did so even when they believed their victims to be suffering immense pain. (The people in the other room were not in fact being electrified; they were actors who did not suffer at all during the experiments.) This suggests that even good people can be easily manipulated into causing great pain to their peers, if only an authority figure instructs them to do so. People who hold that we are easily corruptible also sometimes invoke Lord Acton's precept that "power tends to corrupt, and absolute power corrupts absolutely."[10] If the principle is correct, then those who gain power will change morally: at the very least, they will take advantage of other people and, at the worst, they will oppress them. Those who emphasize people's moral malleability or corruptibility may also point out

---

9. Stanley Milgram, "Behavioral Study of Obedience," *Journal of Abnormal and Social Psychology* 67, no. 4 (1963): 371–378.

10. John Emerich Edward Dalberg-Acton, "Letter to Bishop Creighton," in *Historical Essays and Studies*, ed. John Neville Figgis and Reginald Vere Laurence (London: Macmillan, 1907), 504.

that it seems easy to train people from a young age to do terrible things. A Holocaust survivor whom I knew when I was a teenager told me that he believed that if he or I had been born in the relevant years in Nazi Germany, and had been educated according to Nazi principles, we too would have eagerly joined the Hitler Youth and aspired to serve the Führer, committing the very same type of atrocities that my interlocutor and his family had suffered. Material destitution, too, can very easily and quickly motivate people to cheat, steal, or worse. And rhetorical manipulation seems highly effective as well: it is easy to lead a crowd to feel angry and a little threatened by telling it that a certain other person or group of people despises and endangers that crowd; those feelings can then easily be turned into intense hatred, which can in turn be easily channeled into violent action.

But it is not clear how true these claims are. According to Milgram's own description, 35 percent of the subjects of his experiments refused to continue to inflict pain on peers even though an authority figure was telling them to do so.[11] Moreover, there were different variations of the experiment, and according to Gina Perry, "In over half of all his variations, Milgram found the opposite result—that more than 60 percent of people *disobeyed* the experimenter's orders."[12] Perry also contends that Milgram downplayed contradictions and inconsistencies in his findings.[13] Furthermore, the experiment examines whether people obey instructions of authority figures only to inflict pain, not whether they obey instructions of authority figures to cause any other type of harm. Milgram himself reports that the participants were assured that although

---

11. Milgram, "Behavioral Study of Obedience," 376.

12. Perry's emphasis. Gina Perry, *Behind the Shock Machine: The Untold Story of the Notorious Milgram Psychology Experiments* (New York: New Press, 2013), 9.

13. Perry, *Behind the Shock Machine*, 9.

those in the other room would suffer pain, their health would not be harmed.[14] According to Don Mixon, as cited by Perry, when subjects "were presented with the unambiguous message that the shocks were harmful, they stopped giving them."[15] Mixon suggests that this shows that what Milgram's experiments in fact measured was the faith that people put in experts rather than their readiness to do evil when ordered to.[16] Perry also suggests that a significant number of the subjects suspected that the experiment was a hoax.[17] Finally, the experiments examined only *immediate* obedience to authority. According to Milgram's report, almost all participants showed extreme degrees of tension and discomfort with what they were doing.[18] They did not like it at all, and it is not clear that, had they been given more time (say, a day) and the opportunity to reflect on what they were doing, they would have gone on with the experiment.

I am also not sure how accurate Lord Acton's principle is. There are indeed many cases in which power corrupts, and absolute power corrupts absolutely. But these cases do not show that power corrupts all or even most. Those who are in power are sometimes those who are power hungry anyway and therefore, perhaps, more corruptible than others; some of those who are in power and are corrupt may well have already been amenable to corruption before they came to power. They are certainly not a representative or an arbitrary sample of humanity. And even within this group, one can see that many who are in positions of power do not humiliate or oppress others as much as they could, or at all, even if there is no price that they would

14. Milgram, "Behavioral Study of Obedience," 373, 374.
15. Perry, *Behind the Shock Machine*, 62.
16. Perry, *Behind the Shock Machine*, 60–63.
17. Perry, *Behind the Shock Machine*, 45, 138–140, 173, 213.
18. Milgram, "Behavioral Study of Obedience," 375, 376, 377.

have to pay for it afterward. On the contrary, many people in a position of power behave fairly or perform occasional acts of goodness even if they have nothing to gain from it.

It is also unclear that the Holocaust survivor I mentioned was right to believe that in the right context we could all have been educated to be Hitler Youth. As educators and parents know too well, and frequently to their chagrin, education has its limits; those being educated frequently do not turn out as their educators wished (sometimes that discrepancy is for the worse; sometimes it is for the better). The former USSR, along with other Communist countries, presents an interesting example of the limits of education and of social control. Notwithstanding deliberate indoctrination and the propaganda pervading all types of media, a significant part of the population was estranged from the ideology. The preponderance of delinquents and criminals in all countries also shows that social control has its limits. Just as some criminals are harder to reform, so some good people are harder to corrupt. Material hardship, too, does not have the same effect on all people. Some are very restricted in their material means yet do not join a subculture of emotional, mental, or behavioral destitution, and do not accept a distorted value system. The same holds for rhetorical manipulation, which affects some people more than others. Thus, I would not give up on humanity, certainly not on all of it, too quickly. Some people are less morally flexible than others.

But, for the sake of argument, let us grant that most people are indeed extremely morally malleable. They need favorable external circumstances to hold them in a relatively upright moral position, since they do not have a strong enough moral backbone of their own to withstand pressure; external circumstances can quite easily make them behave in both radically good and radically bad ways. But if this is indeed true—as I am not sure that it is of all people—then this is not only bad news. It means that people are not only easily corruptible but also easily corrigible. They have great potential not only to do evil but also to do good. And this is also good news. We know what to do now. If children can be educated to do both evil and good, then we have good reason to try to educate them in such a way that they will do good. In many countries, education is indeed geared toward doing just that. If laws that grant too much power to individuals lead to corruption, we should, of course, see that laws do not grant absolute or too much power to any individuals. In many modern countries, a balance of powers is in place to prevent such abuse. If poverty produces human degeneracy, that gives us another good reason to combat poverty. Some countries have already succeeded in doing so to an impressive extent. If certain laws and social conventions produce bad behavior, that gives us a strong incentive to try to change those laws and social conventions. More generally, if external circumstances indeed have such power over people's behavior, then we can be hopeful. We know, more or less, what needs to be done, and it may well prove effective. It may well lead many people to live good, moral, fruitful lives.

It is probably incorrect to generalize about human nature. There is an enormous variety in the ratio of good and evil in people (and that ratio also goes up and down for any given individual throughout life), as well as in their moral flexibility. Hence, claims such as "People are essentially good," "People are essentially bad," or "People are morally flexible" are likely to be false just because they are too broad. But it seems true that at least some people have the potential to be both very bad and very good. There are many who could lead either very terrible or very meaningful lives. That means that we should be both fearful and hopeful; acknowledging people's potential for both good and evil, we should try to create the conditions that help realize the former and restrict the latter.

5

Even if most people were, in general, as evil and morally ugly as some arguments paint them to be, we still could, in many cases, lead meaningful lives. We can do so by, for example, keeping company with people who are generally not evil, who do things that are not manipulative and oppressive, who engage with what is beautiful, and so on. It is frequently possible to do so because the world is very diverse; even if it shows an unsatisfactory *average* level of goodness, we may be lucky enough to be in, or wise and active enough to direct ourselves to, those parts that are good. Even in an overall evil world, there are enclaves of goodness. Of course, we cannot always direct ourselves to them. Sometimes evil will not let us go our own way. For example, in contemporary North Korea, those who do not cooperate with the regime by spying and reporting on others are punished severely. But sometimes it is possible for us to distance ourselves sufficiently from other people's evil so that we can lead a good and meaningful life. In some cases, to find and maintain goodness and beauty we even have to remain in our own homes, or in our own inner mental space. True, when we learn of the atrocities that some human beings have visited on others we at times feel that humanity at large has been contaminated, and that includes us. But humanity is made up of many distinct, very different individuals, and other people's immoral behavior does not make our own behavior less moral, just as our own moral behavior does not make other people's behavior less immoral.

Furthermore, the extent of evil in the world can be changed. It is wrong to treat the current amount of evil there is in the world as some kind of metaphysical necessity. It is possible in some cases, through struggle, discussion, empathy, or compassion, to diminish the severity and extent of evil in the world, or at least in certain parts of it. In other cases, after the evil has done its work, it is at least possible to diminish and to some extent mend the harm that it has done. It is very important for those who can diminish evil and suffering to try to do so. Doing this is a good and important way of dealing with evil.

As noted at the beginning of this chapter, I am not advocating naiveté by suggesting that we stop seeing the bad as bad. I am only suggesting that we also make a point of seeing the good as good. The two do not contradict each other. On the contrary, they complement each other in our efforts to see reality as it is. We should acknowledge the bad for what it is; but in the same way, we should also acknowledge the good for what it is, and be as intensely thankful for and happy about the latter as we are sad and angry about the former. Some of those who are highly sensitive to the evil and painful parts of reality but not to its good parts like to think of themselves as realistic, sober-minded, or clear-eyed. But I do not think they are. It is unrealistic to see only the bad parts of reality, just as it is unrealistic to see only its good parts. The inability to see and thoroughly enjoy the good parts of life but only to suffer from the bad parts of life is neither realism nor soberness, but just another type of self-delusion, even if, in this case, it runs in the opposite direction from the self-delusion in which many others engage. It is unfortunate to allow the existence of the bad elements of life to keep us from seeing the good ones. The next chapter points out a few phenomena that blind some people to the good aspects of reality, leading them to see life in general, or their own life, as "nastier" than it really is.

Chapter 14

Why We Are Blind to Goodness

1

As I have suggested throughout the book, perfectionism is one major cause for people's blindness to the goodness and value to be found in their and others' lives. Perfectionists refuse to recognize goodness or worth if it is not perfect goodness or worth, and thus miss much. The previous chapter discussed also how news media can lead people to overlook the positive and dwell on the negative.

There are also common views that lead some people to see themselves and others as worse than they really are. Some hold that people's behavior in a crisis is an indication of their true nature, rather than merely an indication of how they behave under difficult and rare conditions. The same is true of anger; it is sometimes supposed that what people say in times of anger shows what they really think, rather than simply showing what they think when they feel attacked, rejected, or cheated. (Lovers, especially, can fall into the mode of accusing each other of exposing their true thoughts in times of anger.) But these suppositions are problematic. We are complex, having within us many elements that pull in different directions. Different circumstances elicit different responses and behaviors, none of which are more real than the others. Some circumstances bring out the worst in us; others bring out the best. It is wise to create or maintain the circumstances that bring out the best in us and to change or keep away as much as possible from circumstances that bring out the worst in us. (Of course, when we cannot avoid circumstances that elicit bad reactions, we should make very serious efforts to contain or change our reactions.) But the supposition that our problematic reactions in times of crisis or anger are somehow more indicative of the "real" us is incorrect.

2

Many have a tendency to judge themselves too harshly or to refrain from forgiving themselves, and this too interferes with their ability to recognize goodness, in this case specifically their own goodness. They employ a double standard that causes them to discriminate against themselves; they judge themselves more harshly than they judge others and do not forgive themselves for what they would have forgiven in others.[1]

Sometimes people judge themselves harshly and do not forgive themselves for things that are not their fault at all, since one cannot be at fault for, or be guilty of, things over which one has no power. An acquaintance of mine tortured himself for what he saw as his blameworthy failure to prevent the death of his twenty-six-year-old son in a car accident. My acquaintance was not in the car when the accident happened. The accident occurred in another country; his son was not driving; and the person who caused the accident was the driver of the other car. Nevertheless, the father held that parents have the responsibility to protect their children from all harm at any

---

1. For some other cases in which people discriminate against themselves see chapter 3.

time and under all circumstances, and therefore felt that he had failed his son, his family, and himself by not fulfilling his responsibility. In blaming himself for not protecting his son at all times and under all circumstances he was, in fact, blaming himself for not being God. It was only when he realized that if something similar had happened to another family, he would not have blamed the father for an event over which that father had absolutely no power (and that, in general, we cannot be blamed for events over which we have no power), that he was able to see things differently. Another person I knew could not forgive herself for having been sexually abused as a teenager, and only began to see things differently when she was asked whether she would blame another teenager for suffering similar abuse. I know several people who blame themselves for failing to prevent the pain and the deaths of loved ones who were terminally ill, although there was no way of preventing that pain or those deaths. All of these events are painful. There are good reasons to be saddened by them. But they involved no fault by the people in question, since those people had no power over the dire events that occurred; thus there was nothing for which they could be condemned or forgiven, just as they could not be condemned or forgiven for Lincoln's or Gandhi's murder.

We can wish something had never occurred, feel very bad about it, be sorry for being involved in it and for having done what we did, or find it very disturbing, all without being guilty of it. This happens if we had no power over the situation or could not plausibly foresee it.[2] Of course, being sad or feeling disconcerted, wishing that something had not happened, and so on, are also difficult feelings

---

2. Collective guilt seems to be an exception to this rule. However, many do not accept it, and even when it is accepted, it does not usually arouse the sharp sense of guilt that undermines people's feeling of self-worth and sense of the meaningfulness of life.

that have to be dealt with and worked on. They too sometimes lead people to see their lives as meaningless. But they differ from feeling *guilty* for what happened, which is a feeling that often diminishes one's seeing oneself as of worth and, thus, diminishes more sharply one's feeling that one's life is meaningful. We should distinguish carefully between guilt feelings and guilt. Just having (or lacking) guilt feelings is not a good indicator of one's guilt. Many people do not have guilt feelings although they are guilty, while others have guilt feelings although they are not guilty. One should try to fit one's guilt feelings to the real degree of one's guilt rather than trust them as evidence for that guilt.

In some other cases people's behavior does involve real fault, but they pass overly harsh judgment on themselves and have excessive guilt feelings. In both legal and moral discourses, there are many exonerating circumstances that are taken into account when considering degrees of guilt. Such factors include the offenders' age at the time of the misdeed, whether they meant harm, whether they understood that the behavior was harmful and how harmful it was, whether they had sufficient information about the matter, whether they had received good guidance, and whether they were acting under various types of emotional pressure. Likewise, when it comes to punishment, we take into account whether the offenders have truly repented, changed, asked forgiveness, or compensated their victims. We accept that the severity of the punishment should be proportional to the severity of the crime and that punishments have not only beginnings but also ends. When the punishment ends, it should indeed be *over*. After offenders "do their time" they should be set free, not kept in prison forever by the force of inertia. Likewise, people should not be punished twice, three times, or forty times for the same offense. Nevertheless, many of those who accept these general principles, and consistently apply them to others, do *not* apply them to themselves when they consider their own faults. They do not take relevant exonerating circumstances into account, and the internal punishments they inflict on themselves are often disproportionate to the crime, in terms of both intensity and duration. Such people often do not take into account their own regret, compensation, or changes of heart and behavior. They also apply punishments that have no terminus or punish themselves many, many times for the same crime. Some punishments that people apply to themselves are barbaric, including the emotional parallels of mutilation, solitary confinement, torture, or hurried execution. Just as people are sometimes more prone to failures in verdict (assigning blame inappropriately) when they judge themselves rather than others, so too are they often more prone to failures in sentencing when they consider their own deeds. Treating themselves more harshly than they would treat anyone else, they mete out punishments to themselves that are unjust and disproportionate. They fail to do unto themselves as they would do unto others.

In reasonable legal systems, legal processes take time and attention. Judges think long and hard before they decide on a verdict and then on a sentence, carefully weighing, over and over, the evidence and the many details of a case. But many of the verdicts and sentences that people apply to themselves are decided upon hurriedly and almost thoughtlessly, subsequently affecting those people's lives for years. Many people, in deciding on their own guilt and punishment, operate more like a lynch mob than a court of justice.

So far, I have discussed cases in which no crime was committed and, thus, there was no need to forgive anything. I then considered cases in which there was an offense and a corresponding punishment, and argued that, just as we do when we judge others, when we judge ourselves we should strive for a just, proportional punishment. But in some cases, especially those that involve genuine regret, compensation, and changes of heart and of behavior, we can also opt for forgiveness: that is, for ceasing to resent a person—in this case, ourselves—although that person has done something wrong.[3] It is painful to see how some people who are ready after some time to cease resenting others, notwithstanding wrongs they have committed, never stop resenting themselves.

Perhaps the most basic and helpful rule of thumb for behaving morally is the Golden Rule, "Do unto others as you would have them do unto you," and, relatedly, "Love your neighbor as yourself." Both phrases usually provide good guidance for most of our interactions with others. But many people also need guidance for their interactions with themselves. The complementary principles, "Do not do to yourself what you would not do to others" and "Love yourself as you love your neighbor," may be of some help. It is not always easy to live by these principles. Following the complementary Reversed Golden Rule involves a decision, requires effort and time, is achieved by degrees, and necessitates the overcoming of reactions that, for many, have become automatic. Indeed, behaving morally, whether toward others or toward oneself, often requires work. But it is work we should be willing to do.

3

Another factor that keeps some people from appreciating goodness and value is the adoption of an excessively critical attitude toward

---

3. This understanding of forgiveness is originally Bishop Joseph Butler's and is cited in many modern discussions. See, e.g., Jeffrie G. Murphy, "Forgiveness and Resentment," in *Forgiveness and Mercy*, ed. Jeffrie G. Murphy and Jean Hampton (Cambridge: Cambridge University Press, 1988), 15; Robert C. Roberts, "Forgivingness," *American Philosophical Quarterly* 32, no. 4 (1995): 290.

much of what is within and around them. There are various motivations for endorsing this attitude. In some groups, it is considered conformist to see the goodness that inheres in what is around and within us, and hence nonconformist to be melancholic, highly critical, or disgusted with everything (including oneself). But just as it is mistaken to be a conformist only for conformism's sake, so it is mistaken to be a nonconformist only for nonconformism's sake. Positions should be accepted on their merits, not because the majority either agrees or disagrees with them. One should also beware of conformist nonconformism: there are conformists; there are nonconformists; and there is the conformism of the nonconformists. Within their own circles, nonconformists are sometimes as dogmatic, inflexible, and subject to herd or pack mentality as conformists are, or even more so.

For some, maintaining a highly critical attitude functions also as a status symbol, signaling to others that one is intellectually superior, deep, or highly cultured. People sometimes employ this attitude to convey to others or to themselves that appreciating what they encounter may be suitable for the shallow riffraff, but *they* have higher standards. Adopting a highly critical attitude may also be a way to signal that they have seen it all and are thus easily bored and hard to impress, unlike the others who are so naive as to see life as good and interesting. An excessively critical attitude can also be presented, along with bitterness and pessimism, as indications of honesty and courage: unlike all those others who lie to themselves, I who am bitter have the sincerity and the guts to look at reality precisely as it is, without beautifying it in any way. I neither repress, nor regress, nor deny. And in some cases of self-criticism the Freudian notion of *Krankheitsgewinn,* or morbid gain, that is, the advantage a sick person enjoys due to the attention and caring that others bestow, may also be at work (although many people also back away when they meet with such an attitude).

Of course, criticism, pain, and suffering are often genuine. Life and the world include many aspects that pain us. Some of those who are not harmed by external events are tortured by genuine internal psychological tensions or chemical imbalances. Moreover, identifying the negative aspects of reality allows us to beware of them and to improve things. But it is important to distinguish such cases from those in which criticism and suffering are feigned, are adopted as status symbols, or are unnecessarily intensified. We should pay attention not only to whether we are being falsely cheerful, but also to whether we are falsely cheerless.

4

Bitterness and an overcritical spirit can also be professional hazards: some professions inadvertently bring out such attitudes. Lawyers, for example, frequently meet people at their worst, when they are suing each other, divorcing, or have committed crimes. Like doctors, who see people when they are ill, lawyers frequently interact with people's pathologies. There is only a little of what is good and healthy in society that lawyers see in their professional lives, and it is easy for them to extrapolate from the segment of life that they see at work to life in general. Police officers, judges, psychologists, and social workers may suffer from a similar problem.

Contemporary academics, too, are in danger of endorsing an overly critical view of the world. In the modern academic system, the number of articles and books a person publishes is by far the main criterion for professional survival and promotion. Whereas a hundred years ago the depth and breadth of academics' knowledge, along with their teaching, were taken to be of high importance, so that some well-respected scholars produced very little new research, today publication matters more than anything else, at most institutions. This has influenced academic life in a plethora of both good and bad ways, but I focus here on one: this system gives academics a strong incentive to be critical. Agreeing with another scholar, or admiring the wisdom in her writings, will not gain one a new publication, whereas disagreeing with and criticizing her may well allow one to publish something. This sometimes creates a mentality in which one does not read to value but to find fault. This overly critical attitude sometimes also affects how students are trained to read new material; they omit the stage of identifying what may be (even partly) right, interesting, deep, or helpful and focus on spotting as quickly as possible something to criticize. Being critical has many advantages in scholarly contexts, but it may also become excessive, and the excessively critical attitude many academics adopt in their professional lives can easily spill over to their lives outside of work, that is, to the way in which they see almost everything around them.

5

Another factor that diminishes some people's sensitivity to good aspects of reality—in this case, the positive aspects of their own lives—is the cultural ethos that treats pride unfavorably. I agree with Nicholas Dixon, among others, that (regulated) pride can be a positive force in life and should be cultivated.[4] Of course, one should beware of excessive pride (which could be called conceit, smugness, snobbery, pompousness, vanity, or arrogance) that leads to complacency, insensitivity, contempt toward other people, and an

---

4. Nicholas Dixon, "Modesty, Snobbery, and Pride," *Journal of Value Inquiry* 39, nos. 3–4 (2005): 415–416.

unrealistic appraisal of one's own achievements and abilities. But all that differs from deserved pride in the right measure. Admittedly, displaying pride carries some risks: in some social contexts, professing one's self-worth beyond a certain point may pain others and arouse envy and even hostility. But one may feel pride without displaying it, or display it while being sensitive to other people's feelings. A lack of proper pride may lead people not to place enough value on the good and worthy aspects of their lives, and thus see their lives as less meaningful than they really are. It is realistic and helpful to recognize and enjoy what is good in life, including the good in our own character and our own achievements. It is usually advisable to be truthful to ourselves, presenting things as they are. But that includes a self-understanding that shows us to ourselves as being just as good as we are, not worse or better than that. This is healthy, helpful pride. It is easy to exceed the degree in which pride is good and helpful, but it is also easy to have too little pride. Some people have been taught so thoroughly to avoid pompousness or vanity that they have lost their legitimate, appropriate pride in themselves.[5]

6

I have discussed in this chapter how people can have a difficulty with noting the good in the world or in themselves because of perfectionism, excessive criticism, overly harsh self-judgment, and the rejection of pride. It is indeed odd to see how torturous people find it to reply in the affirmative when asked whether they think that they are,

---

5. I accept, however, that in many types of spiritual or mystical endeavor it is necessary to try to lose one's ego; thus, in that special type of striving for meaningfulness, an effort should be made to eradicate pride.

all in all, good; or how embarrassed they become when other people characterize them as good.[6] I do not deny, of course, that each of us is a mixed bag. There are many things we should change and improve about ourselves, and these things should be noted and corrected, not hidden. But it is important to recognize the good in ourselves as well, not only to criticize what is bad. In a meeting I attended with people who, like me, had been engaged in some volunteer work, we began discussing the reasons for our volunteering. One person said that volunteering may help him succeed in a career in social work. Another told us that he was a writer and that he would use the experience as material for a book that he wanted to write. Some mentioned the good feeling they had because they volunteered. Yet another talked about a traumatic experience she had and how volunteering was a way to tackle it. No one mentioned that he or she was volunteering out of goodness, although I am sure that that was true of all of them. When it was my turn I said, rather provocatively, that I volunteer because I am a good person. An embarrassed silence followed, as if I had told everyone that I was a cannibal. In the break, some of them tried to save me from myself, pointing out that it cannot just be that I am a good person. I must also be gaining something from volunteering, even if it is only emotional or spiritual. I agreed; I was also gaining from volunteering, and the reason I gave was only part of the story. But so, I argued, were the reasons they gave, since most of them could have gained more easily the advantages they had mentioned in other ways. They were also, I suggested, good people. It was difficult for them to accept that.

I believe that I am a good person. That does not mean that I am perfect; far from it—ask my family and friends. I have many failings, some

---

6. There are exceptions, of course: when people are accused, criticized, or otherwise challenged in public settings, they often insist, sometimes defensively, that they are indeed very moral.

of which I have succeeded in diminishing, through the years, more than others. Nevertheless, when I consider all the things that I do, and all the things that I refrain from doing, I think that, all things considered, I am a good person. I also have much that I would need to improve in order to become a better person. I hope and believe that over time I will make at least some of these improvements. But being a nonperfectionist, I do not think that only those who are perfect are good people.

The readers of this book are, of course, very diverse. When both the good and the evil that they have done in their lives so far will be taken into account and weighed to form an overall judgment on whether or not they are good people, it will turn out that there are both good and bad people among them. Each reader may want to consider this question: is he or she, overall, a good person? I am sure that the readers are not perfect or saints (and even saints are frequently not "saints," but only good people who are above average). I am certain that in the week that elapsed before reading these lines almost all of the readers of this book have lied a few times. So have I. Almost all of them have acted somewhat dishonestly in some ways. So have I. Almost all of them have shown some hard-heartedness. Again, so have I. Perhaps some of them did worse. Perhaps some of them are, secretly, criminals. But I suspect that most readers of this book—although there is still much in their lives that they can, and should, improve—are all in all good people. Goodness around us, and even within us, is more prevalent than it may at first seem, and than some of us are ready to recognize.

7

Some might object that the attitude presented here, which calls on us to recognize the good around and within us, might lead people into complacency or an exaggerated satisfaction, diminishing their motivation to try to improve things. But I am not calling for us to see the bad as good, only to see the good as good. This is in no way inconsistent with seeing the bad as bad and trying to correct it. It seems to me, on the contrary, that a hypercritical or pessimistic outlook enhances despair and discourages people from trying to improve things. It implies that we should cease all efforts to improve the difficult, painful aspects of reality, within and outside us, since everything is radically bleak and nothing good seems attainable.[7] The attitude that I present here, which aims to notice also the many positive aspects of reality, is the one that considers it possible to engage in efforts to improve ourselves and the world.

---

7. Ironically, some social activists who work hard at improving conditions in the world end up focusing so much on the wrongs that they wish to correct (and which sometimes prove difficult to change) that they develop an angry, pessimistic attitude toward the world at large.

Chapter 15

Identifying I

1

Many people lead insufficiently meaningful lives because they hold wrong suppositions about meaningful lives, or endorse perfectionism, or accept arguments suggesting that life can never be meaningful. Up until this point, the book has mostly focused on these issues. But some people have insufficiently meaningful lives also, or mostly, because they do not know what would make their lives meaningful and, hence, do not engage with it. They just continue to pursue whatever they have been pursuing (or what is commonly accepted in their social environment) even if it is of insufficient worth. Some of these people do not even notice that they experience most of what they pursue in life as of insufficient worth. Others are aware of that, but do not know what would be sufficiently valuable and worth pursuing. They are unclear about what would make their lives meaningful because they have not identified for themselves seriously and clearly enough, or at all, what they hold to be meaningful. Many dedicate more thought in one evening to deliberating which restaurant or film they should go to than they do in their entire lifetime to deliberating what would make their lives more meaningful. Here are a few questions that can help people to identify what is meaningful for them.

1. What would make your life more valuable or meaningful? This is the simple, straightforward question to ask. For some, the reply to this question, once asked seriously and deliberately enough, appears quite clearly. Oddly, however, only relatively few ask it.

2. Which elements in your life do you already take to be meaningful? Increasing the degree of the elements that one already takes to be meaningful in one's life may well increase its meaning. However, caution is advisable, since enhancing these elements beyond a certain degree could be too much. The optimal degree of a meaningful element is frequently not the maximal one.

3. What should be removed from your life in order to make it more meaningful? This question, which focuses on negative values, is important to consider, since the degree of meaning in many people's lives is highly affected not only by what they need to do but also by what they need to stop doing: as in health or in love, an important part of what we need to do to improve does not involve adopting new behaviors but refraining from or moderating old ones. It is not only what is absent in some people's life that makes it meaningless, but frequently, and to a significant degree, also what is present in it.

4. What characteristics in other people lead you to consider them as having meaningful lives? What do you respect and appreciate in others? If you find, for example, that you greatly appreciate people who help other people, you can learn from this that helping others is something that you find valuable. If you feel great respect for people who know a lot, then you can learn from this that knowledge is something you value. I, for example, noticed at a certain point in my life that although I respect people such as Kant (since I teach philosophy, I have a high professional regard for his immense achievements), Einstein, Bach, or Rembrandt, I especially admire people

such as Mother Teresa, Albert Schweitzer, and Gandhi. I inferred from this that, for me, a good way to increase meaning in life was to engage in benevolent activity. It is important to remember, however, that not everything that we appreciate in other people is appropriate for us. We may appreciate other people's musical ability, for example, but not be musical ourselves. Some of what we respect in other people, then, may not be part of what will make our own life meaningful.

5. What has worked for others? What do various traditions see as meaningful? Could those things be meaningful to you as well? Asking these questions assumes that people are often not that different from each other and that they can learn from others' experience. If others have found some things to be meaningful for them, those things may well turn out to be meaningful for us as well. Caution and a critical spirit are necessary here as well. What others have found to be meaningful or what various traditions consider to be meaningful may well not in fact be meaningful, or may not be meaningful for us. But other people's positive and negative experiences and tradition may be worth serious consideration.

6. The first of two deathbed questions: Suppose that you were on your deathbed, and that you had the presence of mind and the time to look back on your life. What would you be happy or sorry to have done and not to have done?[1] You can think of this question as relating to your life in general (what, on your deathbed, will you be sorry or happy to have done and not done in your life as a whole), but also as relating to more

---

1. Cf. Elisabeth Kübler-Ross, *Death: The Final Stage of Growth* (Englewood Cliffs, NJ: Prentice-Hall, 1975), xix: "Live, so you do not have to look back and say: 'God, how I have wasted my life.'"

limited units of time: if you are contemplating spending the next hour, or week, or year in a certain way, do you believe that on your deathbed you will be glad that you had spent it that way, or think that it was a wasted hour, week, or year of your life? It is important to think of this question as relating not only to things we are doing or are about to do but also to things that, for all sorts of reasons, we refrain from doing.

7. The second deathbed question: suppose that you knew that you had only ten more days, or six more months, to live. What would you decide to do in that time?

2

The list above is not exhaustive. There may well be other questions that are helpful as well. Furthermore, these are not perfect or cut-and-dried criteria that will allow us to reach precise and decisive conclusions; as already mentioned in chapter 2, that kind of clarity and certainty cannot be found and should not be expected in the sphere discussed here. The questions are only aids or, at best, rules of thumb to help people arrive at greater knowledge about what is meaningful to them. Answering the questions does not present readers with a comprehensive framework for understanding the meaning of life.[2] However, by pointing out issues of worth and ways of increasing meaning in life, the questions can help to make a heretofore meaningless life into a meaningful one or a meaningful life

2. I disagree here with Taubman–Ben-Ari's claim that "The concept of the meaning of life . . . refers to individuals' attempts to relate to their own existence and to the world *on the basis of a comprehensive view* which dictates their perception, beliefs, priorities, goals and actions" ("Is the Meaning of Life Also the Meaning of Death? A Terror Management Perspective Reply," *Journal of Happiness Studies* 12 [2011]: 394–395; emphasis added).

into an even more meaningful one. Even for the same individual, the seven questions may not all yield the same results, and different people may find different questions to be more or less helpful. The questions should be used, then, with some caution.

The two deathbed questions, questions 6 and 7, should be considered with special care. They have both advantages and disadvantages. Let us start with the advantages of the first deathbed question (What, on your deathbed, will you be sorry or happy to have done and not done in your life?). The question reminds us that life is limited, and that since we cannot do everything in our life, we have to prioritize. The question also encourages us to note that, as with business, education, or health, so with meaning, it is worthwhile to plan not just for the immediate future but also for the distant future and to keep long-term consequences and goals in mind. Current issues seem more important to us just because they are contemporary. The deathbed perspective can correct this tendency, to a certain extent, and help us to see the meaning of things (or lack thereof) in the larger context.

The first deathbed question also emphasizes an important fact that many ignore when they are considering how to go about their lives: we only get one chance, and it passes quickly. If we miss it, it is gone. This specific combination of genes, upbringing, historical era, and social culture who is you or me will never appear again. It is unique. Since you only get one chance, you had better use it well. It is well worth remembering the saying that this is not a dress rehearsal; this is the thing itself. We should beware of living a life that is only, to use Yeats's words, "a preparation for something that never happens."[3] We are not just preparing now for something else that has not started yet and will come in the future; it is already happening, right now, and

---

3. W. B. Yeats, "Reveries over Childhood and Youth," in *The Autobiography of William Butler Yeats* (New York: Collier, 1965), 71.

is passing by every second. We cannot do it better in some other life, trying to live more meaningfully then; this is the only opportunity we get. Just as money (for most people) is limited, so is life. And just as in spending our money there are things that it is wiser or less wise for us to buy, so it is with our life: it can be frittered away. One may suddenly discover, when it is too late, that much of one's time has passed and has not been used well. Wasting one's life is a great sin against oneself, and the deathbed question can help awaken us to this danger.

Furthermore, this deathbed question allows us to see that we are freer than we thought. We often tell ourselves that we are not free to make various changes. For example, if asked whether they want to go have coffee in the middle of the day, many people would answer that they *cannot* leave work, since it is not yet the end of the workday. This may not be just a figure of speech; they indeed feel that they *cannot* leave work. Similarly, they often feel that they just cannot study music, leave everything and go to Nepal, fail to show up at their second cousin's wedding, or change a career. The deathbed question, through the special perspective it employs, helps us to see that this is wrong: in many cases, we *could* do things differently. There would of course be a price to pay. The price may be too great and we may therefore decide that it is wise not to pay it. But frequently we do have the choice, and it is prudent to at least consider whether or not the price is indeed too great. The option of doing things differently *is* frequently there, and it is a good idea to remember this, as some choices we fail to make might turn out to be well worth the price.[4] The deathbed question may help see in a number

---

4. See Jean-Paul Sartre, *Being and Nothingness*, trans. Hazel E. Barnes (London: Methuen, 1966), 328, 438, 441, 488, 495, 509, 555. However, this discussion, while borrowing heavily from Sartre's views of our extensive mental and emotional freedom, does not aim to represent his thoughts on the issue in a full or accurate way. Note also that Sartre does not relate the issue of freedom to awareness of our future death as is done here.

of ways that we are freer than we think. First, acknowledging our future death may shock us strongly enough to help us overcome our habits or our proclivity to automatically act the way we always have. Second, the knowledge that we have only one chance to live, which it would be a crime not to make very good use of, and the resulting necessity to prioritize, may also press on us hard enough to push away some of our fears of other people's reactions, our worries that we might fail, or our habits, indecisiveness, and laziness. Third, the perspective of our whole life, which the deathbed question exposes, puts other people's possible disapproval in its place.

However, one should also note the disadvantages of thinking in terms of what, when we are about to die, we would be sorry or happy to have done and not done in our lives. For obvious reasons, it can arouse tension, fear, and uneasiness. Further, many are not, in fact, in a state in which they will likely die very soon.[5] Thus, entertaining the question may cause us to sense a false urgency in whatever we choose. And since many things seem trivial in comparison to death, entertaining the deathbed question may lead us to treat some things as less important than they really are. For example, the deathbed perspective may turn out not to be sufficiently sensitive to the meaning we can derive from the enjoyment of the small events of everyday life; there is a danger that in the face of death, only large, dramatic events will count, while all the rest, such as playing checkers with our child, cooking and eating nice meals with friends, and going to a show, will seem trivial. Unless we remind ourselves that in the face of death we may well be glad that we did not miss out on the small joys of life, the deathbed question might tempt us to devalue and therefore forsake those joys. It is important to remember that the small things are a very

---

5. Although some people, such as those in active war zones or in disaster- or hunger-stricken areas, are in fact in that position.

important component of a meaningful life; small things are what life is made of, and they can contribute a great deal to its meaning.

Adding to its drawbacks, the deathbed question may lead some to be insufficiently attentive to the need to engage also with things that, while not meaningful in themselves, are nevertheless necessary for achieving meaning. It might seem at first that on our deathbed we would regret the time we had spent, say, in training to acquire a new skill, or in working to provide for our family, since the training or work may not have been meaningful in itself but merely an instrument for something else that was meaningful. But deeper consideration suggests that even from the deathbed perspective, we may well be glad that we had resorted to these necessary means for meaningfulness (if, indeed, they were necessary). The deathbed question does not call on us to do only what is meaningful in itself at every moment, but rather whatever will increase the overall meaning in our lives. That may well include many activities that, when isolated from the context in which they are performed, do not seem meaningful.

Lastly, the deathbed question may stress our freedom too much while being insufficiently sensitive to the price we may have to pay for some choices. Asking ourselves what we would have wanted to do, if we were looking back on our life from its end, does free us from peer pressure to a certain extent, but it should also be remembered that some of the things that we value in life, and that need to be balanced against other factors, are our relationships with other people. Moreover, as will be argued in the next section, although most of us are much freer than we allow ourselves to see, we are not as free as it may at first appear. Hence, decisions made only from the deathbed perspective, if they are not combined with considerations brought forth by asking other questions and with looking at things also from other perspectives, may be problematic. This perspective, like all perspectives, calls our attention to some issues and conceals others. It would be wrong, then, to employ *only* this question when considering the meaning of life. One has to balance it with considerations arising from other questions.

Much of what has been said here about the first deathbed question is also true of the second one, which asks what we would choose to do if we had only a few more months, weeks, or days to live. That question, too, reminds us that life is not eternal and hence that we should make good use of it and see that we do not waste it. The imagined scarcity of life in this thought experiment forces us to distinguish between what is of higher value to us and what is of lower value, and thus to prioritize. The second deathbed question also reminds us that people sometimes do die early, in some cases with little or no prior notice, and thus miss out on doing what was of the most value to them. Asking ourselves this question may counter our inclination to endlessly delay important things, putting them off to some hazy future—sometimes called "soon" or "one day"—that may never arrive.

Again, however, it would be wrong to employ only this question when considering what is meaningful to us. Like any other single question, it too prompts us to think about some important and often neglected issues, but allows us to neglect others. If we relied on this question alone we would never plan for projects that require more than several months, and yet many projects of worth to us (such as finishing a course of study) take much longer. The perspective that this question offers also blocks our understanding of the importance of the many small details that make up life. We do not want to spend our whole lives doing only the things that we would do if we only had ten days, or six months, to live. For example, we might not go to any movies if we had only ten more days to live, since we might choose to spend those days doing only what is absolutely urgent and important. But we do not want to spend our lives always doing only what is absolutely urgent and important; we also want to go to the movies, try out new recipes, and spend time relaxing with friends. For most of our lives, for all we know, we have more than just a few more days or months to live. This question, then, is helpful, but again, only when used with caution, and alongside other important questions.

3

When identifying or deciding on the locations of meaningfulness in our lives, we need to acknowledge reality. Decisions about increasing the meaning of one's life should take into account temperament and inclination, natural gifts and abilities, as well as environment, resources, and circumstances. We all have our specific talents and strengths as well as limitations and weaknesses. A person who has no gift for music cannot find the meaning of his life in great musical performances. Some people may be interested in medicine but unable to study it because it is not taught where they live and they have no money or ability to move to a place where it is taught, or because they do not have the necessary intellectual capacity. Likewise, those who have no inclination to read, and cannot change this lack of inclination, should not try to find the meaning of their life in literature. On the other hand, those who are gifted in mathematics and are disposed toward it should take this into account, and those who have great ability in and inclination for love should consider finding, or creating, significant parts of the meaning of their life in that sphere. Just as we cannot choose to live in just any way we wish, we also cannot choose to give meaning to our lives in any way we wish. We are not God, and are unable to mold either the world or ourselves exactly as we would like, not only in the physical but also in the mental and emotional spheres. Although we oftentimes have more freedom than we realize, it is not unlimited, and we can often transcend what we are only to a certain degree, after investing a lot of work, and not in any way we please.[6]

For these reasons, we should opt not for the most meaningful life possible but for the most meaningful life possible *for us*. And when we look back at our lives thus far, we should ask ourselves not whether we have lived in the best possible way but whether we have lived in the best possible way given our abilities and limitations, including our fears, inhibitions, and insecurities, our capacity to endure pain, uncertainty, and loneliness, and our gifts or lack thereof. (True, some of these conditions can, under certain circumstances, be changed to some degree.) It is also important, of course, not to yield too quickly, and to investigate thoroughly whether we might after all be capable in the area that interests us, and whether obstacles may be surmountable. We should expect early failures and difficulties, and should not see them as proof that a certain direction is wrong for us. Moreover, sometimes the efforts themselves are worthwhile, even if they do not bear fruit.

Because of differences in temperament and inclination, abilities and circumstances, it is only to be expected that different people will identify and choose different things as meaningful. Just as different people require different medications on the basis of their specific conditions, strengths, or ailments, different people also have to

6. I disagree here with what, according to a common interpretation, is Sartre's view (see note 4 and, for a criticism of his views on our radical freedom, chapter 18 section 5), as well as with Frankl's claim that "Man . . . always decides what his existence will be, what he will become in the next moment . . . every human being has the freedom to change at any instant." Viktor Frankl, *Man's Search for Meaning* (New York: Washington Square Press, 1985), 154; see also 86–87.

choose for themselves what is most suitable for them according to their strengths, weaknesses, and the specific circumstances of their lives.[7] If our decisions are genuine, they may well differ from other people's genuine decisions. Hence, although we may well learn from other people's experiences when trying to increase meaning in life, we cannot just copy what others do. We have to decide for ourselves. This is also why it is usually not fruitful to ask the general question that people most commonly ask: "So what is the meaning of life?"

Some people take what has provided meaning in their lives and present it as necessary, sufficient, or both for humanity at large. This kind of free extrapolation or induction is problematic. I have found this tendency to be more frequent among those who follow religious or spiritual paths toward meaning. They sometimes treat spiritual or religious options different from theirs, or nonspiritual and nonreligious options, as inferior.[8] Love, moral activity, learning, art, and other engagements seem to them barren and insufficient. The urge to find meaning for everyone only in what they themselves find meaningful is very strong for some people, but not very helpful.

7. Frankl (*Man's Search for Meaning*, 130–131) suggests that it is wrong to ask the question "What is the meaning of life?" just as it is wrong to ask what the best move in chess is. Different contexts of the game call for different "best moves," and it is wrong to consider one of them as the best move in general.
8. Cf. Leo Tolstoy, *Confession*, trans. David Patterson (New York: Norton, 1983), 85.

Chapter 16

Identifying II

1

Once we have considered the questions that can help identify what would add meaning to our lives, we are likely to find that, because our time and capacities are limited, we cannot engage with everything that we find meaningful. For example, there are many people with whom we could form bonds of love or friendship. But we befriend or love only some of them, making them especially dear to us. We cannot love or befriend everyone in a sufficiently deep way. Similarly, we may value many types of art, but find that we can create better art, or reach a deeper degree of understanding, in only some of them. We may find many fields of learning to be very interesting, but we cannot learn about all of them deeply. What will be meaningful to us is a subset of what could be meaningful to us. This choice to focus on some pursuits among others involves deepening our engagement and committing ourselves to them; we personalize our relation to those issues of value, making them especially dear and important to us.

2

Although different people will find different pursuits meaningful, I should note two categories of activity that turn out to impart worth to the lives of many. The first of these is helping others.[1] This is not true for everyone, but my experience is that for many people, engaging in helping others makes a significant difference for the better in their own lives. Many of us value helping others more than we recognize. Not all types of helping activities suit all potential helpers, and trial and error are frequently needed to find the type of help that suits the helper best. Moreover, for those who are not used to it, some guidance, effort, and practice are necessary, especially in the beginning. But many people who try helping others say that, once they have experienced the effects of doing so, they are surprised that they did not recognize sooner what it would be like. Many people who feel that life is meaningless can make it significantly more meaningful by helping others or, more generally, improving the world.

The other activity that can impart a great deal of worth to the lives of many is avoiding or decreasing their own suffering and increasing their own pleasure.[2] Enjoyment is an important element of worth in our lives, and for most people and in most cases, suffering beyond a relatively low degree powerfully detracts from worth. Those who succeed in identifying what makes them discontented and what makes them contented, and act on those findings, are

1. An interesting and powerful exploration of this option is found in Peter Singer, *How Are We to Live?* (Oxford: Oxford University Press, 1997).
2. I am in disagreement here with Robert E. Adams, "Comment," in Susan Wolf, *Meaning in Life and Why It Matters*, with commentary by John Koethe, Robert M. Adams, Nomy Arpaly, and Jonathan Haidt (Princeton, NJ: Princeton University Press, 2010), 78–79: "It seems very doubtful that feelings, good or bad, without intentional content enter into the meaning of meaninglessness of one's life."

likely to feel significantly more meaning in their lives.[3] Many people do not work hard enough to prevent themselves from suffering or to enjoy pleasures. This includes simple pleasures, among them important bodily pleasures such as those received from food, sex, and good sleep. Other types of enjoyment have to do with watching films, listening to music of various kinds, spending time in the company of people whom we like, and playing games or sports, as well as aesthetic enjoyment. Admittedly, as pointed out in chapter 12, some people can lead a meaningful life even if they do not experience much fun or happiness. This is true, for example, of some ascetics, who experience mostly suffering rather than fun but still feel a high degree of meaningfulness, or of some of the concentration camp inmates, discussed by Frankl, who managed to retain meaningfulness while suffering. But many others cannot. Although it is usually insufficient by itself and should not come at the expense of all other worthy dimensions of life, most people do need at least some pleasure in their lives. It does not always have to be a radical degree of fun, but for most it should not drop below a certain threshold for any lengthy period of time.

One can have a life in which there is too much fun and therefore not enough meaning, but also a life in which there is too little fun and therefore not enough meaning. The model of the playboy—who goes through every possible pleasure but nevertheless, or even because of this overindulgence, feels empty or meaningless—does sometimes hold. Some people value enjoyment too much (or are just attached to it without even valuing it) and fail to pursue what they know will make life meaningful because continuing what they have been doing is more comfortable and fun. But the other extreme

3. In fact, these two processes—decreasing suffering and increasing pleasure—are distinct, but I will treat them in this context as one.

is problematic as well. There is a danger that the suggestions in the previous chapter could lead people to try ever harder to develop only those aspects of meaningfulness that they do not enjoy at the expense of enjoyable activities that do not seem to them respectable enough, thus worsening their condition by the very means they take to improve it. Clearly, we should not pursue only what is fun in life without giving any consideration to other issues of worth. But for most people, it is also very important to regularly experience simple, lighthearted fun.

3

Most people need to give thought periodically, every several years (and in some cases, months), to identifying what it is that would maintain or increase meaning in their lives. There are various reasons for this. First, the issues are complicated: they include many aspects and levels, are not clear-cut, and sorting them out requires introspection and sensitivity to oneself. Second, as is also true for love, religion, artistic endeavors, and work, sometimes people discover that even with careful thought and consideration, they have chosen a course of action that proves unsatisfactory; increasing meaning in one's life, as in those other domains, involves trial and error. When a certain direction does not prove sufficiently meaningful, people should acknowledge their mistake and consider their options anew; sometimes a partially or even wholly new direction has to be chosen. Deciding to devote time periodically to thinking about what it is that would maintain or increase meaning in one's life may alert one to such cases.

Third, people sometimes find that what they had expected to be meaningful is not so because they themselves have changed.

Changes occur not only in our teens or twenties, but also in our sixties and nineties. Because of such changes, even if we made no mistakes in our initial choices, it is helpful to think anew, periodically, about maintaining or increasing our life's meaning. Relatedly—this is distinct from changes in personality, and just as important—people sometimes get to know or understand themselves better over time. This too is a reason for reevaluating what makes life meaningful.

Finally, in some cases the changes are not in us but in the circumstances in which we live; when these change, what hitherto gave meaning to our lives may also change. In extreme cases, what had given meaning to our lives may be destroyed. Some people's dear ones suffer accidents, maladies, deaths, or changes of heart. Sometimes we are fired, or we cannot find a livelihood. Some workplaces close, economic and political systems collapse, and organizations or social movements become corrupt and harmful. Natural, political, economic, and military catastrophes occur. It is important to fight those changes if one can, and if possible to overcome them. But if we do not overcome them, we should reconsider what it is that will now maintain or increase the meaning of our lives.

The last point (mentioned also in chapter 2) needs some expansion. Although it is often hard to find new sources of meaning, it is frequently possible to do so. Most of us are quite flexible when it comes to meaning, and when we fail to achieve something of value, or it is destroyed, or it turns out not to be as meaningful as we had expected, we can often compensate or regenerate meaning by enhancing some other, already existing aspects of value or finding completely new ones. For example, if our love life is not working out well we can try to compensate for that, to an extent, by increasing the value of our volunteer work or our career. If our career is not going well, we can compensate for that with deep aesthetic experiences, volunteer work, or personal relationships. Since some of what we value in life is almost certain not to realize itself, to be destroyed over time, or otherwise change, it is very important to do this work of compensation or regeneration although, in some cases, it requires a great effort.[4] The most difficult period of time is that during which the value we used to count on is now absent from our lives and we have not yet found or created a new value to take its place. But it is frequently the case that, as time goes on, we can heal the lack of meaning in our lives.[5]

To find or generate new meaning, we have to accept that our familiar sources or ways of doing so are now insufficiently (or not at all) helpful, and that we have to engage in new types of work. Paradoxically, in some cases new and challenging situations lead people to a higher degree of meaning than they previously had, since the new conditions sometimes block out distractions, make peer pressure irrelevant, force people to focus, develop their courage, and invite them to rise to challenges.

4

The discussion above has suggested, among other claims, that maintaining or increasing meaning frequently requires us to dedicate a lot of thought, on repeated occasions, to what makes our life meaningful; that our efforts to increase meaning in our lives will not

---

4. Some people refuse to do so. Sometimes they lack the energy that such a feat requires. But in other cases they seem to find it romantic to hold on to the loss more than necessary, or they refuse to find or create something new in order not to lose a habit, a sense of identity, or other people's sympathy.

5. Most people, however, should give themselves sufficient time to mourn a loss before engaging in the effort of finding or creating a new source of meaning. And they should expect that, although life can become very meaningful again, some of the pain of their loss will always persist.

always be successful; that we and our circumstances may change; and that trial and error are sometimes necessary. But these conclusions also suggest that we should be cautious with a romantic model for increasing meaning or for moving from a meaningless to a meaningful life. Call it "the Strickland model," taking its name from the character Charles Strickland in Somerset Maugham's *The Moon and Sixpence*.[6] The book, which is loosely based on some of the details of the life of the painter Paul Gauguin, describes how Strickland, a London stockbroker, one day leaves his work and family in order to become a painter in Paris. He severs all ties with his family and his previous environment. Then, after spending some time in Paris, he moves to Tahiti, where he continues to paint until he dies. His pictures are posthumously recognized as masterpieces.[7]

The Strickland model, to a certain extent the secular analogue of a complete mystical or religious conversion that leads one to be "born again" and "see the light," is characterized by a radical break with the past. When people follow this model, they aim to increase meaning not by making local improvements or by mending what already exists but, rather, by undergoing a complete personal revolution: the source of meaning they focus on is new and very different from whatever they have been doing up to that point. The change is not only radical, involving a move to a wholly new sphere of meaning and a complete rejection of the past, but also abrupt. It is also frequently irreversible. The search for meaning in this model often focuses on only one issue and is strongly committed to nothing less than excellence. However, the various specific characteristics of this model do not entail each other. We

6. W. Somerset Maugham, *The Moon and Sixpence* (Harmondsworth: Penguin, 1944).

7. Maugham adds more ingredients to the story, such as the immoral aspects of Strickland's new behavior. For the purpose of the present discussion, however, I will be ignoring these and other elements of the story.

could, for example, make a radical change that is reversible, is not abrupt, is not focused on only one issue, or is not committed to excellence. Life changes could follow the Strickland model to varying degrees. Here, however, I will mostly discuss the model in its complete form.

There are some cases in which it is indeed necessary to opt for the Strickland model. Sometimes one's social, ideological, or religious environment is so intolerant and unforgiving that any change must be irreversible. For the same reasons, we are sometimes unable to try out various degrees of a new option before we adopt it because any testing of the new option would lead our social environment to ostracize us. And in some cases, multiple aspects of our previous life strongly cohere with and even lead to each other, so that in order to change one problematic aspect of our life we also have to make changes in all or most of the others. For example, a person who grows up in a narrow-minded and oppressive society but wants to test some other options may need to leave that society and her former way of life completely and irreversibly. Likewise, in some cases, in order to cease doing drugs one must also stop seeing one's friends, move to another city, change one's occupation, and adopt new habits and a new way of life. Some aspects of life do come in packages and do need to be replaced together. Furthermore, changes sometimes need to be sharp, complete, and irreversible because the familiar has an enormous power on us: the habitual and known draws us very strongly, sometimes in unnoticed ways, to continue what we have been doing. There are also cases in which all or most of what we have been doing is quite meaningless, and we therefore wish to increase meaning in many aspects at the same time; the change, in such cases, must be considerable and quite encompassing. When these and similar conditions hold, it may indeed be necessary to follow the Strickland model.

But when conditions such as those above do not hold, the Strickland model should be considered with caution. It can carry some significant disadvantages. When the model is typified by focusing on only one sphere or project of meaning, or by committing oneself to nothing less than perfect meaning, the problems with these behaviors (mentioned in chapters 2 and 3) apply. Because it focuses on radical changes, the model is highly demanding, and thus may cause some people to give up trying to change at all, dissuading them from making the small or gradual changes they could have opted for with much gain. Because of the model's commitment to wholesale changes, it also carries a higher probability of failure. Since it is committed to a radical break with the past, the model is completely blind to the worth of what we already have. The abruptness endorsed by the model does not allow us to experiment by trial and error with the new situation (for example, by painting four hours a week in our hometown), to see whether the life of, say, a painter in Paris is in fact that much more valuable for us. When the change is irreversible, it closes many options.

Lastly, the Strickland model is frequently based on an incorrect view of what needs to be changed. We often feel the urge to employ this model when we sense a deficiency in a certain aspect of meaning in our lives. But when sensing a deficiency, we are frequently not good judges of whether we need only that deficient element or how much of it we need. For example, when we are very hungry, we frequently feel that the only thing in the world we want is to eat. Our hunger conceals from us all other problems, deficiencies, and cravings, and we sometimes feel that if only we could satisfy our hunger, we would be completely happy. When we are very hungry we also think, wrongly, that we want to eat huge quantities of food: that we will never want to stop eating. The same is often true for other deficiencies, including deficiencies in aspects of meaning: sensing a lack of religiousness, for example, may lead us to feel that religious activity will solve all our problems; that we would always want to engage only with it; and that the more of it the better, forever. Likewise, sensing a lack of artistic activity in our lives may lead us to feel that artistic creation will solve all our problems; that we would always want to engage only with it; and that the more of it the better. In this state of deficiency, or craving, it is difficult for us to see that in the future we may want the element now painfully absent from our lives only to a certain degree beyond which it would seem to us exaggerated and overbearing, and that we will also need some other things, including those that we already have now but may destroy or forsake if we follow the Strickland model.

Most of us need many different elements of meaning in our lives. Some of these elements exclude others when they appear in their most extreme or radical degree but can coexist with other elements when they appear in moderate degree. We need some degree of altruism and some of egoism, some degree of individualism and some of sociability, some degree of physicality and some of spirituality. Many people who feel that their lives are meaningless have a degree of meaning in their lives that is just below a threshold of sufficient meaning; all they need is to increase that meaning a little bit so that it can pass that threshold. And to make that happen, what they often need is merely to correct the imbalance between the different aspects of meaning in their lives. Their lives are not meaningful enough not because everything they do is wrong but because they do too much of some things or not enough of others. To fix the problem, they have to balance the elements better; they need to diminish some elements or increase others rather than obliterate completely what there is and create something wholly new. In many cases, even fine tuning and a small change can make an important difference, just as a small change in one of the spices in a stew can make it tasty. It may be, for example, that the only thing some people need in order to make their lives meaningful is to help others, or to help others more than previously; or to learn more about art; or to enjoy natural beauty. They do not need to opt for a sharp break with everything. Similarly, in some cases, a meaningless life results from failing to avoid a few things that insert meaninglessness into one's life. In such cases, too, what is needed is only to obliterate or even just to diminish the intensity of one or a few things; what makes life meaningless need not be something wrong in all the aspects of that life, and not all of them might need to change. The Strickland model, however, calls for a radical and complete change that focuses on one element. Thus, the model may just move us from an old imbalanced position to a new, as yet unfamiliar but also imbalanced position, disconnecting us from sources of meaning that have fed us up to now. It may lead to diminishing rather than to increasing the meaning in one's life, exacerbating the problem it aims to solve.

There are times when we must resort to the Strickland model. But notwithstanding its popularity, for most people it is not the right model for increasing meaning in life. It is important to remember the availability of less radical options as well, and to see which is the most suitable. Even those who need to act in accordance with the model would do well to distinguish between those aspects of it that are indeed required and those that are not. For example, even if we have to make a complete change, we may not need to go about it abruptly; or if the change needs to be both complete and abrupt, it may not need to be irreversible, and so on. Those who need to operate by the model would also do well to distinguish among several degrees of irreversibility, abruptness, and so on, and opt, if at all possible, for the lower ones. For example, it may not be necessary to cut off all contact with one's previous environment or end all relationships: it may be sufficient to separate oneself from only some of them, or perhaps reduce the intensity of the relationships rather than end them completely. Likewise, it may be possible to make changes somewhat more gradually than seems necessary at first.

A life that does not follow the Strickland model makes for a less interesting story; it is less focused, intense, and dramatic than a life in which we overthrow everything in pursuit of what might matter more. But the material from which good stories are made is often not the material from which good or meaningful lives are made. In many cases, quite the contrary.

5

Of course, we should act on our choices. If we see that, in order to make our lives more meaningful, we need to change our lives in various ways, then that is what we should do. Considerations such as those explored thus far in this chapter ought not remain on the theoretical level, but be seen as guidelines for improving the meaning of life. Some people will find that they need to make very few changes or none; but those who need alter various aspects of their lives should do so.

Chapter 17

Recognizing

1

Some people who have overcome their perfectionism, combated successfully arguments for the impossibility of leading a meaningful life, identified what they take to be meaningful, and changed their lives accordingly (when one or all of these were necessary), still find their lives insufficiently meaningful because they do not *feel* the value in their lives. They accept that some things are highly valuable, but merely in a theoretical or academic way, which leaves them feeling empty. They only acknowledge value in an impersonal and detached manner, not in an engaged, personal one, similarly to the way one accepts that something is interesting without feeling any interest in it, that something is funny without being in any way amused, or that something is beautiful without enjoying its beauty. In some cases, people's insensitivity to value is so strong that they do not feel the value at all; in other cases, they feel it, but numbly, as through a transparent coating. People in this condition sometimes say that they accept that various things in their lives are highly valuable, or even meaningful, but still do not see "the point of it all" or the point in living. Yeats describes this condition in his poem "What Then?"

His chosen comrades thought at school
He must grow a famous man;
He thought the same and lived by rule,
All his twenties crammed with toil;
"What then?" sang Plato's ghost."What then?"

Everything he wrote was read,
After certain years he won
Sufficient money for his need,
Friends that have been friends indeed;
"What then?" sang Plato's ghost."What then?"

All his happier dreams came true—
A small old house, wife, daughter, son,
Grounds where plum and cabbage grew,
Poets and Wits about him drew;
"What then?" sang Plato's ghost. "What then?"

"The work is done," grown old he thought,
"According to my boyish plan;
Let the fools rage, I swerved in naught,
Something to perfection brought";
But louder sang that ghost, "What then?"[1]

Overcoming this numbness to value will be called here *recognizing*. Some of the discussions in the previous chapters can serve as good starting points for discussing it. Chapter 12, for example, dealt with Schopenhauer's asymmetry arguments. According to Schopenhauer, we are more sensitive to what is unpleasant than to what is pleasant.

---

1. *The Collected Poems of W. B. Yeats* (New York: Macmillan, 1951), 299–300.

We sense fear, but not a feeling of security; we remember bad events better than we remember good events; we have weak positive feelings when unpleasant events end but strong negative feelings when good events end; and so on. As we saw, Schopenhauer's claims are in fact not true for many people. But I also argued that it is frequently possible for people to change the degree to which they sense or enjoy the good aspects of the world. Sensing the worthy aspects of the world more acutely is recognizing.

Another starting point could be the discussion of human goodness in chapters 13 and 14. Those chapters argued that many find it difficult to acknowledge fully the positive aspects of the world and themselves, and accept that they are, all in all, good people. Unlearning the habit of only seeing the negative, and forming the habit of acknowledging the good both inside and outside us, is also a way of recognizing.

A third starting point could be the discussion of the paradox of the end (chapter 11). Those who suffer from the paradox of the end are those who cannot recognize the value of what they have achieved and hence have to achieve again and again. And a fourth possible starting point could be the discussions of perfectionism in chapters 3 and 4. Perfectionists cannot see the value that inheres in what is not excellent or hard to achieve. Some of the literary and artistic works mentioned in chapter 4 could be seen as examples of recognizing what, to many, is regularly invisible. Nick Adams's fishing in "Big Two-Hearted River" and Siddhartha's work and life as a humble ferryman in the last chapters of the eponymous book are instances of the recognition of the value that can be found in these activities. Nick and Siddhartha recognize value without any trumpets and drums, since recognizing is, indeed, often not a flashy process but involves developing a certain sensitivity to the valuable, beautiful parts in oneself and others.

Recognizing not only allows us to sense meaning that we had not perceived earlier but also increases meaning; the fact that one senses meaning in one's life is in itself a good and valuable thing that increases meaning in life. Furthermore, by noticing meaning we had earlier thought to be absent, recognizing diminishes the desolation we might otherwise have experienced. But again, the fact that one is not desolate is in itself a good and valuable thing that increases meaning in life.[2]

2

But why do we fail to recognize? We have already considered theories such as Schopenhauer's about the painfulness of existence, the view that people are completely evil, our overcritical or cynical attitudes that hold us back from valuing what is valuable, the dynamics that lead us to experience the paradox of the end, and the perfectionist ideology that keeps us from seeing the worth of anything that is less than perfect. Some people reject these views and attitudes on the theoretical level but still, sometimes unawares, continue to endorse them emotionally. For example, some, notwithstanding their efforts to get rid of their perfectionism, and sometimes without realizing it, are emotionally perfectionist about the meaning of life.[3] Likewise, some reject various presuppositions about the meaning of life and arguments for the meaningless of life only on the intellectual level. But there are also other factors that diminish our sensitivity to value.

2. See Robert Audi, "Intrinsic Value and Meaningful Life," *Philosophical Papers* 34, no. 3 (2005): 344.

3. Occasionally a vicious circle emerges: people's explicit or latent perfectionism prevents them from sensing the value in what is valuable, and this insensitivity to value, in turn, leads them to suppose that only extremely high or perfect value can be sensed.

In some cases, powerful experiences or emotions lead us to focus so strongly on one aspect of life that we stop noticing others. For example, intense love, success, anger, sadness, or pain can make us inattentive to much of the rest of what is valuable to us. Pain is particularly powerful in this respect. Some of the characteristics of the experience of severe pain are similar to those of a mystical experience: when a burn or a wound hurts very much, often it is as though there is neither reason nor language, neither past nor future, neither I nor the world. There is only pain.[4] In some cases, pain hinders recognizing even when it is numbed; people who have experienced pain sometimes develop numbness so as not to feel the pain, but this numbness can be nonselective, so that they find themselves insensitive to all things. Likewise, since valuing increases the risk of disappointment, some people who have been bitterly disappointed in the past adopt, as a precautionary measure, an attitude that makes it difficult for them to value anything.

There are also cases in which people who habitually consider everything in a rational manner become so accustomed to the detached and cautious disposition typical of some rational attitudes

---

4. This is true not only for physical but also for emotional and mental pain. See Haim Omer and Avshalom Elitzur, "What Would You Say to the Person on the Roof? A Suicide Prevention Text," *Suicide and Life-Threatening Behavior* 31 (2001): 130. As Omer and Elitzur point out, it is for this reason very difficult for people who are in pain and considering suicide to see things in context and proportion. Since there is only pain, it is difficult to remember that it is very plausible that in two hours, two weeks, or two months it will not hurt as much. One is just filled with pain, as if there is nothing else. It is hard to remember in this situation that there are and will be worthwhile aspects of life that do not have to do with the present pain.

People who consider suicide sometimes also say that they want to die. But that is often incorrect. They do not want to die; they just want that pain (which arrests all their attention) to stop. Not knowing how to stop it except by obliterating the life that allows the pain to exist, they undercut both, as if accepting a bad package deal, without noting that there are often ways of obliterating only the pain (or of diminishing it to a bearable degree, or of waiting for it to pass) without also destroying life: that is, there are ways that could allow people to continue to live, and allow them, moreover, to find, later on, both meaning and joy.

that they find it difficult to value things in a sufficiently personal or unreserved way. And as already mentioned in chapter 11, another important source of insensitivity to value is habit and familiarity. We often overlook the worth of what is a regular part of our lives, such as the knowledge we have acquired, our love, or our persistent, everyday courage, simply because we are used to them. It is principally because of habituated familiarity that the beauty of the picture on the wall of our room disappears (often along with the picture itself), and that many people who live in very beautiful areas of the world do not enjoy or even see that beauty after some time.[5]

Value that has partly or completely disappeared, however, can reappear. Sensitivity to value is also a matter of decision. There are various ways of intentionally resensitizing ourselves to value. We can just try to be more aware of this blindness of ours. That in itself already helps. We can also address the theoretical sources of our numbness to value, such as perfectionism or the view that we or the world are bad through and through. Another way of resensitizing ourselves to value is to make small changes in what has become habitual and familiar.[6] It is also possible to try to see what is around us as if it were new and fresh, thus defamiliarizing ourselves with it.

---

5. There are probably biological sources for this tendency: it is instrumental for animals' survival to be highly alert to changes in their surroundings, since such changes frequently indicate the arrival of a predator or of prey (or of other dangers or opportunities) in their environment. Like some other biological tendencies (e.g., our tendency to behave as a herd, to succumb to those more powerful than us, or to solve conflicts by aggression rather than by discussion), this one, too, has also many disadvantages for those who want to have a better and more meaningful human life. Here, as in many other cases, the biological urge has to be used and even developed in some circumstances and restrained or at least managed in other circumstances.

6. It is odd to see how people sometimes search for a major change although what they already have is of high value, occasionally even of much higher value than that of the new alternative. Often they do so, unawares, as a recognizing technique, hoping to sense value again.

At the beginning, it may even help to pretend to ourselves that what we are looking at is indeed new.

We can also make ourselves attentive to value time and again. Just as we can decide to be attentive within the next two hours to the color red, to birds, to our studies, our work, or the needs of a child, so too can we decide to be attentive to goodness, beauty, or worth in general in ourselves and in the world. A close yet distinct way is to take up consciously an attitude of appreciation and valuing. One, then, does not only try to be more open to the value or allow oneself to be more impressed by it (as in many of the previous strategies), but also to adopt an attitude of valuing toward what one knows to be valuable. To do so, one may try to engage oneself in a more involved and personal way with the valuable aspects hitherto noticed only in a theoretical and detached way, or even to try to stimulate in oneself, artificially at first, a valuing attitude toward the issue at hand. The latter attitude should be adopted with caution as there is, of course, a danger of falling into artificial valuing, which should be discontinued. But in many cases the initially artificial attitude becomes after some time genuine and develops "a life of its own."

Recognizing worth is not very different from recognizing beauty. Just as though we were using the volume knob on a radio or an old-fashioned television set, we can increase and decrease our awareness of the beauty of beautiful objects or scenes that seem plain to us. We can look at a view and allow ourselves to feel its beauty more, or less. The beauty we sense in some photographed objects seen in films or pictures is frequently nothing more than that: a long, concentrated look that opens up for us something that we usually pass by. That concentrated look allows us to see beauty in a photograph because we expect it there and are ready for it. But if we are ready to do so, we can see the beauty in the real world as well. Much of what has been said here about sensitization to beauty is also true of sensitization to value in other spheres, as well as value in general.

Many people find doing all these things to be counterintuitive at first, but achievable. If we engage with these methods frequently and persistently enough, they become habits and second nature; we can train ourselves, through effort and practice, to follow them. Most can, by means of persistent awareness, immensely diminish their blindness to value.

3

Value that has become invisible to us can also reappear when it is endangered, when it either worsens or improves, or after it has been destroyed. (In the case of its destruction what we notice is its past existence and its absence: that is, that it was valuable and that we do not have it any more.) For example, people are more aware of their health when they are anxiously waiting for lab results, when they find it either harder or easier than before to climb the stairs, or after they or people they know have become paralyzed. This is a partial explanation for the meaning many people find in performing philanthropic or altruistic work. In addition to their knowledge that it is a worthy and noble activity, helping those who are in need detrivializes, for the helpers, the value of what they already have.

This may also partly explain some of our attraction to tragedies in literature, onstage, or film, although they depict loss, destruction, and other terrible and sometimes monstrous events. There are various explanations for this attraction, including Aristotle's classic discussion of catharsis, the emotional purification or discharge of fear and pity that happens when witnessing the terrible events that appear on stage.[7] But I suggest that another explanation may be that the loss and destruction we see onstage give us a better appreciation for what is normally around us. This may also explain to some extent the attraction some people have to other depictions of unpleasant and difficult events in literature and film, and the attraction to sad or negative news in written and broadcast media. It may be, then, that the media's focus on bad news has conflicting effects on us. It may lead us to form a negative view of the world, which diminishes our recognition of the value in it (discussed in chapter 13), but it may at the same time also sensitize us to the value of what we have by reminding us that it cannot be taken for granted.

A similar explanation may also partially account for the attraction some people feel to doing dangerous, difficult, and sometimes harmful things to themselves or to others. Doing dangerous and harmful things may be a way of making themselves feel again the things to which they have become numb, sensitize themselves to their value, and thus make the meaning of life reappear. It allows people to see that what they have cannot be taken for granted; it could be much worse, or completely lost. But danger and harm (much like the focus on bad news in the media) can also have conflicting effects on the meaning of life. Danger and harm can also lead to trauma, pain, incapacitation, or complete loss. We may well not want to put in harm's way our life, love, health, or anything else that is valuable to us.[8]

---

7. *Poetics* VI, 1149b28.

8. I have not found reliable data on whether, on average, people whose lives are financially secure find life to be less meaningful than do people whose lives are financially hazardous. But if this is the case, then the absence of danger in the life of the former may help to explain this. Since what they have is not endangered, its value becomes invisible to them. Other possible explanations of this fact (if indeed it is a fact) may be that among those who achieve financial security there is a higher percentage of perfectionists (chapter 3) and of people who experience the paradox of the end because of workaholism, radical competitiveness, and an excessive tendency to delay gratification (chapter 11). People

This may also partly explain the Stoic recommendation that we keep in mind that everything that is around us may be destroyed. Marcus Aurelius, for example, mentions approvingly Epictetus's suggestion: "When you kiss your child you should say silently to yourself, 'Tomorrow, perhaps, you will meet your death.'"[9] This suggestion, then, is the very opposite of what is called today positive thinking. Thoughts about what life would be like if we lost what we now have may help us to appreciate it more while we do have it, again detrivializing it and clarifying to us that it should not be taken for granted. Here, too, however, the effects can contrast with one another. Such thoughts, if not held in the right way and to the right degree, may also have negative results, as they can lead some people to experience tension, fear, and even anxiety and despair.

4

One can recognize the value of not only what happens in the present, but also of what happened in the past, that is, sensitize oneself to the value that continues to inhere in achievements, good deeds, times of personal closeness, and other events that occurred in earlier

who grew up in financially secure and protected conditions may also feel more shock and incomprehension when, notwithstanding planning, the arbitrary and contingent aspects of the world strike them (chapter 1 section 5). Further, people from less shielded and less financially secure backgrounds, having frequently grown up in rougher, more arbitrary and contingent circumstances, may have not developed expectations that, at a later age, are shattered.

If it is true that in the modern era people sense life as meaningless more than people in earlier eras did (again, I have found no reliable data on this), the considerations above can help explain that too.

9. Marcus Aurelius, *Meditations* XI 30, trans. Robin Hard (Hertfordshire: Wordsworth, 1997), 111. See also X 34, p. 101.

periods of one's life.[10] Our life as a whole is meaningful, or mean-ingless, also because of what happened in the past. Just as a terrible deed of ours does not cease to affect negatively the overall value of our lives just because it happened in the past, so does a good deed continue to affect the overall value of our lives positively even if it happened in the past. This is also true in cases in which what has been meaningful is now destroyed; we can continue to remember it, be affected by it, and be grateful for the value it has bestowed on our life at large. The current nonexistence of what has been destroyed is sad, even tragic, but need not undermine our relationship to it now.

A close relative of mine who lost her thirty-six-year-old son said at the grave that she was very sad, but also very grateful for having had the relationship with her son for thirty-six years. The common saying that someone's death need not end our relationship with that person is correct. The same is true for other things that have been destroyed. For example, the corruption of an organization or a movement for which one has sacrificed a great deal is very sad. That is not how we would have wanted things to turn out. But we may be grateful for the many years when things were good. There is a great deal of worth in those years as well. They were not just instruments for a future that did not happen; they had a worth of their own. We should recognize what has now been destroyed, hold it in our hearts, and cherish it, finding in it the appropriate happiness or well-deserved pride.[11]

10. I have heard it said that we should live, or see ourselves as living, only in the present, since the past does not exist anymore, and the future does not exist yet. However, following Heideggerian intuitions, I believe that this is incorrect. Our present is made also of our past achievements, failures, memories, things that we learned, experiences, regrets, pride in what we have done, etc., on the one hand, and of our hopes, fears, plans for the future, etc. on the other hand. Moreover, our plans affect our memories, to an extent, and our memories affect our plans. Our future and past, then, are intertwined and very much part of the present.

11. The suggestions made here as regards recognizing the value of what has been destroyed complement the suggestions made in the previous chapter for creating new sources of meaning after what has been meaningful has ceased to exist.

5

I have, up to this point, focused more on cases in which people theoretically acknowledge, but do not sense, various issues in their lives as valuable, and have suggested that recognizing can help overcome this difficulty. However, improving one's capacity and tendency to recognize also allows one to become sensitive to the great value in many of the common things in life, a value that is often not acknowledged even theoretically. Many of us, much of the time, are partly or wholly numb to the value in being alive; in being conscious; in our ability to breathe, sense, know, and care; in our continuous courage and perseverance in face of disappointment, hardship, and pain; or in the raindrops on the leaves near the window or the bird that hovers near the tree.[12] We regularly ignore much of this worth, as if it hardly existed at all. If asked about it, many of us would, after some bewildered hesitation, admit that many of the things that we have ceased to see are indeed worthy, even extremely worthy. But we would feel that the question and the reply were odd, as though they involved a silly mistake whose nature has not yet been made clear. However, I do not see this as a mistake. The mistake, I suggest, is rather in failing to see the worth that persists in so many ordinary things, and thereby ignoring an important part of reality. Perhaps what seems odd about noting such worth has to do with the feeling that it is just stating the obvious, as if someone were one day to point at the table that had long stood in the room and exclaim that there is a table in the room. But the obvious is frequently not

---

12. Some items in this list, such as our ability to breathe or to sense, may be claimed to be only of instrumental value, that is, to lack any value in themselves and to be valuable only because they are a means to achieving something else of value. I need not enter into this issue here because I take both numbness to instrumental value and numbness to intrinsic value to be unfortunate.

obvious at all. Instead, it has often completely disappeared from our view. The table is frequently not present; it is physically there, but otherwise gone.

The worth we regularly fail to notice is considerable. Some indication of that can be found in our readiness to make sacrifices for formerly invisible things the moment they are endangered. We are generally just as ready to make sacrifices in order not to lose our health, our love, our life, or the knowledge that we have acquired as we are to make sacrifices for what we do not yet have and wish to achieve. Another indication of the worth of what has become invisible to us is that we are frequently very, very sorry when it is destroyed. We are often as sorry to lose things that we have had and that have been invisible to us for a long time as we are over failing to achieve what we do not yet have; sometimes we are even sorrier about the losing.

This suggests that most people already have a great deal that is valuable, or meaningful, in their lives. Nevertheless, many people do not appreciate it. Although most people reply in the affirmative when asked whether they value the ability to touch a leaf, walk, spend time with friends and family, or sleep without pain, their general attitude suggests that many of them hardly perceive the worth of those aspects of life, if at all. Many are like a person who has accounts in several banks. He is now in dire need, but because he has forgotten that he has other bank accounts in which there are plenty of funds, he thinks that he is very poor. Or they are like a person who has fallen into dismal poverty and does not realize that the old, beautiful vase in the attic is actually very valuable. Many walk the paths of life as if blind to much of what is meaningful; they misperceive, or ignore, important aspects of reality.

I suggested in section 2 of this chapter that sensitizing ourselves to worth is not very different from sensitizing ourselves to beauty.

But if we sensitize ourselves enough to beauty, we can see how it inheres not only in magnificent pictures or natural sceneries. If we focus and open up enough, we can see and enjoy the great beauty of even simple things, such as the somewhat concave lines of the chair, the folds on the bedspread, the way the leaf on the plant near the window quivers and then stops, just standing out from the stem without movement.[13] If we lift the veil of numbness that usually covers us and look for a few seconds at the curves of the kettle, the roundness of the tea glass, the cylinder of tea standing inside it, or the patterns of lines in the wooden tabletop, we can see a significant degree of beauty there, as we could almost anywhere. Take the kettle on the table. We would not usually call it beautiful, since its level of beauty is not extremely high and, thus, the beauty is not salient. But even if the kettle is not extremely beautiful, it does have *some* degree of beauty. Try to notice that beauty, in whatever degree it is there, for a second or two. Then try to do so, one by one, with some other objects around you. Or try to imagine the common objects on the table, such as the tissues, the lamp, or the keys, as if they are within a frame.

Part of the reason that we sense aesthetic pleasure in museums is that we adopt an aesthetic attitude when we enter them. We decide that now, for a certain period of time, we will focus on and respond to the beauty of things. Thanks to this attitude, we sometimes find ourselves, when in museums, taking aesthetic pleasure even in very common objects that we normally would not enjoy outside the museum.[14] But we do not need to enter a museum in order to adopt

13. See W. H. Davies's poem "Leisure," in *The Oxford Book of Modern Verse, 1892–1935*, ed. W. B. Yeats (New York: Oxford University Press, 1937), 131. The poem begins with "What is this life if, full of care / We have no time to stand and stare."

14. In some cases we may even find ourselves taking aesthetic pleasure in objects that the artists who positioned them in the museum only intended to use as statements about the nature of art, without intending for us to take in them any aesthetic pleasure.

this attitude and sense aesthetic pleasure. We can take that museum attitude out into the world with us; we can turn the world into our museum, modifying our way of perceiving very simple and common artifacts around us. What has been said here about sensitization to beauty or aesthetic worth is also true of sensitization to value in other spheres, such as other people's and our own goodness, everyday courage and persistence, or health. We can also notice the worth in the fact that the human body is so complex and delicate or that any given individual organ, such as the eye or the hand, is such a complex, delicate system and yet it usually works well.

In chapter 4 I mentioned the requirement in some religions to express thanks for, and notice, the merit in worthy but mundane things like having food on the table or waking up alive. A robust example of this propensity is found in the book *The Practice of the Presence of God*, a collection of sayings by Brother Lawrence, a monk in a Carmelite monastery in Paris in the seventeenth century.[15] The sayings were collected posthumously by another monk, since Brother Lawrence himself was illiterate; because of that, he remained a lay brother and held a rather humble position in the monastery, working, until he died in 1691, first in the kitchen of the monastery and then as a sandal repairer. Yet the book recounts his happiness at the presence and love of God in everything he did, all the time, including, for example, picking up a straw from the ground. He trained himself to find the presence of God everywhere. But such practices need not be restricted to the religious sphere, and the great worth in simple things can be valued without being related to transcendent worth. Nonreligious people, too, can learn to sensitize themselves to what they might otherwise take for granted,

15. Brother Lawrence, *The Practice of the Presence of God*, trans. John J. Delaney (New York: Doubleday, 1977).

such as being alive, having food and shelter, having good—or even not so good—health, or knowing people who care about them. Of course, Brother Lawrence was a genius in what he did. Hardly anyone can reach this very high degree of recognizing. But with respect to recognizing, too, we do not need to be perfectionists. Much lower degrees of recognizing are also very valuable, and sometimes all we need is to pass a certain threshold. Recognizing just a little more of the value that has become invisible to us can often do a great deal.

As mentioned at the beginning of this chapter, recognizing is the converse of being detached or alienated—that is, not really being present, or being insensitive to many aspects of life, and feeling it as if through a transparent coating. Recognizing is a way of being more present, or experiencing what is around us as more present. It makes us more aware of the world, so that we experience it more intensely and, in a sense, are more alive.

6

Most people, when considering increasing meaning in life, think of changing reality by achieving various ends that have been identified as meaningful (perhaps by following the guidelines discussed in chapters 15 and 16). They usually think of increasing meaning by, for example, forming a loving relationship or a friendship, creating a work of art, doing a good deed, or learning a language. According to this paradigm, one increases meaning in life by introducing into it new value (sometimes replacing thereby value that dwindled or was destroyed). This is indeed a good way of increasing meaning. But it is important to remember that it is also possible to increase meaning by recognizing more sharply the value that is already there. To employ an analogy, if we want to increase our experience of beauty in our home, we have two main ways of doing so. The first way is to buy new and more beautiful things (such as nicer pictures or furniture) for the house to replace the less beautiful ones we have now. The second way is to learn to notice again the beauty in what we already have, but to which we have become numbed over time.

Both ways are helpful, and they need not be seen as competing ways of enhancing meaning. In many cases we have the time and energy to engage with both without having to choose between them, and together they can enhance meaning more than either one or the other would. We can achieve and recognize at the same time, working toward achievement while simultaneously recognizing the worth of the effort, of what is achieved, and of what we already have. Moreover, using one of these strategies can stimulate the use of the other. Recognizing value can boost our optimism and energy to achieve more, and the anticipation that after we achieve something we will have more to recognize can give us even more incentive to achieve. In the other direction, what has been newly achieved is frequently easier to recognize, and success in achieving things can give us optimism that we will also succeed in recognizing. Those who are more proficient in one of these ways of enhancing meaning should examine whether they do not also wish to develop the other. Both are good, and both contribute to the meaning of life.

But in some cases, when time and energy are limited, recognizing and achieving can compete against each other and will need to be balanced for the combination that yields most value in a given case. Circumstances are highly important: some things (such as new or attractive things) are easier to recognize than others (such as familiar or less attractive things), and some things are easier to achieve than others. Different people should strike the balance that is right for them, according to their personalities and their circumstances, between achieving and recognizing.

In general, however, we underappreciate and underemploy recognizing. Fairy tales, movies, the marketplace, and what might be called the current general ethos promote achieving something one does not yet have over recognizing what one already has. Most people are ready to invest much more effort in acts of achieving and in developing their achieving abilities than in acts of recognizing and in developing their recognizing abilities. Many are ready to make great sacrifices, forsake old habits, develop new ones, and dedicate huge efforts against mammoth obstacles in ventures that seem almost sure to fail in order to achieve, but are not willing to dedicate even a fraction of that in order to recognize. Most people I know are highly unbalanced in favor of achieving. Whenever they have the chance to opt for either recognizing or achieving, they opt for the latter. That is a pity since if they devoted to recognizing only a small part of what they have devoted to achieving, that would greatly enhance the meaning in their life. The trivialization of what is common and of what we already have is a very important factor in making people feel that their life is meaningless. We can frequently increase considerably the meaningfulness of our lives without achieving anything new at all, just by recognizing what we have. Recognizing is often sufficient by itself to make a life extremely meaningful.

Those who value achieving more than recognizing may think that recognizing what is within and around us, or what we have already achieved, is second best, maybe just a consolation prize, for those who fail at achieving more. Even if that were true, recognizing should be seen as valuable because it supplies a worthy way of increasing or maintaining meaning in life when the other, preferred way fails (just as a transplanted heart is very valuable although we would prefer that the one we were born with had continued to function). But it is wrong to see recognizing as second best to achieving. It makes just as much sense to see recognizing as the last resort of those who fail to achieve as it does to see achieving as the last resort of those who fail to recognize. Achieving can be seen as a fallback option because when people fail to appreciate the worth they have already achieved, they have compulsively to achieve more and more new things. It goes both ways: those who prefer either of the two options resort to the other when their first choice does not work well. Those who think that recognizing is a second best to achieving may also be assuming that recognizing is much easier than achieving. I do not think that the difficulty of an activity is an indicator of its worth, but even if it were, in many cases, and for many people, it is recognizing that is more difficult. Much depends, of course, on one's experience and inclination, the specific types of achievements and of things to be recognized, and the degree of recognition and of achievement that is being attempted.[16]

Recognizing, then, is not inferior to achieving, and in many circumstances in which it is possible to opt either for the one or for the other, I would choose recognizing. It is a very good way of enhancing or maintaining meaning in life. What I have written here is not of course meant to belittle or oppose achieving. I emphasize recognizing here only because it is commonly underestimated and, to many, counterintuitive, with the result that many people barely use it at all as a way to increase meaning in their lives.

16. Some people ask themselves what the worst situation is that they could be in and still be able to see their life as meaningful, or, in other words, what is it that, if it happened to them, would not allow them to live a meaningful life. A person who is very advanced in recognizing value would probably reply that as long as she had consciousness, or awareness, life could still be meaningful. She would be able to value things and have a meaningful life. Of course, for most people this would not be easy at all.

Chapter 18

Conclusion I

1

Thus far this book has dealt with some presuppositions concerning meaningful lives, argued against perfectionism, criticized arguments for the meaninglessness of life, and presented some ways of increasing life's meaning. I hope that readers have found these interesting and helpful. By way of conclusion, this and the next chapter will explore some general issues relating to the claims made in this book.

2

Does this book discuss meaning in life or our *perceptions* of meaning in life? In other words, does it aim to show that many people's lives *are* (or could be made) meaningful or that many people's lives could be *seen* as meaningful? The reply is that the book explores both. Moreover, the two are often interconnected; when discussing mistaken presuppositions about what meaningful lives must be like (chapter 2), perfectionism (chapter 3), and arguments for the meaninglessness of life (chapters 5 through 14), the book argues that some lives are, or can become, meaningful, even if they are not believed to be so, and of course also calls us to notice this fact. Chapter 17, which discusses recognizing value in life, emphasizes that some of what is meaningful is often not considered as such, and calls for considering it so, but since, as pointed out in the beginning of that chapter, recognizing value is also valuable in itself, when we recognize we not only discern existing but hitherto unnoticed value, we also make our lives more valuable.

It may also be asked whether this book calls on us to find meaning or to create meaning. Again, the answer is "both." In some cases, the book suggests, meaning is already present, and we just have to recognize it (chapter 17), or to reject certain misguided presuppositions (chapter 2), especially perfectionism (chapters 3, 4, and to an extent many other chapters in the book), that prevent us from seeing the meaning that is already present in life. Chapters 5 through 14, which reject arguments for the meaninglessness of life, also aim to show that life may be meaningful just as it is. Thus, many of the chapters call on us to find meaning.

But chapters 15 and 16, which suggest ways of identifying what is meaningful to us in order to then pursue those ways and increase meaning, discuss the creation of meaning. And since, as argued in chapter 17, recognizing meaning also increases meaning in our lives, it too relates not only to finding but also to creating meaning. The same is true of chapters 2 through 4: they are helpful not only for finding meaning but also for creating it. Rejecting the presuppositions discussed in chapter 2 and perfectionism (chapters 3 and 4) allows us to see what we need *not* aim for when trying to increase meaning in life and, by implication, what is plausible to aim for when trying to enhance meaning. Most people should aim at both finding and creating meaning, and this book discusses both of these avenues for enhancing and maintaining meaning in life.

3

A number of authors, including John Cottingham, William Lane Craig, and Lois Hope Walker, have argued that if certain religious beliefs are untrue, life cannot be meaningful.[1] Some of the arguments for this claim are that if we do not, or if what we produce does not, continue to exist forever, in some form of afterlife, then there cannot be any worth to our life or actions; that if we were not created by a God, according to a design, but are instead a product of chance evolutionary processes, then our feelings, actions, and relationships cannot have value; that if God does not vouch for the absolute certainty of what we believe in, then we cannot hold that it is true that what we see as worthy is indeed so; and that if there is no plan or reason that justifies the suffering and evil in this world or restores justice in the next, by allotting rewards and punishments, then our life cannot be taken to be of value.

Readers will have noted that such arguments, advanced by religious authors who believe that life is meaningful only if certain religious tenets are correct, bear a strong resemblance to the arguments advanced by those who believe that life must be meaningless (let us call them here *pessimists*) and criticized throughout this book. This

---

1. John Cottingham, *On the Meaning of Life* (London: Routledge, 2003), esp. 103–104; William Lane Craig, "The Absurdity of Life without God," in *The Meaning of Life*, ed. E. D. Klemke, 2nd ed. (New York: Oxford University Press, 2000), 40–56; Lois Hope Walker, "Religion Gives Meaning to Life," in *Philosophy: The Quest for Truth*, ed. Louis P. Pojman, 6th ed. (New York: Oxford University Press, 2006), 551–555. Cottingham does, however, qualify his claim by saying that "perhaps there are some who can achieve a systematic responsiveness to these values without the kind of focus provided by the disciplines of spirituality" (103).

may at first appear surprising, since pessimists and religious authors usually have opposing views about the meaning of life: the former believe that life is meaningless, while the latter that it is meaningful. But many in the two groups seem to share the basic presupposition that if our lives or achievements do not persist; if we are products of chance evolutionary processes; if we have no certain knowledge; if there is unjustified suffering in this world and so on, then life is meaningless. Pessimists believe our lives indeed do not persist, we are products of chance, and so on, and that therefore life is meaningless. Religious thinkers believe that lives persist, we were created by design, and so on, so that life is meaningful. But because their basic presupposition is the same, the arguments presented in this book, if correct, reply not only to pessimist but also to religious claims. The arguments presented in this book, if correct, show also that even if many religious beliefs are untrue, life can be meaningful. Meaning in life is not to be found only within religion. Religion is just one of several possible ways of making life meaningful.

This does not mean, of course, that we have to avoid religion when we are seeking meaning in life. On the contrary, religion can be a very good source of meaning. Meaning has to do with value, and religions typically take certain entities, such as God, to be of extreme value. This value then diffuses into various objects (such as books, relics, or symbols), activities (such as praying or fasting), and time periods (such as holy days), thus suffusing many aspects of life with meaning. Depending on details, religions may also offer answers to many of the problems discussed above, such as those related to death (we are not annihilated when we die, only transformed), our minuteness in the face of the cosmos (even though we are tiny, God attends to us and may approve of us and of what we do), the goal of life (living a religious life; being under God's grace), the paradox of the end (if God is transcendent, we will never arrive at full knowledge of or similarity to him), relativism and skepticism (God vouches for the objective correctness of our views), and suffering and evil (they have a purpose or reason, and everything is punished or rewarded in the afterlife). Many religions also include established procedures (such as confession, fasting, or repentance) through which one can periodically be forgiven for the wrong one has done, a burden with which nonbelievers have to cope on their own. In some religions, God also looks after or loves the believers, again a burden that nonbelievers have to carry themselves.

Another advantage of many religions is that they often include strong nonperfectionist elements. Admittedly, some of what religions propose is rooted in the idea of perfection: one is not annihilated in death but goes on to live forever; the afterlife (in heaven) is often described as flawless; some views are absolutely true and can be known with complete certainty; the world is managed by God in a perfectly just way (although we may not always understand exactly how). But in order to live forever in a perfect afterlife and know with perfect certainty, one does not need to be perfect oneself, to work exceptionally hard, or to be extraordinarily talented and successful. It is true that the faith one has to maintain and the religious duties one has to fulfill do require some effort (although these are also frequently presented as joyous): periodically fasting, praying, and so on, is not always easy. But it is a burden that even quite ordinary people can manage. It is not an exceptional feat, suitable only for geniuses. You do not have to be a religious Einstein in order to reach a satisfactory religious status, be blessed, saved, loved by God, or enter heaven. As mentioned in chapter 4, if one does become a member of the clergy, a saint, or the like, one's religious status is even higher. But even a person who just properly fulfills the ordinary duties demanded of the rank and file is often considered to have achieved a completely satisfactory religious status. More is better, but not necessary: the ordinary person gets full points, even if the saint gets extra points. This system, then, offers believers an excellent deal: they can acquire very high meaningfulness (e.g., eternal life, perfect bliss in the afterlife, a just world) for the price of easily performed deeds. A high degree of meaning is accessible to all who are ready to invest a moderate effort; it is not reserved just for the select few who are exceptional achievers. Many religions are nonperfectionist also in their emphasis on human frailty and insufficiency without God, and on the categorical difference between God and humans. Monotheistic religions, for example, emphasize that humans are created beings whose nature differs from that of God, the Creator. And as already noted in chapter 4, many religions also include habits aimed at sensitizing believers to the worth of ordinary, common aspects of life.

However, although these are good avenues to meaning, they are not exclusive. Those who do not adopt a religious outlook are not condemned to meaninglessness. They can find meaning in completely secular settings. The arguments presented throughout this book suggest that atheists, too, can cope successfully with such issues as annihilation, the vastness of the cosmos, contingency, skepticism, relativism, the paradox of the end, suffering, and evil.

4

Some might claim that meaning and meaninglessness are solely a matter of moods, emotions, and other psychological states. Hence, philosophical and rational discussions such as those presented in this book are irrelevant. According to this view, issues relating to the meaning of life should be dealt with by psychologists, who focus mostly on emotional attitudes (related, perhaps, to the subconscious) or by psychiatrists, who focus mostly on the chemical imbalances that produce certain emotions and attitudes.

I disagree. Views and decisions regarding the meaning of life may well have psychological or psychiatric aspects but, for many people, they also have important philosophical features. There are some good reasons or arguments and some bad reasons or arguments for seeing life as meaningless or meaningful. Many people, without being exposed to any psychological or psychiatric treatment, change their views about the meaning of life after hearing philosophical or rational arguments about the topic, just as they change their views after hearing rational arguments about renting a certain apartment or choosing a certain profession. Moreover, changes in our views due to philosophical considerations frequently affect our emotions: many of us feel worse when we find ourselves convinced by arguments for the meaninglessness of life and feel better when we are convinced by arguments for the meaningfulness of life, just as our feelings would change in response to arguments suggesting that we have good or bad chances for winning a scholarship. This suggests that philosophical considerations about the meaning of life are frequently relevant and effective. Many intellectual events also have emotional or chemical counterparts, but that does not show that the former should be reduced to the latter or that we should only use psychological or psychiatric tools to deal with views about the meaning of life.

Even if we were to accept that the issue of the meaning of life is mostly an emotional one, philosophical discussions of the meaning of life would remain highly relevant, because emotions frequently have an important cognitive component. For example, we may feel angry because we believe that a friend has mocked us; jealous because we believe that a colleague has achieved more than we have; or loving because we believe that our beloved is a kind person. But once we learn that the friend was referring not to us but to a literary character in a novel; that our colleague has not in fact achieved more than we have; or that our beloved is a cruel person who enjoys torturing animals, our anger, jealousy, and love, respectively, dissipate. Our views about the facts of a case or about the way the world is, based on better or worse evidence and argument, frequently determine our emotions. Even under more emotive understandings of the meaning of life, then, there is a need for reasoned discussions such as those presented in this book.

True, there are also cases in which emotional responses seem unaffected by rational considerations. For example, a person suffering from agoraphobia may know rationally that there is nothing particularly dangerous in open city squares, yet still sense acute discomfort in such places. Similarly, some people feel depressed to such a degree that no argument of the type presented in this book will lead them to see things differently. But even in such cases, philosophical arguments such as those we have explored are relevant. The agoraphobe will agree to receive psychological help relating to the irrational aspects of her fear only if she accepts that, from the rational point of view, open spaces are not in fact harmful or dangerous. She would not want to enter into psychological treatment to change her emotional reaction to open spaces if she believed that it is, in fact, dangerous to stroll through them. Similarly, people who are depressed and believe that life is meaningless may refuse psychological treatment if they believe that their attitude is a plausible reaction to what is in their view the real meaninglessness of life. They may well hold that there is nothing wrong with them; that they are just seeing reality as it is, without cheating themselves. They may hold that, things being as they are, it is only appropriate and rational to be depressed and there is no

sense in toiling away with a psychotherapist to identify uncon-
scious patterns from the distant past. Noting that there are some
good and perhaps convincing arguments that suggest that life is
not irredeemably meaningless, however, may lead those who suffer thus to try therapy, and address their feeling of the sourness of
life also in a psychological way.

Most of these points about arguments and emotions are also
true for arguments and chemical imbalances. Just as changes in
our chemical conditions can affect our views, changes in our
views can also affect our chemical conditions. In some cases,
then, arguments such as those discussed in this book can affect
people's attitude to the meaning of life even when the chemical
aspects of their attitude are acknowledged. As above, there will
also be cases in which philosophical discussions alone will be of
no avail, and chemical intervention might be helpful. In these
latter cases, too, some of those who suffer may refuse to accept
the medication that could help them, since they believe that they
are simply seeing life as it really is (that is, as meaningless) and
therefore prefer to remain sad but authentic rather than happy
but inauthentic. Showing such people that there are good reasons to believe that life is not, in fact, inherently or irredeemably
meaningless may convince them to take the medication they had
ceased, or refused, to take.

Thus, although I have defended here the importance of the intellectual consideration of questions relating to the meaning of life,
I also note that, in some cases, it alone will not suffice. In such cases,
our views about the meaning of life also have a lot to do with our
emotional habits, personality traits, early education, deep-seated
traumas from the past of which we may not be fully aware, or chemical imbalances. In such cases, discussions with psychological or
psychiatric professionals are advisable and can be extremely helpful.

5

Many people consider existentialist philosophy to be a good source of knowledge and guidance for increasing or maintaining meaning in life. However, while there is much to learn from existentialism, if what is presented in this book is correct, several central themes in major existentialist philosophies are misguided and even harmful to those who want to promote meaning in their lives.

I should stress that the themes I will discuss are not present in all existentialist philosophies. I will focus mainly on Nietzsche (considering him here as an existentialist), Kierkegaard, Heidegger, Sartre, and Camus, but some of my points will not hold for several other existentialist writers (and almost none of what I write here holds for, say, Buber). Moreover, many of the points I will make here apply only to one or several of the five authors I have named. Furthermore, their philosophies are complex and sometimes also include themes that are opposite to those that I emphasize, and are amenable to more than one interpretation. Nevertheless, because the themes that I will discuss appear (under many readings) in some major existentialist theories, people who wish to promote meaning in their lives should approach existentialist thought with some caution.

Some existentialist thought is perfectionist. As already pointed out in chapter 3, Nietzsche envisages his Overman as very different from almost all people, whose regular identity and mode of being, he writes, should be completely overcome. The Overman's superior qualities are very hard, if not impossible, to achieve. Kierkegaard writes that, although he has been looking for many years, he has not found even a single authentic instance of what he calls a *knight of faith*, and he is uncertain that anyone in his generation has reached what he considers to be faith.[2] Sartre argues that "man is fundamentally the desire to be God."[3] Camus's explanations, in *The Myth of Sisyphus*, of what makes life absurd and his descriptions of the absurd hero all present ideals that are very difficult or next to impossible to attain.[4] These authors seem to despise common practices, ordinary enjoyments, and the simple lives of most people. To arrive at what these authors say they seek, people would have to detach themselves from the ordinary and become different and special. Almost all of us, almost all of the time, are insufficient—the existentialist analogue of living in sin—whatever we do, and will remain hungry for meaning all our lives. But this approach conflicts with the nonperfectionist attitude espoused in this book, according to which meaning can also be found in much of what is ordinary. A meaningful life is easier to attain than many people (perhaps under the influence of such existentialist writers) believe it to be. To lead meaningful lives, we do not have to be geniuses or heroes.

Another problematic theme in the writings of prominent existentialist thinkers such as Sartre and Camus is the view that life is inherently absurd or meaningless (and that those who do not notice this absurdity are insincere, cowardly, or dimwitted).[5] They suggest various coping strategies that we may wish to adopt, within this meaningless existence, in order to deal with it better. But human existence, for them, is and will ever remain absurd. I have argued

2. Søren Kierkegaard, *Fear and Trembling [and] Repetition*, trans. Howard V. Hong and Edna H. Hong (Princeton, NJ: Princeton University Press, 1983), 34, 38.

3. Jean-Paul Sartre, *Being and Nothingness*, trans. Hazel E. Barnes (London: Methuen, 1966), 566.

4. I should note that this (and much else of what I say here) is not true of all of Camus's other writings. Albert Camus, *The Myth of Sisyphus*, in *"The Myth of Sisyphus" and Other Essays*, trans. Justin O'Brien (New York: Vintage, 1991), 17, 21, 38, 58, 60, 64–65, 70, 101, 113, 115, 117.

5. Sartre, *Being and Nothingness*, 479–481, 539–541; Camus, *The Myth of Sisyphus*, 17–21, 31.

throughout this book, however, that this is incorrect. If we do not adopt perfectionist standards (which, as I have shown, there is no need to adopt), life often emerges as meaningful. There are some events in life that, for some people, can undermine the meaning of life. But not all people suffer from these events. Moreover, some of these events can be prevented or moderated ahead of time, or the damage from them partly or wholly healed afterward.

Some existentialists are also insufficiently averse to suffering and not committed enough to diminishing it. Nietzsche writes that the discipline of suffering, moreover great suffering, is the cause of the enhancement of humanity.[6] Kierkegaard points out that much suffering is involved in religious existence.[7] Heidegger takes authenticity to involve anxiety.[8] Sartre explains that freedom, and therefore also what he calls human reality, necessarily involve anguish, suffering, unhappiness, and despair.[9] Camus recommends a painful life: from this pain, he believes, we can generate a type of happiness, but one that will still involve considerable frustration.[10] None of the existentialist authors mentioned here appropriately value plain, simple happiness or see it as a sufficiently important aspect of life. They are not adequately interested in condemning and diminishing the suffering or pain that so many people go through.[11] But as

---

6. Friedrich Nietzsche, *Beyond Good and Evil*, §225, trans. Judith Norman (Cambridge: Cambridge University Press, 2001), 116–117. See also *Thus Spoke Zarathustra*, trans. Adrian Del Caro (Cambridge: Cambridge University Press, 2006), 234.

7. Søren Kierkegaard, *Concluding Unscientific Postscript*, trans. David F. Swenson and Walter Lowrie (Princeton, NJ: Princeton University Press, 1944), 386–414.

8. Martin Heidegger, *Being and Time*, trans. John Macquarrie and Edward Robinson (Oxford: Blackwell, 1962), 309–311.

9. Sartre, *Being and Nothingness*, 38, 90, 627.

10. Camus, *The Myth of Sisyphus*, 31, 38, 88.

11. Nietzsche, Kierkegaard, Heidegger, Sartre, and Camus also seem to be deadly serious. They are completely blind to the lighter aspects of life. Sometimes they employ irony and sarcasm, but hardly ever humor.

suggested in chapter 16, although happiness is not a necessary or sufficient condition for meaning in life, it is, for many people, an important contributing factor, and its absence very frequently takes away meaning.

I also take the existentialists mentioned above to have a problematic understanding of truthfulness, sincerity, and authenticity. They do not see that sincere, authentic people, who understand life correctly, should also take into account what is good and comforting in the world and in themselves. What these existentialist authors point out and call on us to note if only we are sincere enough has to do mostly with the difficult, tense, and painful aspects of life. In their writings it is difficult to find any discussions of the joyful, satisfying aspects of human existence. As I suggested in chapters 12 through 14, however, it is important to be realistic and to acknowledge both the bad and the good in life.

Yet another theme that I find problematic in the work of some major existentialists is their hostility to society and community. The existentialist hero is frequently a loner who reaches the state he is aiming for by himself, after having distanced himself from others. They hardly mention the support and empowerment that close personal relationships or a community could offer. Nietzsche characterizes almost any social or communal activity as herd mentality.[12] Kierkegaard is very hostile toward what he sees as the crowd.[13] Camus's absurd hero develops without any company. For them, solidarity, togetherness, empathy, kindness, friendship, and love hardly play a part in what endows life with meaning. But this existentialist predisposition can lead some people, unnecessarily,

12. E.g., *Beyond Good and Evil* §201, pp. 88–89.
13. Søren Kierkegaard, *The Point of View*, trans. Howard V. Hong and Edna H. Hong (Princeton, NJ: Princeton University Press, 1998), 106–112, 277.

to seclude themselves from close personal relationships or from society and, thus, decrease meaning in their lives. For most people, loneliness is torturous and unhelpful. Some of the most meaningful experiences in life involve interactions with other people, and lack of company can enormously decrease meaning. Most of us are social beings, and other people's support can frequently help us to improve ourselves and our lives. We often grow through interaction with others. Thus, for those who want to increase or maintain the meaning of life, it is often helpful to try to find or build a community. (Of course, not all others are helpful for increasing or maintaining life's meaning, and we should try to stay away from those who are harmful.) Admittedly, some people can, and some even need to, increase the meaning in their lives through solitude. But this is only one option out of many, and for most people not a good one, unless it is supplemented by some kind of communal activity. Thus, many of those who have been convinced by Nietzsche, Kierkegaard, and other existentialists to distance themselves from society in order to enhance the meaning of their lives find it instead weakened by this act. Like perfectionism, excessive distancing of oneself from any community is counterproductive. Some people adopt it in an effort to increase meaning in their lives, but thereby very often decrease it.

Related to the aversion to society is the tendency to judge issues in a personal rather than impersonal way, and to refrain from judging oneself in a detached fashion, as one would do when seeing oneself as just one among many or when judging another person. However, this book suggests that people who take their lives to be insufficiently meaningful frequently discriminate against themselves, and that in order to cope with this tendency they should try to judge themselves as they would judge others.

Another difference between the approach of some existentialists and the one offered here has to do with the basic attitude to the meaning of life. This book has made an effort to take the meaning of life off its pedestal. Meaning is presented here as not very different from quite plain things we value. Meaninglessness, similarly, is presented as not very different from quite plain things we take to have negative value, such as a toothache: there are various activities that can decrease the probability that it will occur, and we should learn what they are and undertake them, even if performing them is sometimes boring. Also like a toothache, meaninglessness, if it does occur, can in many cases be healed or at least moderated. It is not a necessary part of life. Meaning and meaninglessness are quite accessible to simple reasoned argument or even common sense, and to experimentation through trial and error; there is nothing especially mysterious or exalted about them, and there is no need to treat them with romantic fervor or awe. Nietzsche, Kierkegaard, Heidegger, Sartre, and Camus, however, treat what they see as the meaning of life as something special, exalted, and somewhat mysterious, difficult not only to attain but also to grasp.

I also find the Sartrean notion of radical freedom problematic. Sartre argues that although we are not absolutely free when it comes to the physical and material circumstances in which we find ourselves, we are completely free in our feelings and thoughts about them.[14] For example, although a person who has no legs is not free to walk, she is absolutely free in her interpretation of and attitude toward her physical condition.[15] And because we are absolutely free, we are also absolutely responsible.[16] But I believe that this is incorrect. As suggested in chapter 15, people have various mental and psychological limitations. In some cases, people cannot change the way they feel or interpret

14. Sartre, *Being and Nothingness*, 438, 441, 550, 555.
15. Sartre, *Being and Nothingness*, 328. See also 488–489, 505.
16. Sartre, *Being and Nothingness*, 509.

situations; in some other cases, it takes considerable effort and guidance to succeed in making such changes.[17] This Sartrean view is not only incorrect but also unhelpful, since it may lead people to suppose that they can increase meaning in their life by making emotional and psychological changes that, in fact, they cannot, or that they can make these changes without needing time, hard work, guidance, and support that some of these changes require. Then, if they fail, they undermine meaning in their life even further by accusing themselves for not having exercised their alleged absolute freedom, holding themselves absolutely responsible for some things they do not, in fact, have much or any power over. We should not underestimate the degree of our freedom, but also not overestimate it.[18]

This book also differs from some central existentialist accounts in that it presents a pluralist conception of the meaning of life. Although it does not hold that all behaviors are meaningful or that all people have meaningful lives, it suggests that there are multiple ways, in multiple spheres, of attaining or increasing meaning. However, existentialists frequently present the meaningful life and the way toward it as much more specific and exclusive. Thus, their accounts are significantly less pluralistic than that presented in this book. They would see much of what I take to be meaningful as meaningless.

This very short discussion cannot do justice to the richness and complexity of the philosophies mentioned above. It is important to emphasize that many of them also involve some elements with which this book agrees and that are opposed to those criticized

17. For a more elaborate discussion of this issue see my "Sartre's Absolute Freedom in *Being and Nothingness*: The Problem Persists," *Philosophy Today* 56 (2012): 463–473.
18. For similar reasons, popular sayings such as "The sky's the limit," "You can be whoever you want," or "The only limit to your achievements is the reach of your dreams and your willingness to work" are also false, again leading some people to reprimand themselves for not changing what they cannot in fact change. People often can improve on what they do, but not in all spheres, and not in any way and to any degree.

here.[19] I do not have the space to discuss here how such contradicting assertions should be interpreted, how conflicting strands can cohere (when they do), or how, on balance, the overall attitude of these philosophies toward the issues discussed here should be understood. In the present context, I must be content with noting that there is a large enough difference between what this book suggests and central themes in some important existentialist philosophies, so that if what this book claims is correct, then the existentialist philosophies discussed above should be approached with great caution. Because I of course subscribe to what I have argued for in this book, I take the existentialist themes that I have laid out here not to enhance the meaning of life but to diminish it: I believe that they unnecessarily instill negative feelings in people, suggesting to them that their lives are less meaningful than they really are and, often, that they are by and large worthless beings. If what I have written in this book is correct, then some of the central and commonly cited discussions in existentialist thought, although they aim to improve people's condition by showing them a way of making life more meaningful, or of functioning well in an absurd world, actually exacerbate the problem they aim to solve.

---

19. For example, notwithstanding the many perfectionist themes in Nietzsche, he also writes that he supports an affirmation of the world as it is (*The Will to Power*, §1041. ed. Walter Kaufmann, trans. Walter Kaufmann and R. J. Hollingdale [New York: Vintage, 1968], 536) and that in some cases it is preferable not to try to change oneself but, rather, to accept oneself as one is (*Ecce Homo*, in *"The Anti-Christ", "Ecce Homo", "Twilight of the Idols", and Other Writings*, ed. Aaron Ridley and Judith Norman, trans. Judith Norman [Cambridge: Cambridge University Press, 2005], 82). Likewise, much of what I have written about Camus is not true of his novel *The Plague*, for example, and notwithstanding the many perfectionist themes in his *Sisyphus*, he also writes there that he wishes to solve the problem of suicide without appealing to eternal values (*Sisyphus*, v), and that those he calls *conquerors* can successfully cope with the absurd while knowing their limitations (*Sisyphus*, 88–89). For a general appraisal of the degree of perfectionism in *Sisyphus* see my "Perfectionism and Non-perfectionism in Camus's *Myth of Sisyphus*," in *On Meaning in Life*, ed. Beatrix Himmelmann (Boston: de Gruyter, 2013), 139–151.

Chapter 19

Conclusion II

1

It has been argued throughout this book that to see life as meaningless or insufficiently meaningful is to see it as lacking a sufficient number of aspects of sufficient value. This is not how many people who find their lives to be meaningless describe the meaninglessness of their lives, however. One sometimes hears people saying that they feel that their lives are "wrong" or that they feel their life as an unfulfilled promise. Others, when describing their feeling of meaninglessness, say that the world, or their life, feels like one big lie, or deception. Many remark on their feelings of general despair, anxiety, or guilt without being able to identify the sources of these feelings, sometimes referring to them as existential despair, anxiety, or guilt.[1] Some report going through life with a persistent sense of

---

1. What will be said here of these general feelings of despair, anxiety, and guilt is not true of some specific employments of these terms by, for example, Kierkegaard, Heidegger, and Buber. See Søren Kierkegaard, *The Sickness Unto Death*, trans. Alastair Hannay (London: Penguin, 1989); Martin Heidegger, *Being and Time*, trans. John Macquarrie and Edward Robinson (Oxford: Blackwell, 1962), 227–235; Martin Buber, "Guilt and Guilt Feelings," in *Martin*

missing something crucial or of having something important to do but not being able to recall what it is. People also discuss a sensation of "not being at home" in life, or describe a meaningless life as a big bad joke, as a farce, or as ridiculous. Can the analysis of meaninglessness suggested in this book cohere with, or even make sense of, such descriptions?

I think it can. The analysis suggests that to see life as meaningless or as insufficiently meaningful is to see it as a life with an insufficient number of aspects of sufficient value. In other words, those who take life to be meaningless feel that there is a gap between their expectations and reality: a gap between the degree of value that life should have and the degree of value that it actually does have.[2] Noting that meaninglessness has to do with this gap can help explain the descriptions and perceptions mentioned above. Take, again, some people's description of their meaningless lives as "wrong." This sense of wrongness may have to do with the discrepancy between their expectations and reality; life is taken to be wrong because it does not include a sufficient number of aspects of sufficient value. It is "wrong" because it is not the way it "should" be. For similar reasons, some describe life as an unfulfilled promise. They feel as though they were promised, perhaps implicitly, possibly by parents or early educators, that there would be a sufficient number of aspects of sufficient value in their lives, but this did not happen (sometimes in spite of the fact that they did what they were told would be necessary to make that happen). The same is true of people who, when describing their

Buber on Psychology and Psychotherapy: Essays, Letters, and Dialogue, trans. Maurice Friedman (New York: Syracuse University Press, 1999), 110–138.

2. See Albert Camus, *The Myth of Sisyphus*, in *"The Myth of Sisyphus" and Other Essays*, trans. Justin O'Brien (New York: Knopf, 1955), 29–30, and, following Camus, Thomas Nagel, "The Absurd," in *Mortal Questions* (Cambridge: Cambridge University Press, 1979), 13.

sense of meaninglessness, say that the world or life feels like one big lie or deception. It is as if they had been told that life would meet certain standards or have certain qualities, but then it did not. In some cases people also use these expressions to indicate that, for them, continuing to live this insufficiently valuable life as though it were valuable enough involves deceiving, lying, or pretending.

The above is also true of the general feelings of despair, anxiety, or guilt that people occasionally experience without being able to identify the sources of these feelings, sometimes referring to them as existential despair, anxiety, or guilt. Despair frequently has to do with unsuccessful efforts to achieve something. After repeatedly unsuccessful efforts, one gives up, experiencing loss, powerlessness, and failure. Some of those who walk around with a general feeling of despair, but have difficulty explaining to others and themselves why they are despairing or what they despair of, may have consciously or unconsciously adopted, and then repeatedly failed to fulfill, expectations about sufficient value in their lives. Likewise, many of those who experience anxiety that has no specific object, especially anxiety related to the feeling that life is meaningless, may feel that way because of an expectation of a certain level of value that is not met. This is also true of existential guilt. Similarly, some report an unsettled feeling throughout their lives of missing something crucial or of having something important to do but not being able to recall what it is. Often what they feel uneasy about "missing" or "forgetting" is an expectation concerning value that is both unfulfilled and unclear. I would explain in a similar way the general sense of not being at home in life. Those who describe their feeling that way often do not sense in life the familiarity or comfort of a home because (according to their expectations) life is not as it should be. Hence, they also feel alienated.

Some also refer to the meaningless life as a big bad joke, as a farce, or as ridiculous. Jokes present situations that challenge our expectations. This is true both of slapstick jokes (it is undignified to slip on a banana peel in front of everyone) and of sophisticated plays on words (where the meaning of a word is intentionally twisted). Life, for such people, is a joke because what happens in life does not match their expectations. Sometimes people who use this term to describe their meaningless life feel that a joke is being played on them, as though someone has pulled their leg: they were told that their life would turn out a certain way, they believed that it would, but then it did not. Similarly to a joke, a farce represents reality as being far beneath our expectations of the way it should be. And when we find something to be ridiculous we think that it is considerably inferior to what it should be; ridiculing something conveys that we think it is of poor quality.

2

One way of eliminating or reducing a gap between expectations and reality is to change expectations. In this book, this way is followed in, among others, the critiques of some common presuppositions about the meaning of life in chapter 2, such as that only a life focused on one issue can be meaningful. Likewise, chapters 3 and 4 critique perfectionism, and chapters 5 through 14 critique some perfectionist presuppositions in arguments for the meaninglessness of life, such as those that claim that only an immortal life, or a life that impacts the entire universe, or a life in which absolutely certain knowledge is achieved, can be meaningful. In terms of the descriptions of the feeling of meaninglessness presented in the previous section, this book suggests that those who experience life as wrong would do well to consider the possibility that it is their expectations, rather than their lives, that are wrong. Those who do not feel at home in their life can try to change their life so that they will feel at home, but should also consider whether their notion of home might be problematic. Perhaps their lives are already very good "homes" as they are, and these people feel desolate only because they are perfectionist and, thus, will not settle for anything less than ideal as an acceptable "home."

The same is true for the other expressions mentioned above of the feeling that life is meaningless: if I see my life as a promise unfulfilled, perhaps I should examine whether a promise was actually made, who made it, and whether there were good grounds to make it and suppose that it could ever be fulfilled. Those who sense existential despair, anxiety, or guilt because they have invested the greater part of a lifetime trying and failing, over and again, to achieve the unachievable (sometimes without being fully aware that that was what they were doing) may wish to consider relinquishing their perfectionist expectations.[3] Likewise, if we walk around with the feeling of missing something crucial or not recalling something important, we may try to identify it and, then, consider whether we really need to realize it or can accept and enjoy life as meaningful

3. Note, however, that some degree of despair, anxiety, or guilt about various specific issues is frequently appropriate. I, for example, am guilty of certain misdeeds, and it would be problematic if I were not to feel some guilt about them. But this is different from a deep, general, and pervasive feeling of guilt (or despair, or anxiety) about failing to achieve something that it is neither necessary nor possible to achieve. Note also that not all cases of despair, anxiety, or guilt whose sources are unknown have to do with perfectionist ends, and not all of them should be interpreted as "existential despair," "existential anxiety," or "existential guilt." Sometimes people experience despair, anxiety, or guilt without knowing the source of these feelings because specific harsh events and circumstances of their lives have remained unnoticed or repressed and, hence, unaddressed. To solve these problems, they need not renounce perfectionist ends but rather attend to the specific harsh events, sometimes by seeking counseling. The same is true also of the other feelings discussed here, such as that of not being at home in life.

without it. And if we feel that our life is ridiculous, farcical, or a joke, we should examine not only whether our life can be changed so that it is no longer ridiculous, but also whether we need to continue upholding the standards that render it ridiculous.

A second general way of closing or narrowing a gap between expectations and reality is, of course, to change reality. Chapters 15 and 16 suggest ways to identify what to pursue so as to increase meaning in our lives. Those who feel that life is wrong, then, may make it right by changing how they live, and those who feel that they are not at home in their life may amend some of its aspects so that it will be more homelike. Those who feel that they have missed or forgotten something very important and basic can attain that which they now understand or "remember" to be valuable in life. Similarly, we can sometimes actively work to realize promises we feel should be kept, eliminate feelings of guilt, despair, or anxiety for not having done what we believe we should have done by doing it, and improve a ridiculous life, "a joke," or "a lie," until it becomes nonridiculous, a nonjoke, or a nonlie.

A third general way of coping with gaps between expectations and reality is to examine whether they are indeed genuine gaps rather than merely perceived ones. For example, chapter 11 shows that the paradox of the end is a fixable psychological problem rather than an inherent flaw of the human condition. Chapters 12 through 14 argue that the ratios of pleasure to suffering and of goodness to evil in some human lives, or in the world, differ from what some people perceive them to be. Chapter 17, which discusses recognizing, suggests that, in many cases, there is more meaning in our lives than we notice. According to the discussion in these chapters, then, some people who experience life as wrong, who do not feel at home in life, who sense that a certain fundamental promise has not been fulfilled, or that life is just one big lie or a joke, may have an incorrect understanding of reality.

Of course, these three general strategies for dealing with the feeling that life is insufficiently meaningful may be combined. One could, for example, both conceive some aspects of reality anew and at the same time change other aspects, or do both of these while also lowering expectations. Some chapters indeed apply more than one of these principal strategies. For example, chapters 8 through 10 claim that determinism, contingency, skepticism, relativism, and the absence of an external end to which life is a means do not exclude meaning (the third strategy), *and* suggest that we avoid perfectionism (the first strategy). Likewise, chapter 17 discusses how recognizing not only notices but also enhances meaning in life (the second and third strategies).

Thus, the claim made throughout this book, that a meaningless life is one in which there is not a sufficient number of aspects of sufficient value, does correspond with, moreover can explain, many people's seemingly unrelated descriptions of their meaningless lives. I hold that many people who thus describe their lives could find the arguments and suggestions made in this book helpful.

3

The book may well be read by those only interested in the topic academically, as a merely theoretical text. But it was written with the hope that it would also be useful for people who take their lives to be insufficiently meaningful. Those who do wish to use it in a practical manner in order to increase meaning in their lives, however, should bear in mind that merely understanding intellectually what is said in this book would likely be insufficient. Practical work, beyond a theoretical understanding, is usually indispensable for countering long-entrenched assumptions about the meaning of life, perfectionist inclinations, arguments for the meaninglessness of life we have become used to, and emotional habits that cause us to experience the paradox of the end or to notice only the bad in everything. Likewise, identifying what is meaningful to us and pursuing it, or what I have called recognizing, requires effort that goes beyond scholarly comprehension.

Not everyone has to work equally hard in order to have a meaningful life. There are better and worse starting points, and there is a lucky minority that does not have to put in any conscious effort at all. Of course, the latter also have to act in various ways in order to have meaningful lives, but thanks to nature, nurture, or both, it is relatively effortless, automatic, and intuitive for them to act in ways that make their lives meaningful, sometimes without even being aware of this. Most people do, however, have to put in at least some conscious effort in order to increase or maintain the meaning of their lives. As with many other types of work, this one, too, is much more difficult at the early stages. If engaged in frequently and persistently, it can become second nature and is much easier. But even then, an investment of effort is almost always needed.

Yet some people find it hard to accept that they need to invest work in order to enhance or maintain the meaning of their lives. This is surprising, since most people accept that improving or maintaining their health, happiness, love, artistic abilities, knowledge, or even more concrete and immediate things such as their financial situation or the cleanliness of their home requires work. It is odd, then, that when it comes to living a meaningful life, they adopt a passive attitude, as if they expect that it will happen by itself, complain bitterly when it does not, and invest no real effort in making their lives meaningful. They find distasteful the notion that meaning has to be worked for. They would prefer it just to show up.

Note, however, that although most people need to work in order to have meaningful lives, more work is not always better.[4] As in friendship, dancing, poetry writing, jogging, love, and enjoying music or natural beauty, so with the meaning of life, the optimal degree of effort is frequently not the maximal one. It is not always wise to try to work as intensely as one can, since trying very hard can be counterproductive. Maintaining or increasing meaning should also include an element of letting things be, trying things out and following intuitions, using what is already there and enjoying it, and in some cases only making some small, sensitive changes that tune up what already exists and is good. This suggestion, which is also informed by nonperfectionism, does not of course mean that one should just lazily let things happen and not work at all.

One might also think (perhaps under the influence of certain interpretations of Sartrean discussions of freedom) that increasing or maintaining the meaning of life cannot have to do with automatic behavior, routine, or habit, but needs to be freely and consciously chosen each time anew; that one should always try to break one's mechanical habits in order to have a meaningful life. But certain habits and automatic reactions can be very helpful. A painter may paint very well thanks to practices and habits she has acquired and which are now no longer chosen. Musicians work hard on drills so that some actions will become automatic; then they can play well, elegantly, and enjoyably. Players who improvise, too, have at the basis of their improvisation, and as a necessary condition for

---

4. The notion that there is great value to the relentless effort to improve is a significant theme at the end of Goethe's *Faust*. As the angels who save Faust (although he had sold his soul to the devil) explain, while taking him to heaven, "Whoever strives in ceaseless toil, him we may grant redemption" (11936; Johann Wolfgang von Goethe, *Faust*, ed. Cyrus Hamlin, trans. Walter W. Arndt, 2nd ed. [New York: Norton, 2001], 339).

it, some automatic behaviors that are carried out mechanically and without conscious thought, thus allowing them to focus their attention on their improvisation. We try to form useful habits in many other contexts as well: reading habits and working habits, listening habits and exercising habits. Of course, some habits are obstacles to a meaningful life and should be eliminated. Habits should be adopted or maintained with some caution: we should use them, not allow them to control us, and when they are unhelpful we should try to unlearn them and develop others. But habits that are helpful should be kept, and we may well wish to work hard at forming more that are helpful.

Some also presume that the work we undertake toward increasing meaning in life must itself be meaningful and pleasant and cannot be repetitive, tedious, or a nuisance. However, although the paths toward increased meaning may be meaningful and pleasant themselves, it is highly probable that at least some parts of them will not be so. This should not be surprising: preparing a meal is in itself not tasty, and bringing a house to a pleasant state of cleanliness involves dealing with a lot of dirt. Likewise, producing an interesting philosophical paper requires a great deal of technical and sometimes boring work, and learning to play a musical instrument beautifully involves tedious and unmelodious practice, especially at the beginning. The same applies for the meaning of life: some of the work required for making life more meaningful may well not be meaningful and fun, but more like drudgery. Therefore, in most cases, one cannot have a completely meaningful life. There may be some minutes, hours, days, or weeks that are completely or almost completely meaningful, but since it is rare that meaning comes without work and that work for meaning does not involve some tediousness, a meaningful life will often also include some nonmeaningful aspects.

But nonperfectionists will accept that one's life can be meaningful even if it is not purely and absolutely meaningful.[5]

4

Sometimes people who have worked hard and have succeeded in making their lives meaningful find themselves falling back into the feeling that life is meaningless. How should such reversions be treated? I believe that they do not show that life is, in fact, meaningless, that perfectionism is the correct attitude to have toward the meaning of life, that the responses to arguments for the meaninglessness of life are mistaken, or that identifying what is meaningful, pursuing it, and recognizing were in vain. Here, too, we should beware of perfectionism. Views and intuitions that we have been socialized to accept from a young age, that we have entertained for many years, and that may also be held by those whom we care about are difficult to erase completely. It is only reasonable to expect that we will occasionally fall back into them out of habit. And as pointed out in chapter 16, because both we and the circumstances surrounding us often change, what was once meaningful for us sometimes ceases to be so and should be reconsidered. In addition, some people do not persist in working for meaningfulness as much as they once did, or as much as they should. But all of that can be corrected. Thus, the reappearance of old thoughts and feelings about the meaninglessness of life does not attest to their truth or mean that the work we have done was futile. Occasional relapses into former patterns

5. Nevertheless, since tedium and boredom diminish the meaning of life, they should be minimized as much as possible. They should be tolerated only as far as they are necessary means to achieving meaningfulness.

of thought and intellectual and emotional habits should be seen for what they actually are: occasional relapses.

5

Of the practical guidelines that this book lays out, which ones do I take to be the most important? The first, of course, is *Avoid perfectionism*, a theme that informs many chapters of this book. A corollary is the common-sense principle that, surprisingly, many fail to follow: *If it is impossible to achieve something, do not try to achieve it.*[6] Another corollary is *If it is impossible to achieve something, do not blame yourself for not achieving it.* And yet another corollary is *Do not ignore the good just because not everything is good* (or *Do not ignore the good just because there is also bad*).

A second important guideline is *Do not discriminate against yourself.* As mentioned in chapters 3 and 14, we think mostly about issues of discrimination against others. However, many people who see their lives as meaningless discriminate against themselves. A group of corollaries of this principle reverse the Golden Rule. The Reversed Golden Rule (mentioned in chapter 14) could be phrased as *Treat yourself as you treat others,* or *Do not treat yourself as you would not treat others.* Other versions are *Treat yourself as you would want others to treat you,* or *Do not treat yourself as you would not allow others to treat you.*

A third important guideline is the common saying, *This is not a dress rehearsal* (see chapter 15). Although in life we often need to make preparations for things that will come later, the life we have is

6. The exception to this is, again, aiming for regulative ideals, that is, guiding ideals that direct our efforts while we know that we will never reach them.

not (from a secular point of view) in itself a preparation for something else that might come later. Thus, we should not defer our life. We have one opportunity to live a meaningful life, and it is a great pity to waste it.

A fourth important guideline, mentioned in chapter 3, is *Do not be cruel to yourself*. We have duties to ourselves as well as to others, and one of those duties is not to be cruel. Cruelty is odious in relation to anyone, including ourselves. We should immediately cease all acts of cruelty. It is forbidden to be cruel to oneself.

And a fifth important guideline is *Work*. Only few people can have a meaningful life without working.

All of these principles are so obvious that pointing them out seems almost silly. They sound as if they could be part of a joke ("And then the old sage in the cave said: *If it is impossible to achieve something, do not try to achieve it*"). Yet a surprisingly large number of people seem not to follow them. It may be that many are unaware of these principles and, therefore, do not follow them, precisely because they are so obvious that they have become invisible. The practice of recognizing may be useful here as well.

BIBLIOGRAPHY

Abernathy, Ralph David. *And the Walls Came Tumbling Down: An Autobiography.* New York: HarperPerennial, 1990.

Acton, John Emerich Edward Dalberg. "Letter to Bishop Creighton." In *Historical Essays and Studies*, edited by John Neville Figgis and Reginald Vere Laurence, 503–507. London: Macmillan, 1907.

Adams, Robert M. "Comment." In Susan Wolf, *Meaning in Life and Why It Matters.* Commentary by John Koethe, Robert M. Adams, Nomy Arpaly, and Jonathan Haidt, 75–84. Princeton, NJ: Princeton University Press, 2010.

Aquinas, Thomas. *Summa Theologica.* Translated by Fathers of the English Dominican Province. New York: Benziger, 1948.

Aristotle. *Nicomachean Ethics.* Edited and translated by Roger Crisp. Cambridge: Cambridge University Press, 2000.

Aristotle. *Poetics.* Translated by Ingram Bywater. Oxford: Clarendon, 1925.

Audi, Robert. "Intrinsic Value and Meaningful Life." *Philosophical Papers* 34, no. 3 (2005): 331–355.

Aurelius, Marcus. *Meditations.* Translated by Robin Hard. Hertfordshire: Wordsworth, 1997.

Ayer, A. J. "The Meaning of Life." In *The Meaning of Life and Other Essays*, 178–197. London: Weidenfeld and Nicolson, 1990.

Baier, Kurt. "The Meaning of Life." In *The Meaning of Life*, 2nd ed., edited by E. D. Klemke, 101–132. New York: Oxford University Press, 2000.

Balaguer, Mark. *Free Will as an Open Scientific Problem.* Cambridge, MA: MIT Press, 2010.

Ben Ze'ev, Aaron, and Ruhama Goussinsky. *In the Name of Love: Romantic Ideology and Its Victims.* Oxford: Oxford University Press, 2008.

Blackburn, Simon. *Being Good*. Oxford: Oxford University Press, 2001.

Boghossian, Paul. *Fear of Knowledge: Against Relativism and Constructivism*. Oxford: Clarendon, 2006.

Bond, E. J. *Reason and Value*. Cambridge: Cambridge University Press, 1983.

Brickman, Philip, Dan Coates, and Ronnie Janoff-Bulman. "Lottery Winners and Accident Victims: Is Happiness Relative?" *Journal of Personality and Social Psychology* 36, no. 8 (1978): 917–927.

Brogaard, Berit, and Barry Smith. "On Luck, Responsibility and the Meaning of Life." *Philosophical Papers* 34, no. 3 (2005): 443–458.

Brother Lawrence [Nicolas Herman]. *The Practice of the Presence of God*. Translated by John J. Delaney. New York: Doubleday, 1977.

Buber, Martin. "Guilt and Guilt Feelings." In *Martin Buber on Psychology and Psychotherapy: Essays, Letters, and Dialogue*, translated by Maurice Friedman, 110–138. New York: Syracuse University Press, 1999.

Camus, Albert. *Caligula*. In *Caligula and Cross Purpose*, translated by Stuart Gilbert, 27–98. Harmondsworth: Penguin, 1965.

Camus, Albert. *The Myth of Sisyphus*. In *The Myth of Sisyphus and Other Essays*, translated by Justin O'Brien, 1–138. New York: Vintage, 1991.

Čapek, Karel. "The Makropulos Case." In *Four Plays*, translated by Peter Majer and Cathy Porter, 165–259. London: Methuen, 1999.

Cavafy, Constantine. *The Complete Poems of Cavafy*. Translated by Rae Dalven. New York: Harcourt Brace Jovanovich, 1976.

Cohen, Stewart. "How to Be a Fallibilist." *Philosophical Perspectives* 2 (1988): 91–123.

Cottingham, John. *On the Meaning of Life*. London: Routledge, 2003.

Craig, William Lane. "The Absurdity of Life without God." In *The Meaning of Life*, 2nd ed., edited by E. D. Klemke, 40–56. New York: Oxford University Press, 2000.

Dagan, Avigdor. *Der Hahnenruf*. Frankfurt am Main: Ullstein, 1980.

Davies, W. H. "Leisure." In *The Oxford Book of Modern Verse, 1892–1935*, edited by W. B. Yeats, 131. New York: Oxford University Press, 1937.

Diener, Ed, Richard E. Lucas, and Christie Napa Scollon. "Beyond the Hedonic Treadmill: Revising the Adaptation Theory of Well-Being." *American Psychologist* 61, no. 4 (2006): 305–314.

Dixon, Nicholas. "Modesty, Snobbery, and Pride." *Journal of Value Inquiry* 39, nos. 3–4 (2005): 415–429.

Dostoevsky, Fyodor. *The Brothers Karamazov*. Translated by Richard Pevear and Larissa Volokhonsky. San Francisco: North Point Press, 1990.

Edwards, Paul. "The Meaning and Value of Life." In *The Meaning of Life*, 2nd ed., edited by E. D. Klemke, 133–152. New York: Oxford University Press, 2000.

Emerson, Ralph Waldo. "Experience." In *The Complete Essays and Other Writings of Ralph Waldo Emerson*, edited by Brooks Atkinson, 342–364. New York: Modern Library, 1950.

Epicurus. *Letter to Menoeceus*. In *Epicurus: The Extant Remains*, translated by Cyril Bailey, 82–93. Hildesheim: Georg Olms Verlag, 1975.

Fara, Michael. "Masked Abilities and Compatibilism." *Mind* 117 (2008): 843–865.

Feinberg, Joel. "Psychological Egoism." In *Reason and Responsibility*, 6th ed., edited by Joel Feinberg, 480–490. Belmont, CA: Wadsworth, 1985.

Fischer, John Martin. *The Metaphysics of Free Will*. Oxford: Blackwell, 1994.

Fischer, John Martin. "Why Immortality Is Not So Bad." *International Journal of Philosophical Studies* 2, no. 2 (1994): 257–270.

Frankfurt, Harry. "Freedom of the Will and the Concept of a Person." *Journal of Philosophy* 68 (1971): 5–20.

Frankfurt, Harry. "On the Usefulness of Final Ends." *Iyyun: The Jerusalem Philosophical Quarterly* 41 (1992): 3–19.

Frankl, Viktor E. *Man's Search for Meaning*. New York: Washington Square Press, 1985.

Frankl, Viktor E. *The Will to Meaning*. London: Souvenir, 1971.

Frederick, Shane, and George Loewenstein. "Hedonic Adaptation." In *Well-being: The Foundations of Hedonic Psychology*, edited by Daniel Kahneman, Edward Diener, and Norbert Schwarz, 302–329. New York: Russell Sage, 1999.

Fujita, Frank, and Ed Diener. "Life Satisfaction Set Point: Stability and Change." *Journal of Personality and Social Psychology* 88, no. 1 (2005): 158–164.

Goethe, Johann Wolfgang von. *Faust*. 2nd ed. Translated by Walter W. Arndt. New York: Norton, 2001.

Haack, Susan. *Evidence and Inquiry: Towards Reconstruction in Epistemology*. Oxford: Blackwell, 1993.

Hanfling, Oswald. *The Quest for Meaning*. New York: Blackwell, 1988.

Headey, Bruce. "Life Goals Matter to Happiness: A Revision of Set-Point Theory." *Social Indicators Research* 86, no. 2 (2008): 213–231.

Heidegger, Martin. *Being and Time*. Translated by John Macquarrie and Edward Robinson. Oxford: Blackwell, 1962.

Hemingway, Ernest. "Big Two-Hearted River." In *In Our Time*, 133–156. New York: Scribner, 1970.

Hepburn, R. W. "Questions about the Meaning of Life." In *The Meaning of Life*, 2nd ed., edited by E. D. Klemke, 261–276. New York: Oxford University Press, 2000.

Herbert, Zbigniew. *Selected Poems*. Translated by John Carpenter and Bogdana Carpenter. Oxford: Oxford University Press, 1977.

Hesse, Hermann. *Siddhartha*. Translated by Susan Bernofsky. New York: Random House, 2006.

Hetherington, Stephen. "Fallibilism and Knowing That One Is Not Dreaming." *Canadian Journal of Philosophy* 32, no. 1 (2002): 83–102.

Heyd, David. *Supererogation: Its Status in Ethical Theory*. Cambridge: Cambridge University Press, 1982.

Hitchens, Christopher. *The Missionary Position: Mother Teresa in Theory and Practice.* London: Verso, 1995.

Hoffmann, Yoel. *The Heart is Katmandu.* Translated by Peter Cole. New York: New Directions, 2001.

Hooker, Brad. "The Meaning of Life: Subjectivism, Objectivism, and Divine Support." In *The Moral Life: Essays in Honour of John Cottingham,* edited by Nafsika Athanassoulis and Samantha Vice, 184–200. New York: Palgrave, 2008.

Hume, David. *Essays, Moral, Political, and Literary.* Edited by Eugene F. Miller. Indianapolis: Liberty Fund, 1987.

Hurka, Thomas. *Perfectionism.* New York: Oxford University Press, 1993.

Huxley, Aldous. "Swift." In *Do What You Will,* 73–84. London: Watts, 1936.

James, Laurence. "Achievement and the Meaningfulness of Life." *Philosophical Papers* 34, no. 3 (2005): 429–442.

James, William. *The Varieties of Religious Experience.* New York: Modern Library, 1902.

Joske, W. D. "Philosophy and the Meaning of Life." In *The Meaning of Life,* 2nd ed., edited by E. D. Klemke, 283–294. New York: Oxford University Press, 2000.

Kane, Robert. *The Significance of Free Will.* New York: Oxford University Press, 1996.

Kierkegaard, Søren. *Concluding Unscientific Postscript.* Translated by David F. Swenson and Walter Lowrie. Princeton, NJ: Princeton University Press, 1944.

Kierkegaard, Søren. *Fear and Trembling [and] Repetition.* Translated by Howard V. Hong and Edna H. Hong. Princeton, NJ: Princeton University Press, 1983.

Kierkegaard, Søren. *The Point of View.* Translated by Howard V. Hong and Edna H. Hong. Princeton, NJ: Princeton University Press, 1998.

Kierkegaard, Søren. *The Sickness unto Death.* Translated by Alastair Hannay. London: Penguin, 1989.

Klemke, E. D. "Living without Appeal: An Affirmative Philosophy of Life." In *The Meaning of Life,* 2nd ed., edited by E. D. Klemke, 186–197. New York: Oxford University Press, 2000.

Kübler-Ross, Elisabeth. *Death: The Final Stage of Growth.* Englewood Cliffs, NJ: Prentice-Hall, 1975.

Kushner, Harold S. *When Bad Things Happen to Good People.* New York: Schocken, 1983.

Landau, Iddo. "Perfectionism and Non-perfectionism in Camus's *Myth of Sisyphus.*" In *On Meaning in Life,* edited by Beatrix Himmelmann, 139–151. Boston: de Gruyter, 2013.

Landau, Iddo. "Sartre's Absolute Freedom in *Being and Nothingness*: The Problem Persists." *Philosophy Today* 56 (2012): 463–473.

Landau, Iddo. "The Meaning of Life *Sub Specie Aeternitatis.*" *Australasian Journal of Philosophy* 89, no. 4 (2011): 727–734.

Lenman, James. "Immortality: A Letter." *Cogito* 9 (1995): 164–169.

Lucretius. *On the Nature of Things.* Edited and translated by Anthony M. Esolen. Baltimore: Johns Hopkins University Press, 1995.

Lutyens, Mary. *Krishnamurti and the Rajagopals*. Place of publication unmentioned: Krishnamurti Foundation of America, 1996.

Mancini, Anthony D., George A. Bonanno, and Andrew E. Clark. "Stepping Off the Hedonic Treadmill: Individual Differences in Response to Major Life Events." *Journal of Individual Differences* 32, no. 3 (2011): 144–152.

Maugham, W. Somerset. *The Moon and Sixpence*. Harmondsworth: Penguin, 1944.

McDermott, John J. "Why Bother: Is Life Worth Living?" *Journal of Philosophy* 88, no. 11 (1991): 677–683.

Metz, Thaddeus. *Meaning in Life: An Analytic Study*. Oxford: Oxford University Press, 2013.

Metz, Thaddeus. "Recent Work on the Meaning of Life." *Ethics* 112, no. 4 (2002): 781–814.

Milgram, Stanley. "Behavioral Study of Obedience." *Journal of Abnormal and Social Psychology* 67, no. 4 (1963): 371–378.

Mill, John Stuart. *Autobiography*. New York: New American Library, 1964.

Morris, Thomas V. *Making Sense of it All*. Grand Rapids, MI: Eerdmans, 1992.

Mother Teresa [Anjezë Gonxhe Bojaxhiu]. *Come Be My Light*. Edited by Brian Kolodiejchuk. New York: Doubleday, 2007.

Murphy, Jeffrie G. "Forgiveness and Resentment." In *Forgiveness and Mercy*, edited by Jeffrie G. Murphy and Jean Hampton, 14–34. Cambridge: Cambridge University Press, 1988.

Nagel, Thomas. "Birth, Death, and the Meaning of Life." In *The View from Nowhere*, 208–231. New York: Oxford University Press, 1986.

Nagel, Thomas. "Death." In *Mortal Questions*, 1–10. Cambridge: Cambridge University Press, 1979.

Nagel, Thomas. "The Absurd." In *Mortal Questions*, 11–23. Cambridge: Cambridge University Press, 1979.

Nagel, Thomas. *The Last Word*. New York: Oxford University Press, 1997.

Nielsen, Kai. "Death and the Meaning of Life." In *The Meaning of Life*, 2nd ed., edited by E. D. Klemke, 153–159. New York: Oxford University Press, 2000.

Nietzsche, Friedrich. *Beyond Good and Evil*. Translated by Judith Norman. Cambridge: Cambridge University Press, 2001.

Nietzsche, Friedrich. *Daybreak*. Translated by R. J. Hollingdale. Cambridge: Cambridge University Press, 1997.

Nietzsche, Friedrich. *Ecce Homo*. In *"The Anti-Christ", "Ecce Homo", "Twilight of the Idols", and Other Writings*, edited by Aaron Ridley and Judith Norman, translated by Judith Norman, 71–151. Cambridge: Cambridge University Press, 2005.

Nietzsche, Friedrich. *The Will to Power*. Translated by Walter Kaufmann and R. J. Hollingdale. New York: Vintage, 1968.

Nietzsche, Friedrich. *Thus Spoke Zarathustra*. Translated by Adrian Del Caro. Cambridge: Cambridge University Press, 2006.

Norris, Christopher. *Reclaiming Truth: Contribution to a Critique of Cultural Relativism.* Durham, NC: Duke University Press, 1996.

Nozick, Robert. *Philosophical Explanations.* Cambridge, MA: Belknap Press of Harvard University Press, 1981.

O'Hara, Frank. *The Collected Poems of Frank O'Hara.* Edited by Donald Allen. New York: Knopf, 1972.

Omer, Haim, and Avshalom Elitzur. "What Would You Say to the Person on the Roof? A Suicide Prevention Text." *Suicide and Life-Threatening Behavior* 31 (2001): 129–139.

Parfit, Derek. *Reasons and Persons.* Oxford: Clarendon, 1984.

Peirce, Charles Sanders. "Fallibilism, Continuity, and Evolution." In *Collected Papers,* edited by Charles Hartshorne and Paul Weiss, 1:58–72. Cambridge, MA: Belknap Press of Harvard University Press, 1965.

Pereboom, Derk. "Free Will Skepticism and Meaning in Life." In *The Oxford Handbook of Free Will,* 2nd ed., edited by Robert Kane, 407–423. Oxford: Oxford University Press, 2011.

Pereboom, Derk. *Living without Free Will.* Cambridge: Cambridge University Press, 2001.

Perry, Gina. *Behind the Shock Machine: The Untold Story of the Notorious Milgram Psychology Experiments.* New York: New Press, 2013.

Plato. *Greater Hippias.* Translated by Benjamin Jowett. In *The Collected Dialogues of Plato,* edited by Edith Hamilton and Huntington Cairns, 1534–1559. Princeton, NJ: Princeton University Press, 1961.

Plato. *Phaedo.* Translated by Hugh Tredennick. In *The Collected Dialogues of Plato,* edited by Edith Hamilton and Huntington Cairns, 41–98. Princeton, NJ: Princeton University Press, 1961.

Popper, Karl. "Science: Conjectures and Refutations." In *Conjectures and Refutations,* 2nd ed., 33–59. London: Routledge and Kegan Paul, 1965.

Popper, Karl. "Truth, Rationality, and the Growth of Scientific Knowledge." In *Conjectures and Refutations,* 2nd ed., 215–250. London: Routledge and Kegan Paul, 1965.

Reed, Baron. "How to Think about Fallibilism." *Philosophical Studies* 107, no. 2 (2002): 143–157.

Roberts, Robert C. "Forgivingness." *American Philosophical Quarterly* 32, no. 4 (1995): 289–306.

Rousseau, Jean-Jacques. *Julie ou la Nouvelle Héloïse.* Paris: Garnier, 1960.

Russell, L. J. "The Meaning of Life." *Philosophy* 28 (1953): 30–40.

Sartre, Jean-Paul. *Being and Nothingness.* Translated by Hazel E. Barnes. London: Methuen, 1966.

Schacht, Joseph. *An Introduction to Islamic Law.* Oxford: Clarendon, 1964.

Schlick, Moritz. "On the Meaning of Life." In *Philosophical Papers,* edited by Henk L. Mulder and Barbara F. B. van de Velde-Schlick, 2:112–129. Dordrecht: Reidel, 1979.

Schmidtz, David. "The Meanings of Life." In *Life, Death, and Meaning*, 2nd ed., edited by David Benatar, 93–113. Lanham, MD: Rowman and Littlefield, 2010.

Schopenhauer, Arthur. *Complete Essays of Schopenhauer*. Translated by T. Bailey Saunders. 7 vols. New York: Wiley, 1942.

Schopenhauer, Arthur. *The World as Will and Representation*. Translated by E. F. J. Payne. 2 vols. New York, Dover, 1969.

Shakespeare, William. *The Complete Works of William Shakespeare*. Edited by William Aldis Wright. Garden City, NY: Garden City Publishing, 1936.

Shaw, George Bernard. *Man and Superman*. New York: Brentano, 1922.

Sher, George. *Beyond Neutrality: Perfectionism and Politics*. Cambridge: Cambridge University Press, 1997.

Shneur Zalman of Liadi. *Likutei Amarim Tanya*. Translated by Nissan Mindel. New York: Kehot, 1972.

Siegel, Harvey. *Relativism Refuted: A Critique of Contemporary Epistemological Relativism*. Dordrecht: Reidel, 1987.

Singer, Peter. *How Are We to Live?* Oxford: Oxford University Press, 1997.

Slote, Michael. "Ethics without Free Will." *Social Theory and Practice* 16 (1990): 369–383.

Smith, Adam. *An Inquiry into the Nature and Causes of the Wealth of Nations*. Edited by R. H. Campbell, A. S. Skinner, and W. B. Todd. Vol. 1. Oxford: Clarendon, 1976.

Spinoza, Baruch. *Ethics*. In *The Collected Works of Spinoza*, edited and translated by Edwin M. Curley, 1:408–617. Princeton, NJ: Princeton University Press, 1985.

Spinoza, Baruch. *Letters*. In *Complete Works*, edited by Michael Morgan, translated by Samuel Shirley, 755–959. Indianapolis: Hackett, 2002.

Stevenson, Robert Louis. *Virginibus Puerisque*. London: Thomas Nelson, 1932.

Talmud Bavli (Babylonian Talmud): Tractate Bava Batra. Edited by Hersh Goldwurm and Yosaif Asher Weiss. Translator not mentioned. 1st Schottenstein ed. New York: Mesorah, 1992.

Taubman–Ben-Ari, Orit. "Is the Meaning of Life also the Meaning of Death? A Terror Management Perspective Reply." *Journal of Happiness Studies* 12 (2011): 385–399.

Taylor, Charles. *The Ethics of Authenticity*. Cambridge, MA: Harvard University Press, 1992.

Taylor, Richard. "The Meaning of Life." In *The Meaning of Life*, 2nd ed., edited by E. D. Klemke, 167–175. New York: Oxford University Press, 2000.

Taylor, Richard. "Time and Life's Meaning." *Review of Metaphysics* 40 (1987): 675–686.

Thackeray, William Makepeace. *The Luck of Barry Lyndon*. Edited by Edgar F. Harden. Ann Arbor: University of Michigan Press, 1999.

The Seventh Seal. Directed by Ingmar Bergman, produced by Allan Ekelund, distributed by AB Svensk Filmindustri, 1957.

Thoreau, Henry D. *Walden: Or, Life in the Woods*. Mineola, NY: Dover, 1955.

Tolstoy, Leo. *Anna Karenina*. Translated by Richard Pevear and Larissa Volokhonsky. London: Penguin, 2000.

Tolstoy, Leo. *Confession*. Translated by David Patterson. New York: Norton, 1983.

Tolstoy, Leo. *War and Peace*. Translated by Richard Pevear and Larissa Volokhonsky. New York: Vintage, 2008.

Trisel, Brooke Alan. "Futility and the Meaning of Life Debate." *Sorites* 14 (2002): 70–84.

Trisel, Brooke Alan. "Human Extinction and the Value of Our Efforts." *Philosophical Forum* 35, no. 3 (2004): 371–391.

Underhill, Evelyn. *Mysticism: A Study in the Nature and Development of Man's Spiritual Consciousness*. New York: Noonday, 1945.

Voltaire [François-Marie Arouet]. *Candide*. In *"Candide", "Zadig", and Selected Stories*, translated by Donald M. Frame, 15–101. New York: Signet, 1961.

Voltaire [François-Marie Arouet]. "La Bégueule." In *Les Oeuvres complètes de Voltaire*, vol. 74A: *Oeuvres de 1772 (I)*), edited by Nicholas Cronk and Hayden T. Mason, 217. Oxford: Voltaire Foundation / Alden Press, 2006.

Walker, Lois Hope. "Religion Gives Meaning to Life." In *Philosophy: The Quest for Truth*, 6th ed., edited by Louis P. Pojman, 551–555. New York: Oxford University Press, 2006.

Wall, Steven. *Liberalism, Perfectionism and Restraint*. Cambridge: Cambridge University Press, 1998.

Wielenberg, Erik J. *Value and Virtue in a Godless Universe*. Cambridge: Cambridge University Press, 2005.

Wilde, Oscar. *Lady Windermere's Fan*. In *Complete Works of Oscar Wilde*, edited by J. B. Forman, 385–430. London: Collins, 1966.

Wilde, Oscar. *The Picture of Dorian Gray*. In *Complete Works of Oscar Wilde*, edited by J. B. Forman, 17–167. London: Collins, 1966.

Williams, Bernard. "The Makropulos Case: Reflections on the Tedium of Immortality." In *Problems of the Self*, 82–100. Cambridge: Cambridge University Press, 1973.

Williams, William Carlos. *The Collected Poems of William Carlos Williams*. Edited by A. Walton Litz and Christopher MacGowan. Vol. 1. New York: New Directions, 1986.

Wings of Desire. Directed by Wim Wenders, produced by Wim Wenders and Anatole Dauman, distributed by Basis FilmVerleih, 1987.

Wittgenstein, Ludwig. *Tractatus Logico-Philosophicus*. Translated by D. F. Pears and B. F. McGuinness. London: Routledge and Kegan Paul, 1966.

Wolf, Susan. "Happiness and Meaning: Two Aspects of the Good Life." *Social Philosophy and Policy* 14, no. 1 (1997): 207–225.

Wolf, Susan. "Meaning and Morality." *Proceedings of the Aristotelian Society* 97 (1997): 299–315.

Wolf, Susan. *Meaning in Life and Why It Matters*. Commentary by John Koethe, Robert M. Adams, Nomy Arpaly, and Jonathan Haidt. Princeton, NJ: Princeton University Press, 2010.

Wolf, Susan. "The Meanings of Lives." In *Introduction to Philosophy*, 4th ed., edited by John Perry, Michael Bratman, and John Martin Fischer, 61–74. New York: Oxford University Press, 2007.

Wolpert, Stanley A. *Gandhi's Passion: The Life and Legacy of Mahatma Gandhi*. Oxford: Oxford University Press, 2001.

Yeats, W. B. "Reveries over Childhood and Youth." In *The Autobiography of William Butler Yeats*, 1–71. New York: Collier, 1965.

Yeats, W. B. *The Collected Poems of W. B. Yeats*. New York: Macmillan, 1951.

INDEX

absurd 32, 259–60, 265n19
    and meaninglessness 32n6
academics 156, 198–9
Acton, Lord. *See* Lord Acton
Adams, Robert E. 218n2
adolescents 13–14
afterlife 69–70, 80n17, 251, 253–4
aim of life. *See* goal of life
alienation 11–12, 14, 28, 229–30, 240–2,
    244, 269
altruism. *See* helping others
anger 38, 54, 191–2, 233
Anna Karenina 60–1
annihilation. *See* death and annihilation
anxiety 238, 260, 267, 269, 271
appreciation vs. idealization. *See*
    idealization vs. appreciation
Aquinas, Thomas 56n10
Aristotle 17, 137n4, 236–7
Audi, Robert 39n17, 49n1, 72, 232n4
authenticity 10–11, 28, 129–31, 257,
    260, 261
    radical 129–31
    See also realism
Ayer, A. J. 133

Baier, Kurt 36n13, 49n1, 137–42
Balaguer, Mark 106n2
beauty 25, 28, 57, 108, 234–6,
    241–3, 244–5

Ben Ze'ev, Aaron 49–50
bereavement 9, 14–15, 23, 221–2, 239.
    See also suffering
Bergman, Ingmar 61–2
best vs. good 53–4, 59
Big Two-Hearted River 58–9, 231
Bishop Butler. *See* Butler, Joseph (Bishop)
Blackburn, Simon 93–4, 95, 97–8
blame. *See* guilt
Boghossian, Paul 123n3
Bond, E. J. 34
boredom 12, 25, 80–1, 145–8, 160, 167,
    197, 263, 276–7
Brogaard, Berit 6n1, 33
Brother Lawrence 243–4
Buber, Martin 258, 267–8n1
Buddhism 80n17
Butler, Joseph (Bishop) 196n3

Camus, Albert 32, 39, 54n8, 61, 66, 90, 92,
    258–61, 263, 265n19, 268n2
Candide 59–60
Čapek, Karel 79
causality 101–5, 107
Cavafy, Constantine 146n4
certainty 17n2, 18–19, 50–2, 117–18, 208,
    251, 253
challengers. *See* paradox of the end: and
    challengers
chance. *See* contingency

Christianity 55–6. *See also* religion
Cohen, Stewart 51n3
compatibilism. *See* determinism:
    compatibilism
competitive value. *See* value:
    competitive vs. noncompetitive
competitiveness 43–8, 155–6
conceit 41–2, 199–200
    vs. pride 199–200
Confession 7–8, 67–8, 216
conformism and nonconformism 197
contingency 111–16, 159, 251–2, 254
conventionality 28, 80n16, 175. *See also*
    conformism and nonconformism
conversion. *See* identifying: conversion
corruptibility 184–8
cosmic perspective. *See* perspectives:
    wide vs. narrow
Cottingham, John 6n1, 13n11, 49n1, 86n1,
    122n2, 125n4, 136n2, 251
Craig, William Lane 33n7, 36–7,
    113n7, 251
crisis 23, 114–15, 191–2, 221–2, 239
    healing from 23, 221–2, 239
critical attitude 196–9
cruelty 40–1, 171, 177, 279

Dagan, Avigdor 61n20
danse macabre 67n4
Davies, W. H. 242n13
death and annihilation 8–9, 11, 62, 65–92,
    193, 207–8, 209–14, 233n4, 238, 239,
    251, 252
    all equal because of 8–9, 66–7, 75, 77,
        82, 86–7
    deathbed questions 207–8, 209–14
    dying for something 11
    floor sweeping parable 65–6, 75,
        77, 88–9
    myth of Sisyphus 66, 89–90
    Tolstoy's Eastern fable 67–8, 90–1
    See also afterlife; immortality; suicide
delayed gratification 154–5, 159
despair 39, 52, 54, 59, 118, 203, 238, 267,
    269, 271–2

determinism 101–11, 134
    compatibilism (soft determinism) 107
    hard determinism 107–11
    metaphysical libertarianism 106–7
    and moral responsibility 105–7
    and religion 105–6, 111
detrivialization. *See* trivialization and
    detrivialization
discrimination. *See* self-discrimination
Dixon, Nicholas 199
Dostoevsky, Fyodor 173n1
double standards. *See* self-discrimination
dramatic attitude towards life. *See*
    life: as drama
duties towards ourselves 41

Ecclesiastes 8–9, 67
education 153–6, 158–9, 169,
    184–5, 187–8
Edwards, Paul 49n1
Elitzur, Avshalom 233n4
Emerson, Ralph Waldo 49n1
emotion 169, 194–5, 210, 215, 229–30,
    232–3, 254–7, 264, 274
emptiness 16, 145, 171
end of life. *See* goal of life
Epictetus 238
Epicurus 75–6
eternal life. *See* immortality
evil 173–90, 251, 253
    and history 173–4, 176–7
    and human nature 188–9
    and media 173–6
    ways of coping with 177, 188–90
evolution 113–14, 142–4, 251, 252
evolutionary psychology 234n5
existentialism 210, 215, 258–65, 275
expectations 238n8, 267–73
    fulfilled and unfulfilled 267–73
    and reality 267–73
    should be realistic 25, 40, 38–9, 42,
        155, 169
    vs. wishes or preferences 53
    See also perfectionism; realism;
        standards

external perspective. *See* perspectives: wide vs. narrow
extrinsic value. *See* value: extrinsic vs. intrinsic

fallibilism 50–2, 117–18
familiarity 25–6, 156–7, 222, 224, 234. *See also* routine
Fara, Michael 107n3
Feinberg, Joel 181n7, 182n8
Fischer, John Martin 15n14, 80–1, 107n3
forgiveness 40, 169, 192–6, 253
Frankfurt, Harry 6n1, 107n3
Frankl, Viktor 7, 24n5, 27, 52n5, 116, 136n2, 171, 215n6, 216n7, 219
free will. *See* determinism
freedom 129–31, 194, 210–11, 212–13, 214–16, 263–4, 275–6. *See also* determinism
fulfillment 10, 56–7, 253–4

Gandhi, Mohandas Karamchand 177–9
Gauguin, Paul 223
goal of life 11, 135–44, 252
God 13n11, 33, 36–7, 39, 40, 42, 55, 69, 83, 96–7, 105–6, 111, 116, 152, 171, 181, 193, 214, 243, 251, 252–3, 254, 259
Goethe, Johann Wolfgang von 275n4
Goussinsky, Ruhama 49–50
guilt 25n6, 153, 180, 192–6, 264, 267, 269, 271–2
    existential 269, 271–2
    exonerating circumstances 194–5
    vs. guilt feelings 194

Haack, Susan 51n3
habits 153–6, 158–9, 169, 211, 222n4, 224, 231, 233–6, 246, 254, 274, 275–6, 277–8
Hamlet 2
Hanfling, Oswald 33, 143, 150n6, 150n8, 152n10, 159, 163n1, 164
hard determinism. *See* determinism: hard determinism
Hassidism 56–7

heaven. *See* afterlife
hedonic adaptation 151n9
Heidegger, Martin 239n10, 258, 260–1, 263, 267n1
hell. *See* afterlife
helping others 7, 179–81, 201–2, 203, 206–7, 218, 236
Hemingway, Ernest 58–9, 231
Hepburn, R. W. 6n1
Herbert, Zbigniew 57
Hesse, Hermann 60
Hetherington, Stephen 51n3
Heyd, David 55n9
history 173–6
Hoffmann, Yoel 61n20
Holocaust 7, 27, 116, 171, 172, 185, 219
Homer 71–2
Hooker, Brad 49n1
Hume, David 67
humility. *See* pride: vs. modesty
Hurka, Thomas 31n1
Huxley, Aldous 49n1, 133
hypercompetitiveness. *See* competitiveness

idealization vs. appreciation 42, 61, 179
ideals 32, 50, 52–3, 258–9, 271
    and nonperfectionism 35–6
    regulative 52–3, 151–2, 278n6
    See also realism
identifying 117, 205–28, 250, 272, 273, 274, 277
    conversion 223
    deathbed questions 207–14
    and helping others 218
    instructive questions 206–14
    personalizing in 217
    and pleasure 218–20
    pluralism in 215–16, 245, 264
    realism in 214–15
    vs. recognizing 244–7
    requires periodical consideration 220–2
    Strickland model 223–8
    when in crisis 221–2
immigrants 13
immortality 36–7, 62, 78–85

incessancy 25–6, 157
inconsequentiality 65–6, 75, 76, 77,
    82, 88–9
ineffability 13n11
instrumental value. *See* value: extrinsic vs.
    intrinsic
intrinsic value. *See* value: extrinsic vs. intrinsic
irony 260n11
Islam 56

James, Laurence 33–4
James, William 13n11
jogging. *See* running analogy
Joske, W. D. 6n1
Judaism 55–7

Kane, Robert 106n2
Kant, Immanuel 41, 139n5, 152
Kierkegaard, Søren 258–65, 267n1
King, Martin Luther 177–8
Klemke, E. D. 133
Krankheitsgewinn. *See* morbid gain
Krishnamurti, Jiddu 178
Kübler-Ross, Elisabeth 207n1
Kushner, Harold S. 14n13

Lenman, James 83n20
libertarianism. *See* determinism:
    metaphysical libertarianism
life
    balanced vs. imbalanced 226–7
    both wonderful and terrible 92,
        176–7, 190
    as drama 29, 59, 60, 62, 228
    as a journey 142
    wasted 82–4, 87–8, 207n1, 208, 209–10,
        212–13, 278–9
Lincoln, Abraham 180–1
Lord Acton 184, 186–7
love 15, 25, 26, 49–50, 61, 62, 117, 129–30,
    191, 206, 217, 220, 221, 234, 253, 255–
    6, 261–2, 274, 275
Lucretius 77

malleability. *See* corruptibility
manipulation 185, 187

Marcus Aurelius 238
Maugham, W. Somerset 223
McDermott, John J. 176
meaning in life. *See* meaning of life
meaning of life
    can be increased or decreased 19
    clarification of term 6–16
    comes in degrees 20–2
    and creativity 27–8
    does not solve all of life's problems 26–7
    fluctuates in degree 26
    vs. happiness 170–2
    nonmysterious 29
    overromanticized 29, 263
    precision in discussion of 17
    regenerating after crisis 23–4,
        221–2, 239n11
    solace in the face of death 87–8
    uniqueness not necessary for 27–8
    See also meaninglessness
meaningfulness. *See* meaning of life
meaninglessness
    continuum between it and
        meaningfulness 20–2, 34–5
    descriptions of 267–70
    and economic class 237n8
    Frankl's denial of 52n5
    and modernity 237n8
    relapses to 277–8
    threshold between it and
        meaningfulness 21–2, 34–5, 63, 95–6,
        98, 226–7, 244
    See also meaning of life
media 173–6, 187, 191, 237
metaphysical libertarianism. *See*
    determinism: metaphysical
    libertarianism
Metz, Thaddeus 15n14, 49n1, 75, 125n4,
    130n6, 171n8
Milgram, Stanley 184–6
Mill, John Stuart 148–9, 158, 160–1
Mixon, Don 186
modesty. *See* pride: vs. modesty
monism 22–4, 225, 226–7
moral activism 202–3, 206–7, 218, 236
morbid gain 197

Morris, Thomas V. 33n7
mortality. *See* death and annihilation
Mother Teresa 171, 178
Murphy, Jeffrie G. 196n3
mysticism 13n11, 15, 29, 200n5, 233

Nagel, Thomas 7, 11, 73–5, 76, 77n14, 91,
    93–5, 112, 119, 123n3, 268n2
naiveté 190, 197, 203. *See also* realism
Narcissism 41–2
narrow perspective. *See* perspectives: wide
    vs. narrow
neutrality. *See* objectivism
Nielsen, Kai 6n1
Nietzsche, Friedrich 32, 258, 260–3, 264–5
noncompetitive value. *See*
    value: competitive vs. noncompetitive
nonconformism. *See* conformism and
    nonconformism
nonperfectionism. *See* perfectionism
Norris, Christopher 123n3
Nozick, Robert 33, 106n2
numbness. *See* alienation

objectivism 10n9, 118–34. *See also*
    relativism
O'Hara, Frank 57
Omer, Haim 233n4

pain. *See* suffering
parables
    floor sweeping 65–6, 77, 88–9
    should be used with caution 91, 92
    Sisyphus 66, 89–90, 147–8
    Tolstoy's Eastern fable 67–8, 90–1
    the tree 91–2
    See also running analogy
paradox of the end 145–61, 164, 231,
    237n8, 252–3, 254, 274
    can be mitigated 153–9
    and challengers 160–1
    and education 153–9
    explained 145–9
    Schopenhauer's use of 164
    and workaholism 153
Parfit, Derek 77n14

Peirce, Charles Sanders 51n3
Pereboom, Derk 107–11
perfectionism
    arguments against 36–48
    different employments of the term 31n1
    explained 31–6
    in language 47n24, 57n13
    not symmetrically opposite to
        nonperfectionism 53
    and romantic ideology 49–50, 60–1, 62
Perry, Gina 185–6
personalized value. *See* value: personalized
perspectives
    neutral (*see* objectivism)
    vs. standards (*see* standards: vs.
        perspectives)
    wide vs. narrow 93–9
philanthropy. *See* helping others
Plato 33, 38
pluralism 215–16, 245, 264
point of it all 12, 24n5, 43, 229–30
Popper, Karl 51n3
power 184, 186–8, 192–4, 234n5, 264, 269
    assumed in guilt 192–4, 264
pride
    about the past 239
    vs. modesty 154, 199–200
procrastination 154–5, 209–10, 213
psychological egoism 179–84
psychology and psychiatry 151n9,
    254–7, 271n3
punishment. *See* self-punishment
purpose of life. *See* goal of life

questions, wrong 141–2

Ramsey, Frank 94
realism 50, 51, 155, 190, 200, 214–15, 261.
    See also authenticity; expectations:
    should be realistic; naiveté
recognizing 47–8, 53, 55–63, 169, 177, 179,
    190, 229–47, 250, 254, 272, 273, 274,
    277, 279
    both notes and increases meaning 232
    vs. identifying 244–7
    of past occurrences 238–9

recognizing (*Cont.*)
  and pride 200
  reasons for failing in 191–200, 232–4
  veil of numbness 242
  ways of 234–8, 242–3
Reed, Baron 51n3
regenerating meaning. *See* meaning of
    life: regenerating after crisis
regulative ends. *See* ideals: regulative
reincarnation. *See* afterlife
relativism 118–34, 252–3
  and "anything goes" argument 122,
      124–5, 132
  and counterintuitive implications 121–2,
      124–5, 128–9
  debate about irrelevant 131–4
  and rationality 122, 125–8, 132
  and real value 122–3, 128–31, 133
religion 55–7, 69–70, 105–6, 111, 116, 216,
    225–6, 243–4, 251–4
  and determinism 105–6, 111
  helpful for meaningfulness 252–4
  and immortality 69–70
  and nonperfectionism 55–7
  not necessary for meaningfulness 251–2
  See also afterlife; Buddhism; Christianity;
      Islam; Judaism; mysticism
responsibility 105–6, 107, 192–4, 263–4
resurrection. *See* afterlife
Reversed Golden Rule 195–6, 278
Roberts, Robert C. 196n3
romantic ideology. *See* perfectionism: and
    romantic ideology
Rousseau, Jean-Jacques 145
routine 25–6, 55, 157, 234, 275–6
running analogy 43–4
Russell, L. J. 136n2

salvation 55–6, 223
sarcasm 260n11
Sartre, Jean-Paul 210n4, 215n6,
    258–65, 275–6
Schacht, Joseph 56n11
Schlick, Moritz 140n7
Schmidtz, David 17n2, 49n1
Schopenhauer, Arthur 37n15, 145,
    163–70, 230–1

analysis of pleasure 163–5
self-discrimination 37–8, 40–1, 192–6,
    262, 278
self-punishment 194–6
self-realization 10
Shakespeare 2, 54n7, 72, 110, 145
  and Shakespeare* 110
Shaw, George Bernard 146
Sher, George 31n1
Shneur Zalman of Liadi 56n12
Siddhartha 60, 231
Siegel, Harvey 123n3
sincerity. *See* authenticity; realism
Singer, Peter 218n1
Sisyphus, myth of. *See* parables: Sisyphus
skepticism 50–2, 117–18, 251, 253
Slote, Michael 107–11
Smith, Barry 6n1, 33
soft determinism. *See*
    determinism: compatibilism
species, persistence of 142–4. *See also*
    evolution
Spinoza 33, 104
standards
  double (*see* self-discrimination)
  objective vs. relative (*see* relativism)
  vs. perspectives 95–8
  See also expectations; realism
Stevenson, Robert Louis 145–6
Stoa 238
Strickland model. *See*
    identifying: Strickland model
sub specie aeternitatis. *See*
    perspectives: wide vs. narrow
sub specie humanitatis. *See*
    perspectives: wide vs. narrow
suffering 163–7, 218–22, 232–3, 251,
    253, 260–1
  and difficulties to recognize 233
  effects on meaningfulness 218–20
  and existentialism 260–1
  feigned and genuine 197–8
  guilt about 192–4
  vs. meaninglessness 26–7, 170–2
  and suicide 2, 233n4
  See also bereavement; life: as drama;
      realism

suicide 2, 54n8, 233n4, 265n19
supererogation 55–6, 253–4
superficiality 22

Talmud 57
Taubman–Ben-Ari, Orit 208n2
Taylor, Charles 129–31
Taylor, Richard 27n7, 34, 49n1, 143n9
terminal value. See value: extrinsic vs.
    intrinsic
Thackeray, William Makepeace 66–7
The Practice of the Presence of God 243–4
The Seventh Seal 61–2
Thoreau, Henry David 8
thought experiments
    competitive-noncompetitive value 44
    immortality pill 78–80
    radioactive catastrophe 143–4
    ratio of earth to universe changed 99
    Shakespeare* 110
    world destroyed in 300 years 144
time, subjective vs. objective 166–7
Tolstoy, Leo 7–8, 60–1, 67–8, 90–1, 216n8
Trisel, Brooke Alan 39n17, 43, 49n1, 133
trivialization and detrivialization 55, 57,
    231, 234–46. See also recognizing

Underhill, Evelyn 13n11

value
    competitive vs. noncompetitive 44–8,
        83–4, 155–6
    extrinsic vs. intrinsic 137–42, 240n12
    personalized 217
veil of numbness. See recognizing: veil of
    numbness
visual art 62
Voltaire 53–4, 59–60, 147

Walker, Lois Hope 136n2, 251
Wall, Steven 31n1
War and Peace 60–1
wasted life. See life: wasted
Wenders, Wim 62
wide perspective. See perspectives: wide
    vs. narrow
Wielenberg, Erik J. 125n4
Wilde, Oscar 47n23, 146
Williams, Bernard 79–82
Williams, William Carlos 57
Wittgenstein, Ludwig 20n4
Wolf, Susan 6n1, 15n14, 18n3, 49n1, 125n4
work 153–5, 196, 212, 215, 228, 273–7, 279
workaholism. See paradox of the end: and
    workaholism

Yeats, W. B. 209, 229–30